Performance
Histories

Books by Bonnie Marranca

As author

Performance Histories
Ecologies of Theatre
Theatrewritings
American Playwrights: A Critical Survey (with Gautam Dasgupta)

As editor

A Slice of Life: Contemporary Writers on Food
Conversations on Art and Performance (with Gautam Dasgupta)
Plays for the End of the Century
Interculturalism and Performance (with Gautam Dasgupta)
A Hudson Valley Reader
American Garden Writing
American Dreams: The Imagination of Sam Shepard
Animations: A Trilogy for Mabou Mines (with Gautam Dasgupta)
Theatre of the Ridiculous (with Gautam Dasgupta)
The Theatre of Images

Performance Histories

❑

Bonnie Marranca

New York, New York

Performance Histories is published by PAJ Publications, P. O. Box 532, Village Station, New York, NY 10014.

PAJ Publications is distributed to the trade by Consortium Book Sales and Distribution: www.cbsd.com

Publisher of PAJ Publications: Bonnie Marranca

Library of Congress Cataloging-in-Publication Data

Marranca, Bonnie.
  Performance histories / Bonnie Marranca.— 1st ed.
     p. cm.
  ISBN-13: 978-1-55554-077-7
  ISBN-10: 1-55554-077-5
  1. Performing arts. I. Title.
  PN1584.M35 2007
  790.2—dc22

                    2007030976

                First Edition, 2008
          Printed in the United States of America

For Susan Sontag

If we can perceive ourselves in the work—not the work but ourselves when viewing the work then the work is important. If we can *know our response*, see in ourselves *what we have received* from a work, that is the way to the understanding of truth and all beauty.

AGNES MARTIN, "THE STILL AND SILENT IN ART"

Contents

Author's Note

The selections in *Performance Histories* represent for the most part a gathering together of essays, lectures, and interviews that I have completed since the publication of *Ecologies of Theatre* (1996). They include revision and expansion of a few of the originals, namely "Performance, A Personal History," as I have lived with the ideas over a period of time and incorporated them into different formats. As a point of clarification in reading the Endnotes, the contents of this volume have been largely drawn from *Performing Arts Journal*, which was renamed *PAJ: A Journal of Performance and Art* in 1998. My work as a publisher, editor, lecturer, and sometime curator of public events has given me the opportunity to engage on a personal level with many artists and thinkers whose comments on such topics as artistic process, history, and contemporary culture find personal expression in the conversations that flow through the volume, alongside the writings. I am full of admiration for the honesty and risk-taking in their contributions.

I am especially grateful for the exchanges and working relationships I have had over the years with friends and colleagues, here and abroad, whose perspectives have energized my own reflections: Herbert Blau, Alison Knowles, Carolee Schneemann, Mac Wellman, Małgorzata Semil, Jennifer Parker-Starbuck, Joshua Abrams, Claire MacDonald, Stanley Kauffmann, Claire Montgomery, Hanne Jorna, Giovanna Fiorenza, Frantisek Deak, Johannes Birringer, Erik Ehn, Moira Roth, Valentina Valentini, Andrzej Wirth, Meredith Monk, Maria Irene Fornes, Devon Allen, Cynthia Jenner, Erika Fischer-Lichte, Frank Hentschker.

To Steve Luber, the production manager of *PAJ: A Journal of Performance and Art*, and George Hunka, who worked with me to get the manuscript of *Performance Histories* into shape, heartfelt appreciation for their enthusiasm and care in bringing to fruition the current publishing activities of PAJ Publications. A special thank you to Susan Quasha, designer of this volume, for her generosity of spirit.

November 2007
New York City

Preface:
Pressing Tender Buttons or,
How to Write

CLAIRE MACDONALD

I have long been interested in the American essay, written, as it is, in that most fluid of registers, American English. Its foremother, as Bonnie Marranca would be the first to acknowledge, is Gertrude Stein, who, according to poet and critic Charles Bernstein, came to English as a second language, and whose ear for the clear rhythms and phrasing of colloquial American English allowed her to push the horizon of its possibilities.

The American essay appears in many forms, including literary memoir, politics, arts, food, garden and nature writing, and writing about travel—or what Thoreau might have called "awandering"—and it seems to me that, whatever the specificities of the subject, a great many of the best American essayists are women, and that Bonnie Marranca is surely among them. In her work, and that of M. F. K. Fisher, Joan Didion, Elizabeth Hardwick, Martha Gellhorn, Jessica Mitford (an adoptive American), Marina Warner (OK, I am stretching a point but she too began her writing in the United States), Susan Sontag, and of course Stein herself, we read a vigorous, subtle, and persuasive style of public writing, a descriptive poetics that makes what they see, new. They remake the cultural landscape from which they write, giving us not only powerful and accurate narratives, but a reflexive sense of remaking the landscape around them so that its topography is forever changed, and we, literally, see differently.

Bonnie Marranca is a mistress of American essay writing. Her approach is matrilineal rather than feminist, her method genealogical and associative. She disciplines the form and inflects it with a femininity of approach evinced in the quality of her attention to the contours of the emotional life as a legitimate aspect of intellectual practice, and to the formative power of experience. She casts light and shadow before her, illuminating parts of the territory under consideration. For her, writing is part of a conversation about culture that resonates as much among artists as scholars, and her writerly ethics lie in the belief that critical writing can have an equivalent place, but not a governing place, in that conversation.

Historically, her writing emerges from a specific American locale. Hers is the viewpoint of an East coast girl brought up just outside New York in New Jersey (albeit inflected by the Italian ways of her family), and who has lived just over the Hudson for almost all her adult life, in that most vibrant of cities, New York: socially and artistically experimental, vital yet gracious, and utterly old-fashioned. *Performance Histories* is her third book of essays. In common with many people I first came to her work through the extraordinarily radical *Theatrewritings*. Here, in the mid-1980s, was a voice that spoke with such assurance and yet with such clarity about the avant-garde and about experiment in the arts; yet it was a *vernacular* voice, straightforward and vivid and detailed, always gracious about artists and respectful about art as work. My copy of *Theatrewritings* is literally falling apart. It is held together with a large rubber band, so many times has it been read and reread. And it is reread.

When I first came to the United States I was too shy to call her. She had, I imagined, so much to do, so little time. Little did I know that her soup, her pasta, her recommendations for stores and restaurants, and her conversation about cultures and places—Europe, America, and the Hudson Valley among them—would provide more and more reasons for me to come to her table, her desk, and her subsequent books. She is primarily a writer rather than a critic and, in moving between writing and criticism, depicts the imaginative landscape of her interests, beginning in theatre and literature and moving outwards towards other cultural formations and processes, and to the wider tradition of the personal essay. I think here of Thoreau on mountains, Emerson on friendship, and Whitman, whose *Leaves of Grass* refers, of course, to publishing itself.

So what is new in *Performance Histories*? What is different? What has changed since *Ecologies of Theatre*, or, indeed, since *Theatrewritings*? How does this new collection sit within the body of her own work?

This is a book focused on the *idea* of performance history as well as on the history of performance and unfolds from Bonnie Marranca's experience and interests. It is history as *storia* or *histoire*, a form of narration as well as a description of events, that tells us about who we are and where we might go, through instances that show us the way that we have come. Those instances, and the critical imagination that they reveal, act as steps in constructing her approach, and as an *aide memoire* in proposing her view of the arts in their historical context.

For her, art-making is a form of experimental thinking and of poetics—that is, of making, and of making sense. Art-making is a "critical" act, occasioning turning points and shifts of thinking as well as pleasure and reflection. Therefore, what artists do, both materially and through the events they make, is central to cultural process, and rather than being a platform for theoretical posturing art-making needs to be understood as a crucial part of the history of ideas. Her sense of genre is porous. As part of a generation which has grown up seeing the gradual intermixing of the arts, she looks at what *has* happened with an eye to what *might* happen and what, indeed, *should* happen, to what, that is, we might want to pay attention. History is written *to* the future as well as *of* the past, situated on the boundary of what we know and don't know, and her talent for informed conjecture, for speculation if you like, takes seriously the part that we all play, as readers, writers, and viewers, in the construction of the conversation about art's experimental project.

Not all of these essays are new. What *is* new is their curation. She has brought them into new contexts, and in their new settings they read differently. I think, for example, of the interview "Art and the Imagery of Extinction" with the noted author and psychiatrist Robert Jay Lifton, from 1982, which discusses art in relation to the then pressing and terrifying notion of extinction in a nuclear accident or act of war. Reading it in 2007, I am struck by the powerful sense of elegy in so much contemporary Western art now, often combined with a new kind of openness and dialogue, which seems oddly juxtaposed to the turbulence of our times, as if, in the process of becoming *gradually* extinct, rather than being suddenly wiped out, we are reclaiming a sense of the transitory pleasure that we share in the world we have inherited.

In 1977, when Bonnie Marranca wrote about the "Theatre of Images," she referred to theatre that had been produced "in the last dozen years" to describe what was referred to in the 1970s as a "paradigm shift" in the way performance was seen and the way it was made. This shift was evident in a loose grouping of practices, events, and writings that she wanted to attend to critically, and in which she saw a refiguring of literary and visual conventions of representation. In *Performance Histories* that dozen years has stretched to many more and the long view down the past four decades takes in a wider sweep, yet retains its close contact with artists, curators, writers, and what they are doing.

I think that the particularity of *Performance Histories* lies in its understanding of the spiritual as a profound generative force in American art, and especially in the avant-garde. In "Performance and Ethics," a conversation with

Peter Sellars, and in "Art as Spiritual Practice," a dialogue with Meredith Monk, Alison Knowles, Erik Ehn, Eleanor Heartney, and Linda Montano, as well as in the interview with Robert Jay Lifton, Bonnie Marranca comes closest to seeing the production of art within a wide arc, one that considers what we do now against the stark light of ultimate purpose—not that she has an easy answer, or a position to propound. The American avant-garde has been, as she notes, "the place where the spiritual dimension resides in American theatre." She recognized and wrote about this in *Plays for the End of the Century*, in her earlier essays, on Stein, "Presence of Mind," and in "The Mus/Ecology of John Cage," both in *Ecologies of Theatre* (1996), published the same year as *Plays for the End of the Century*, and it has become more apparent that the relationship of art, spirituality, and religion, far from being a side issue, is one of the most pertinent and illuminating issues of the day.

In *Performance Histories*, Bonnie Marranca's strength as a writer lies, as it always has, in her clear eye for detail, in seeing what is *really* going on, and in her ability to write what I called earlier "descriptive poetics," a phrase used by another American essayist and poetic experimentalist, Lyn Hejinian, to describe that discursive register that is able to move horizontally and connect ideas across a wide field, using description in the topographic sense of attending to what is found. It is also that practice to which Susan Sontag (to whom this book is dedicated) first alerted us in "Against Interpretation," holistic and exploratory, almost a form of reportage, intellectually informed, and always focused on the matter in hand.

In this long quarantine of a view, which she discusses in depth in her first essay in the book, "Performance, a Personal History," she focuses on the way in which the relationship between art and life is thought and formed, and rethought and reformed. In "The Economy of Tenderness," her essay on Maria Irene Fornes, she talks about Fornes's "realism," a term she herself used in the late 1970s in *The Theatre of Images* in a revivified sense to refer to the entry into art of the vernacular gesture, the pedestrian movement, the assonant sound, the insertion of the demotic into the heightened, overly mannered world of modern drama, fraught as it was with subterranean psychology and motivation.

From the mid-1960s this new realism began to be expressed scenographically and dramaturgically. It generated a new kind of aesthetics in which space became primary, as well as a new kind of performer, one differently attuned to the possibilities of the stage as a space for rethinking representation and to the world outside the theatre as the source of language and gesture, as well as to a new register of shared experience between audience and artist. In "The Solace of Chocolate Squares," her essay on Wallace Shawn, she writes about his realist sensibility, focusing on his choice of domestic space as the setting and medium for a new kind of spatial arrangement between watchers and watched that emphasizes this sense of connection. Her attention to what might even be called an *ethics* of intimacy in publicly shown work infuses this book, and carries over into her notes on travel and the cities over which she casts an intimate eye—"Barcelona holds a special place in my dreamlife of cities"—as she visits and revisits their performances, and their social and political cultures.

But not all in this book is delicate or gracious. Bonnie Marranca bewails the loss of a publicly engaged form of intellectual writing that includes artists and intellectuals through creating an inclusive, informed, but essentially democratic form of discourse. She rails against those whose "lumpy prose" is scattered like bad seed across the academic field, and wishes for a return to the historical imagination, to creative projects in scholarship that deal with the histories of institutions and with artists' own writings; to projects that attend to translation, and that acknowledge the "sheer pleasure" of the viewer. At times she writes as if she believes that artists, intellectuals, and scholars once shared a utopian vision for the arts, and have lost it. I am not so sure. I think that part of our particular sensibility in the United States (and I count myself here as a part-time, adoptive American) is always to have a sense of a pervading loss, of what we are never sure, what it *is* we want to find out. So progressive are we as a culture, in the literal sense of always moving forward, that we move too defiantly into the future without pause, and yet, we mourn what we leave behind us.

In "Performance and Ethics," she and Sellars discuss his engagement with classical and popular forms in terms of a commitment to expressive language, as well as the power of the creative imagination to act transformatively and the "poverty" of realism on the contemporary stage. In her essay "Performance, a Personal History," she restates the need for a utopian vision for theatre, saying that, "What is needed now are works of the creative spirit that conceptualize not merely document human behavior, works that address public not only personal concerns, works that are more philosophical and poetic discourse than lamentation, even if they must acknowledge the catastrophic imagination."

If she is caustic in her disdain for the ahistorical, hypertheorized world of scholarship that emerged in the 1990s, as performance began to be understood as an episteme, a lens through which to consider social process rather than as an art form, it is because she continues to believe in the utopian project of art. Her strongly expressed viewpoint is that performance scholarship is no longer, quite literally, "in touch" with art. But scholarship is always in flux, and there has recently been a move towards recognizing the voice of the artist, and the significance of artists' writings, as she acknowledges in discussing Kristine Stiles's long essay on art in the exhibition catalogue *Out of Actions: Between Performance and the Object, 1949-1979.*

Where I do not agree with her I commend her polemicism, because it proposes engaged, provocative debate of the kind that I fear at times we lack in the United States today. I say "we" once again as that part-time, adoptive, adaptive creature, the writer between the worlds of the U.S. and the UK. When I first began to read American critical writing, poetry, and fiction, in my teens, I found in American letters an openness to inventiveness and innovation that did not distinguish on class terms between the experimental and the conservative, that had no truck with tradition for tradition's sake, that was always progressive and open to what might come next. It is that inventiveness, openness to the new, and clarity of diction that distinguishes the American essay, and which continues to attract and influence me, as a viewer, thinker, and writer myself.

And so we return to Gertrude Stein—whom I did not discover in my teens but wish I had—and to grace. In the topos of Bonnie Marranca's writing, Stein is an originary point, a recurring theme, trope, and moment. I think it is because Stein, like Cage, lived and still lives, in the enormous room of language, spare and abstract and clear, and that she encourages us to write well just by opening the door. If Virginia Woolf opened the door for British women writers in December 1910, then Gertrude Stein flung it wide in the 1920s and 30s and flooded the room with light. In "Hymns of Repetition," her essay about Robert Wilson's staging of Gertrude Stein and Virgil Thompson's 1934 collaborative theatre work *Four Saints in Three Acts,* Marranca refers to Stein's contribution to what she calls the "vernacular marvelous" in American performance-making, and, in this case, avant-garde music-theatre.

She traces a distinctiveness of style from Stein's modernism to the experiments of Cage and Cunningham and to a group of American composers that includes Laurie Anderson, Steve Reich, John Adams, Philip Glass, and Meredith Monk, all whom, she suggests, continue to search for "new colloquial musical languages." She calls this distinctive tradition in which European modernism and American experiment are fused "the American sublime." It is appropriate that she should locate it in musical form because it is, I think, in music and musicality that an American style and sensibility can be seen most clearly, particularly in its relationship to the cadences of speech and the tones of spoken language. And it is in visual music performance that the collaborative, colloquial, rhythmically complex, painterly, and spatial aesthetics that has characterized so much American experimental work becomes transformative. In *Performance Histories* Bonnie Marranca connects her own writing trajectory to this philosophical and poetic tradition, as she explores the topography of performance in its historical context with insight, seriousness, and grace.

July 2007
London and York

Towards a History of Performance Ideas

❒

Performance,
a Personal History

I

After a century of hybridization in the arts, the concept of "performance" has come to the forefront of contemporary thought on art and culture. The word "performance," whether it describes a live event or personal acting-out; the features of a car, a perfume, a sound system; and whether it refers to history or therapy or the act of mourning, now shapes contemporary thinking about people and things. Some of the chief preoccupations of our time—namely, spectatorship, identity, memory, the body—are framed within the terms of performance. Offering a vocabulary of human action that can be used to shape a view of the world and its events, performance is the condition to which American culture increasingly aspires. Who doesn't want to be an American "idol"? Reality TV shows have brought to the culture the national theatre America has always lacked.

The borders delineating art, culture, and commerce, art and entertainment, and experimental art and popular culture, have been blurred for a long time. Likewise, the separation between visual and theatrical arts has become less pronounced. Museum shows on post-war American art have increased the attention given to performance, video, dance, and sound as part of a larger view of visual culture and spectatorship. To give some performance history perspective, works by Yvonne Rainer, Robert Wilson, Laurie Anderson, Meredith Monk, Joan Jonas, and The Wooster Group are included regularly in museum and gallery shows here and abroad, along with documentation of happenings, Fluxus, performance art, and independent cinema, highlighting their artworld values.

Probably the first group of contemporary American theatre artists whose work demonstrated so openly the commingling of the visual arts, dance, and theatre worlds were Robert Wilson, Richard Foreman, and Mabou Mines, whom I had written about in the late seventies in *The Theatre of Images*. These artists, soon to be joined by The Wooster Group, were shaped equally by the European modernist heritage and the new American arts and pop culture of the post-war period.

3

This theatrical generation had created a theatre that was not based on conventional drama and dialogue. Instead it elaborated the idea that there are many more languages of the performance experience than a text could provide, and that the performing body, space, sound, objects, and images could also be considered as types of language or text. It was understood that the visual image had its own rhetoric. This way of working inspired an interdisciplinary approach that could encompass theatre, music, dance, painting, photography, video, sculpture, and architecture. Thirty years later, it has been absorbed as a basic vocabulary in the new media and new music-theatre—two important new directions in New York performance. In the recent work of such different artists as Cynthia Hopkins, Les Freres Corbusier, and Big Dance Theatre, the impact of Foreman and The Wooster Group was highly visible; the imprint of Wilson's style on opera and theatre in the U.S. and abroad has been evident for some time; and Lee Breuer brought to the *Dollhouse* another exceptional Mabou Mines encounter with a classic.

It would be impossible to measure the impact that two major inspirational figures, John Cage and Merce Cunningham, have had in the last half-century on artists, whether in dance, music, theatre, performance, or video. The powerful Cage/Cunningham model, articulated by Cage in his prolific writings and compositions, is founded on the principle that there are no centers, only multiple perspectives on a field of events, each creating its own "right to space." Music, movement, and design can exist in space as autonomous elements, each with its own vocabulary, even created separately and in isolation from each other. What this vision unfolds is essentially a new ecology for the arts.

Recent commentary on the growing interest in sound art and electronic music, enhanced by new technologies and the availability of world music on the Internet and through distribution by alternative record companies, reflects a certain triumph of Cage's transcultural belief that the whole world "sounds." And Cunningham, who continues to cross new frontiers in the creation of computer-generated dance and dance for video, approaching ninety years of age, proves that to be innovative and cutting-edge does not mean necessarily to be young. You have to be worthy of certain adjectives. The masterful last collaboration in 1994 with his long-time partner, entitled *Ocean*, illumines the paradoxical classic and modernist exchange at the heart of Baudelaire's dream of a modernity worthy of one day taking its place as antiquity. Who cannot imagine the Cunningham dancers spiraling around the cracked shards of a ceramic vase left in the ruins of our civilization would such pieces remain?

The artists who emerged under their tutelage did so in a period of cultural liberalism when, in addition to open-minded audiences and critics willing to educate themselves in new art forms, there was genuine support and encouragement of experimentation in the arts at the national and local levels. In addition, an arts structure devoted to expanding artistic resources, eager funding organizations, and a network of European festivals and commissions welcomed them. Several generations of risk-taking artists generated a high performance energy—stimulating, provoking, and critiquing one another in a vigorous exchange.

What mattered was how an individual experienced a work of art. Emphasis was placed on the perceiving subject, rather than the work as an embodiment of any single, fixed meaning. That is not to say that a work had no meaning, only that it is different for each spectator. Artists valued the play of thought, artistic process; the feeling for real space and real time. Audiences were often turned inward to the private rather than to the social realm. Except in the period when works more overtly protested the Vietnam War, whatever politics existed was framed mainly as a politics of consciousness. Feminism and other emancipatory movements were soon to change all of this. Women have been prominent figures in American performance history from the sixties on, not only in more traditionally women-centered arts such as dance, but in the new democratizing technologies of video as well. They proposed many of the terms of understanding and engagement, eventually influencing the turn from the formalist to the activist, from the impersonal to the autobiographical.

When I began to frequent the avant-garde arts scene in the early seventies, one could still see many Cage/Cunningham events and the Judson dancers who had elaborated a new post-Cunningham dance aesthetic; Philip Glass was giving concerts Sunday afternoons in a Tribeca warehouse, where all of his audience in the world easily fit. The filmmaker/performer Jack Smith, who has been an enduring influence on so many New York artists, showed off his strange brilliance in polymorphously sexual films and highly personal and eccentric slide shows and plays. In the new center of the arts downtown—the Manhattan district known as SoHo—Trisha Brown's company was dancing on the rooftops of its landmark buildings and George Maciunas gave Fluxtours on the main thoroughfare, West Broadway. I even participated in one of them in 1976, reading Virgil's Book IV of the *Aeneid* in front of a prestigious gallery building, 420 West Broadway. Meredith Monk offered performances in her loft. The kind of work characterized as "theatre of the ridiculous"—by John

Vaccaro, Kenneth Bernard, Ronald Tavel, Charles Ludlam—cleverly exposed the dark side of the American psyche and its infatuation with images, celebrity, and the language of "ready-mades," aligning itself with the new glam-rock club scene. Reza Abdoh carried on their legacy before his untimely death.

In the visual arts world, the new forms, called "performance art" and "video art," were attracting crowds in the galleries and alternative spaces, with works of Vito Acconci, Carolee Schneemann, Mary Lucier, the Kipper Kids, Michael Smith, Robert Ashley, Adrian Piper, Charles Atlas, Robert Whitman, and many more too numerous to mention. Everywhere, young dancers were starting up companies. Cross-overs of art, music, video, and performance packed the local clubs and bars. Artists and audiences weren't afraid to define themselves as "avant-garde" because to do so signified an experimental mentality and an attitude of opposition to mainstream culture. But, it was already possible to see that elements of this work linked up with mass culture, especially in a social climate where the worlds of art, business, and politics were becoming increasingly intertwined.

The influence, not only of electronic media, but also of dance, independent film, conceptual art, process art, body art, minimalism, and earthworks was exuberantly present in the "downtown" Manhattan centers, particularly in SoHo and the East Village and elsewhere below Fourteenth Street. This performance activity generated a dialogue with modern art and theatre movements. And while artists wanted to create an "American" art distinct from the European, in the post-war period the performance world of the visual arts was characterized by a great feeling of internationalism. American, European, and Japanese artists, working together, organized worldwide festivals, performances, and conferences focusing on censorship and the politics of liberation, several events taking place in London. In the U.S. and in Europe curators continue to organize expansive histories of performance and visual art, particularly happenings and Fluxus, more frequently incorporating the work of artists of the West, Asia, and Latin America. This globalizing project is long overdue.

As early as the mid-sixties artists had begun to collaborate with scientists and engineers, led by Billy Klüver, in the fusion of art and technology, introducing the discoveries from their experiments in special programs and festivals, such as Nine Evenings: Theatre and Engineering, in 1966, and EAT (Experiments in Art and Technology) the following year, which involved influential artists of the era, such as John Cage, Robert Rauschenberg, James Tenney, Deborah Hay, David Tudor, and Lucinda Childs, though often in experiments that proved disastrous. Where once these patterns of work and organization were identified with avant-garde culture, now they have become part of the mainstream, as the products and interchanges of the entertainment and communications industries demonstrate. Recently, The Builders Association used the Dynovision software created by IBM for *Alladeen* and collaborated with dbox for *Super Vision*. A new program known as Face-to-Face animates one of Ralph Lemon's drawings in *Come home Charley Patton*.

Long before them an example of this transmutation is the career of the acknowledged father of video, Nam June Paik. In the sixties he created the technology for a culture that would give itself over to speed and the globalization of imagery. He more than anyone is responsible for the now-familiar walls of multiple-channel videos with their split-screen rapid sampling of world images and sounds. This border-crossing, high-tech model, drawn from the progressive wing of the arts and organized around performance ideas, has brought us closer to an understanding of contemporary culture and society. It moves toward the kinds of knowledge our globalized Internet consciousness is demanding that we embrace.

What a surprise I had some years ago when I thought I heard a section from Meredith Monk's work *Recent Ruins* underscore a stock market commercial on Sunday morning television. In fact, it *was* her music. And who cannot fail to hear as well the influence of Philip Glass in so much of the music we hear all around us, on television and in film, including the recent *Notes on a Scandal*. More than three decades ago, Glass had to start his own record company because no one would record him. He had to put together his own ensemble because no musicians would play his work. He was back to driving a New York City taxicab the day after the landmark opera *Einstein on the Beach*, which he created with Robert Wilson, closed at the Metropolitan Opera, that November of 1976. Now his sound is simply the sound of our time.

What we have been witnessing is the gradual transformation of the media and popular culture, which has absorbed non-traditional artists and their ideas into the entertainment business, television, advertising, and film. Likewise, entertainment has long begun to take the place of art, confusing the terms of audience engagement. If previously the downtown arts community functioned as a subculture, opposed to the exigencies of the marketplace and populist demands, and reveling in its own intellectual rigor, advanced forms, and vocabularies, by now many of the terms of contention have become irrelevant for younger generations. In the last two decades especially, many artists and audiences have turned toward more activist goals; and, at the opposite pole, "accessible" became the keyword. For quite some time distinctions between a great deal of performance art, solo performance, and stand-up comedy have not been so clearly drawn. In fact, solo performers such as Spalding Gray, Eric Bogosian, and Sandra Bernhard—who eventually made Hollywood movies—came out of the alternative arts scene. Much of what now passes for new work is influenced by television comedy.

No "downtown" artist had achieved what Laurie Anderson did, by mid-career moving into mainstream culture, to bring performance art values to the rock music world. Not long ago she became NASA's first "resident artist." At the same time, in deference to the interplay of artistic vocabulary and cultural politics, "performance art" came to be called "performance" and "video art" was designated "video." By the eighties, the mention of "art" in the description of these forms had made them seem, well, too arty when, in fact, they were now redefined in more culturally activist terms and goals.

Of course, throughout the twentieth century artists themselves have worked to undermine the notion of "Art," long before contemporary theories appeared on the scene to shift it to the periphery. But many artists and critics now express regret at the disregard of artistic values and historical lapses in discussions of art, in addition to the confusion of history and nostalgia on the part of younger generations, particularly as the narratives of this period are starting to take shape and aging artists are concerned with their legacies. It seems we are not quite ready to "un-art" ourselves so completely as Allan Kaprow had proposed.

Notwithstanding, the increased cross-overs and the dividing lines between high and low culture, tradition and experimentation, and avant-garde and mainstream, can be highly troublesome for unprepared audiences and institutions. One of the striking characteristics of the American scene of recent decades is the naïveté of non-traditional artists and institutions, and their lack of a coherent cultural policy, in the struggle of the so-called "culture wars." Vanguard culture cannot pass as mainstream at the national level, especially when public monies are involved, and the subject matter is sex or religion. The confrontation of public opinion, government policy, and artistic imperative over the highly-charged sexual content in the work of Karen Finley and Robert Mapplethorpe, and Andres Serrano's Catholic blasphemies, proved to be a public relations and funding disaster for the arts in an era characterized by political conservatism, pietism, feminist backlash, the infantilization of culture, and the AIDS crisis.

By the end of the century, it had lead to the near dismantling of the National Endowment for the Arts, which has been, to all intents and purposes, vastly disabled. The use of public monies in relation to community standards was played out in the courts. The result of the widespread politicization of American art (from both the left and the right) led to an impoverished arts ecology whose most pronounced features can only have been the demoralization of artists and fragmentation of audiences, the compromise of artistic and funding institutions, and unrelenting distortion and promotional hype, all of which proved unsettling. The persistent conservative attacks on the Public Broadcasting Service is an enduring legacy of this state of affairs.

II

Though there are artists involved in the permanent emancipatory desires of art, given the turn in our time toward the scar, the wound, trauma, and even masochism, we are compelled to address the uneasy questions raised by more disturbing sexual, psychological, and social actions. When does a performance become unwatchable? What will we refuse to look at?

One of the most heartrending events in New York in recent years was the gallery show of photographs of lynchings in the South and Midwest which occurred in the first half of the twentieth century. Not only do they depict the deaths themselves, but the huge crowds who watched what were called "spectacle lynchings" and later bought postcards of the events to send home or to keep as souvenirs. Decades removed from our own time and accusations of exploitation, the photographs function as both political history and the history of cultural spectacle. Surely, these audiences of all-too-ordinary citizens must be some of the most debased of modern times.

In a seemingly merciful though quite disturbing live context, a few years ago Dutch television featured an assisted suicide in its evening programming. The California performance artist, Bob Flanagan, before his death, had his slow, painful deterioration from cystic fibrosis documented in a film called *Sick*. He also spent several weeks in bed in a hospital room which he created for his performance and installation at a few museums around the country. An account of Flanagan's difficult everyday life has been published in his *Pain Journal*.

Several years ago, in a controversial 1994 essay widely criticized, *New Yorker* dance critic, Arlene Croce, attacked the ethics of dancer Bill T. Jones's new work, entitled *Still/Here*. It had been created with the participation mainly of terminally ill individuals who appeared on video in the work. Explaining why she refused to see a performance of what she termed "victim art," Croce wrote:

> I understand that there is dancing going on during the talking, but of course no one goes to *Still/Here* for the dancing. People are asking whether Jones's type of theatre is not a new art form. Dying an art form? ... Jones is putting himself beyond the reach of criticism. I think of him as literally undiscussable.

Before you think the issues are clear-cut, here is another way to look at the conjugation of performance and illness. A dozen years ago the Ronald Feldman Gallery in New York displayed large photographs taken by the visual artist Hannah Wilke, with the help of her husband, documenting her own terminal cancer (lymphoma). She had died the year before. Photos were shown of the feminist artist and performer, known for her beauty, now bald, and striking seductive fashion poses which she had parodied more than a dozen years earlier. Others exposed her body ravaged by chemotherapy, a few strands of hair substituting for a once dark, rebellious mane. Still more showed her with a blue blanket framing her sad face, like a Madonna in a Renaissance painting. In an ironic modern context, her Duchamp-inspired cages of medicine bottles were featured and her sculptures of female genitalia installed on the gallery floor. The name of the gallery exhibition, if one can call it that, was marked by Wilke's signature word play: it was titled *Intra-Venus*.

In my view, her last work did not seem at all exploitative because Wilke was a celebrated artist who in the seventies worked in forms known as "body art" and "conceptual art." She had used her body, in glamorous and teasing come-ons, to comment on the use of the female body in fashion, film, and visual art. Well-versed in the styles of modern and post-war art, she appropriated them in her feminist discourse with art history. Wilke photographed herself in provocative quasi-narrative cinematic frames, predating similar strategies by younger artists like Cindy Sherman and Valie Export, and she created video works of "female" gestures using her own face and hands and sculptured body parts. She covered herself with tiny "found" objects in the *Starification* series, which alluded to the marking of the female body by social codes. Like a number of women of her generation, the artist established rights for the freedom of the body in performance at a time when private and public realms were more rigidly observed.

Wilke's art confronted issues of cultural writing on the body and its commodification. Savvy and wise-cracking, throughout her career she defied common attitudes surrounding performance and sexuality and woman as icon. Seen against this artistic past, then, as a form of documentation her last photographs exhibit a sublime will to truth. They are the ultimate expression of her body art. Wilke was fully experiencing her death as an artist, just as she had been fully present in its most life-affirming artistic moments. In the end, she had the courage to follow the assumptions of her aesthetic to their absolute end, bringing body art as close as it can come to the tragic mode.

This is an approach to art that I have referred to in other contexts as "autobiology." I had first used the term to describe the work of the Los Angeles-based artist Rachel Rosenthal, who linked the aging of the Earth and the aging of her own body in eco-performances centering on Gaia theory, plate tectonics, environmental pollution, and nuclear war. Feminist performers have been at the forefront of addressing the taboo of the aging performing body, in Wilke's case even documenting her own corporeal deterioration and death.

At the end of 2005, another performance artist who ignores the boundaries of life and art, Linda Montano, witnessed the death of her father whose chief caregiver she had become after his stroke a few years earlier. The ritualistic unfolding of this entire process—perhaps performance art's contribution to the probing family dramas of psychological realism—she called "Dad Art."

To be honest, performance has gone to places I never could have imagined when I started seriously thinking about it as a graduate student, and just before the founding of *PAJ*, in 1976. We have come so far from distinguishing between art and life, the personal and political. And yet, the performing body is real and it is really there. What we have been witnessing in the arts in recent years is, I believe, a return to authenticity—to the real, the documentary. In drama, there is a new stripped-down realism of which the playwright Richard Maxwell is the chief exponent, and in visual art, a return to the hand, to drawing, alongside the new technologies and monumentalism. This development comes after years of so-called "postmodern" irony, which is too self-indulgent and alienated an attitude for the world we now inhabit. Certainly one of the most pronounced directions of contemporary drama is the use of Greek tragedy as a source, exemplified in such recent diverse works as Peter Sellars's *Children of Herakles*, John Jesurun's *Philoktetes*, Charles L. Mee's rewriting of several Greek plays, and the video/performance of Joan Jonas, *Lines in the Sand*, which took as its starting point the myth of Helen of Troy, based on H.D.'s work. Perhaps it was Heiner Müller who had led the way toward rethinking contemporary history backwards through the classics with his fierce visions drawn from Euripides and Seneca. Pasolini worked in the same political terrain.

But even as the heat of life and death matters compels our attention, makes us slow down, simultaneously the constant sensory overload hurtles us with tremendous speed in another direction, like Benjamin's angel caught in time. Everywhere, the privatization of experience challenges the temptation to make everything public. In a world that has become performance space, and where image and reality, spectators and actors cross realms freely, what makes one experience, artistic or otherwise, more important than another? And can we still understand the differences between states of being?

Contemporary American audiences take for granted the cross-fertilization of dance, theatre, visual art, music, and pop culture; the self-assured use of imagery, technology, mediated voices; multiple identities, cross-dressing/cross-gendering. They feel at home with the confluence of American/African/Asian/Latin sounds and styles. The proliferation of tastes defines the new fusion cuisine in cities as well. Now at the start of a new century, this non-traditional, and largely artistic, model serves as a point of departure for new ways of understanding and interacting in the world: intertextual, intercultural, intermedial.

III

The performance culture that is America transforms everything into some form of actor-spectacle equation. Can one differentiate any longer between an installation, a theatre set, a window display or interior design? In SoHo, my Manhattan neighborhood, the fluidity of spaces is borne out in designer clothing boutiques, with their minimalist sculptured lines and flat-screen attractions, and the big glass windows of its restaurants, where those dining are simultaneously looking out and being looked at, in a new kind of interface. On the street I've noticed that everyone's gestures seem so much bigger these days, their responses to ordinary events so highly exaggerated, as if they know they are being watched. Probably some of them are wearing copies of the clothes of television characters, now available for sale online as a form of "shopping-enabled entertainment." Even all the gallery- and museum-going these days seems a kind of performance social. One of the most fascinating developments in the triumph of the urban sensibility is—let's call it the "performance marvelous."

By that I mean the celebration of the individual as a staging ground of multiple decentered parts, as repository of excess feeling, the self as a work-in-progress. This is what is understood to be "contemporary."

If at emotionally-heightened moments people used to describe their lives as being like a film, now the same situation is framed within the context of performing. The difference is this: in the film metaphor, a person described him or herself as a "character," that is, someone part of a larger narrative, whereas in the performance scenario, one sees oneself as a "celebrity" of sorts; here there is no narrative context, only a repertoire of morphing positions, playing around. A significant development in the entertainment and communications industries is to blur the distinctions between performers and spectators, artists and celebrities, in the new democracy of spectacle. Strangely enough, the many reality TV shows centered around dancing, succeeding in business, building a house, getting rich, and finding a partner demonstrate that people don't even care if they perform badly, lose, or are humiliated on national television by a panel of "judges." In the performance marvelous, the idea is to be noticed, applauded, rewarded for effort. If once all the arts aspired to music, today longing is directed toward the state of performance. As an essential point of reference, performance contributes increasingly to the analysis of culture, and, at the individual level, redefines itself as a medium of self-empowerment and vainglory.

How is one to sort out the various meanings generated by the concept of "performance"? Neither public nor academic discourse differentiates with any degree of refinement between performance as an ontology and performance as gestural attitude, or performance in social space and performance on the stage. The word "performance," then, is used interchangeably to describe actors playing characters or those doing performance art. It is also called upon to characterize everyday human behavior, ritual, or social interaction. In something of a historical paradox, the often-scorned actor is now the symbolic figure of liberation. Today vast numbers of people want to document personal thoughts and acts for the purpose of disseminating information, images, and texts about themselves on the Internet, which is becoming a chief means of building what is called a "community," when it is actually an undifferentiated "mass."

The great freedom everyone can agree upon in America is the freedom to make yourself up, to be self-made. As an act of self-creation, of possible transformation and imagination, role-playing and constructing oneself as a character has the power to turn anyone into a work of art. On a subliminal level, ordinary people understand that the artist is the last free person in contemporary society.

Intriguingly, the cultural turn that joins the aesthetic realm to the public realm has made representation into a rights issue: every performing body is now a legislative body. In this sense, performance can be viewed as a form of speech. This merging of bourgeois mentality with the protean yearnings of the artist links modernity and its worship of subjectivity to the mass cultural values of democratic pluralism. The idea of performance has become so much a part of contemporary discourse that modernity and theatricality now seem indivisible as organizing themes of the last one-hundred years.

Performance acts allow one to create any number of new images of one-self—in effect, to rewrite one's life and to reshape reality at will. But looked at from another perspective, the individual who is unable to break through to an inner self is fated to recast him- or herself in the image of what is socially or peer-sanctioned behavior and opinion. Roles, performances, the image, the mask, the mistaking of the celebrity for the artist—these are large themes to grapple with. Some of them have been with us for hundreds of years. The idea of the *theatrum mundi* has been expanded to incomprehensible proportions. There is much to be learned from the problematic and profound nature of performance, especially its philosophical implications. The freedom, even euphoria, of self-willed performance acts may be inherent in democracy, but it has led to the cultivation of fascism as well. Twentieth-century history has shown that societies are drawn to theatrical expression at moments of profound identity crisis and myth-making. What we need is more careful thinking about categories of spectatorship and performance, not their uncritical celebration. Where is all of this acting-out behavior leading us?

If it is important to understand the differences between the performing self in daily life and the life of a performer in the theatre, to that task must be added the performer on the Internet, in the era of MySpace and YouTube. What does "live" mean any longer, in relation to the physical body of the performer, instant feedback, telepresence, and forms of mediated presence? And how should we consider the performing body in comparison to the body on a video monitor, or the no-body of a virtual performer? What are the differences between digital reality and theatrical reality, the varying conditions of the real, the performative, the virtual? What defines representation, reproduction, or re-enactment? And what of the varieties of time—real and not-as-real—in the intermingling of the ontological, the social, and the digital? We are now asked to consider our lives as "post-human." There is even the possibility of a Second Life which offers unimaginable license for new narratives. Or LiveJournal where anyone's life can become an open book for the Internet "community." Or Flickr, where you can show your photos to the world in an ongoing documentation of your life. How ironic that in our age dramatic form has lost its stature as a reflection of the human drama, even as today there is such craving for stories—preferably someone else's. And what of the "friends" online who take the place of real friendship in the actual community where one lives and works or goes to school? Where are the theatre writers who can describe how human beings exist in the world today? Where are the new species of criticism that can analyze the levels of reality experienced in contemporary life, and how they may shape our common acts of seeing and listening?

In recent years, the digital arts have been proliferating in media lounges and media evenings created in galleries and universities, helping to introduce the public to the latest developments in computer systems, digital artworks, and projects. Likewise, they take place in major museums where installations, Net art, photography, and video are increasingly impinging on the exhibition space of painting. But the idea of the digital has been generating more excitement than much of the actual work itself. There are those who ask if a lot of the digital art isn't to some degree the redoing of familiar ideas in a new technology.

Even still, much of the discourse around forms of media reveals a direct link backwards to familiar themes from the histories and practices of modernism and the avant-garde, whether on the subject of utopia, the role of the state, or language experiments and hypertext. The renewed interest in sound, suggested by examples of sound art and installations lately in museums and galleries, has demonstrated the enduring legacy and prophetic nature of the Cagean world-view. Indeed, his early proclamation of "distribution" supplanting ownership, when joined to the "library of sounds" at the center of his artistic practice, encapsulates a vision that helps to define the new varieties of perceptual experience and artistic creativity. The audience is regarded as a collective intelligence.

We have yet to see how the world of theatre may be infused by digital media. In the future, how will what I call "mediaturgy" define the new performance? If a decade ago there were relatively few theatre artists exploring these forms in live performance, the move toward media is now one of the most evident trends in theatre downtown, though much of it replicates mass entertainment styles, rather than creating a new conception of performance. The Wooster Group continues to explore performance style as a rhetorical form, demonstrated in their latest work, *Hamlet*. The Builders Association, a theatre generation or so later, had a virtual character share the scene with live actors, teasing the idea of liveness in their recent *Super Vision*. For quite some time, developing technologies have influenced the making of dance for live and virtual performance, using motion-capture, animation, and other imaging techniques, as in the work of Paul Kaiser, Marc Downie, and Shelley Eshkar, with Merce Cunningham, Bill T. Jones, and Trisha Brown. As for film, the public has yet to understand the growing impact of digital film editing and the movie-going experience, which is changing the very texture of viewing.

Sometimes it seems as though our reliance on the realms of knowledge, consciousness, and memory has given way to information systems and emergent realities, and self-expression to interface. The concepts of live, real, and virtual have changed the way we relate to time, which, like space and the text, has collapsed in the digital world. Many of the subjects addressed by artists and by the popular press have special significance for performance as a paradigm of contemporary human interaction.

The digital culture is so new that we are still at a point of raising questions about what is called "interactive" or "performative" in the current vocabularies. Numerous myths about interactivity abound. What will the future of art be? For many, there is also the question of facing the prospect of learning new tools and languages of communication in the move away from literary culture, and its assumptions, to visual culture. Critics are persuaded to re-educate themselves in the developing forms of artistic expression and to evolve new criteria in response to new works. This is a daunting task in any age, even more so in the demands of turning from the real to the virtual and to unforeseeable modes of perception.

How does one distinguish between the territory of art as an expressive medium and interface as art? What of the erasure of professional fault lines between artists, scientists, and technicians, and between art and science? Many artists cannot realize their visions without working with scientists or engineers. The digital arts are so new that there isn't any established critical discourse or terms of engagement. We're all feeling our way in this undefined territory: What am I seeing? What am I hearing? How does it differ from older modes of feeling?

Still very much a new field of serious study, performance thinking lacks a coherent history that is capable of synthesizing a century of theatre and visual arts achievement, and the new mass media and communications industry, into a larger philosophical whole. No history of visual art performance can ever be complete without incorporating the knowledge of theatre history and criticism, shaped by hundreds of years of intellectual scrutiny and debate. And, by the same token, theatre ought to be more conversant with art history, especially the performance dimension of installations, video and digital art, and photography. As performance is increasingly integrated into museum shows constructing the histories of arts activity of the last several decades, it is time that the two different histories of performance that now exist—one in the artworld and the other in the theatre—are brought together for an integrated approach to research. Surely, in the years to come there will develop a more comprehensive view of performance history, so that in time the concept of performance can take its place in the history of ideas.

IV

I had the occasion in recent years to collect the interviews and dialogues with American performers, playwrights, composers, video artists, and critics from more than two decades of *Performing Arts Journal*, which is now in its thirtieth year, for publication in a book entitled *Conversations on Art and Performance*. Many of the topics of these contributions anticipated contemporary thought in ways that now seem prophetic. Even subjects that once were the provenance of art, have lately come to the forefront of American social thought and cultural policy. What surprised me was that in so many of these conversations the artists and thinkers referred to as touchstones of ideas and ideals are repeated over and over. In theatre—Ibsen, Strindberg, Chekhov, Stanislavsky, Pirandello, Stein, Brecht, Beckett, Artaud, Genet, Grotowski, Brook, Williams, Shepard; in visual art—expressionism, surrealism, Duchamp, Picasso, Pollock; in music—Mozart, Wagner, Stravinsky, Weill, Boulez, Cage; in dance—Balanchine, Graham, Cunningham, Judson Dance Theatre; in philosophy—Marx, Freud, Wittgenstein, Foucault; in letters—Thoreau, Rousseau, Yeats, Pound, Eliot, Barthes. And always, the Greeks and Shakespeare.

In any given period serving as a context for discussion, a marked consensus flows around what is important to speak of, and why. Remarkably, and for the most part, traditionalists and avant-gardists, I learned, claim the same artistic heritage. What is also apparent is how much artists learn from each other and how essential aesthetic values and their own work processes are to them. In every sense, the historical continuum their chosen art form inhabits still retains its significance. If the Western canon has been under assault in the university and in arts institutions, the artists themselves unashamedly declare allegiance to surprisingly stable canons.

And, for all the theoretical issues circulating around us, artists and intellectuals, inspired by their constant exposure to art, are largely oblivious to it, educating themselves, as always, in artworks. What is the nature of the performance act? Where does language reside? Performers are still struggling to understand the ecstasy of presence, writers want desperately to live inside words, and everyone is concerned with the varieties of time and space.

What is it that they speak of? In the early years of *PAJ* major preoccupations were consciousness and process, the potentiality of performance space, research and experimentation, the divorce of literary and theatrical culture, and the alienation of theatre from intellectual life. There was talk of the decline of playwriting and the stultification of regional theatres, discomfort with the notion of the "theatrical" in art and theatre worlds, and excitement at the appearance of performance art. There were plenty of inquiries: What is performance space? How does one see? Why is acting not the same as performing?

Over the years the conversations turned from space to text and play to fragment, from the modernist heritage to postmodernism, from group to solo, from art forms to arts funding, from the situation of the object to subject positions, from process to pedagogy, from art to culture, from play to pain. Power, representation, transgression, violence, ritual, gender, race, autobiography, censorship, and the critiques of representation, the image, and the canon were now the subjects that filled new dictionaries of ideas.

At the center of thought: the palpable body, the mediated voice. When is a man a woman? When is the body a text? The emphasis shifted from experience to interpretation, from art to theory, from the impersonal to the political, from high culture to pop, from invention to anger, from joy to trauma. Increasingly, performance space came to be regarded as public space and the individual as social construct. Artists were called "cultural workers" or "activists" and critics considered their writing "performing." The body, once celebrated as the site of pleasure and freedom, was now analyzed as a repository of disease, pain, death, and contested being. These are powerful themes, which raise disturbing epistemological questions about the ever-expanding lyric of performance and an aging avant-garde.

The contrast of attitudes in the last three decades was brought home to me when I began teaching contemporary performance and observed the difficulty students demonstrated in understanding the use of the nude body, even the innocent fun and sexual exuberance, that characterizes much performance of the sixties. More interesting is the case of the pioneering feminist performer

Carolee Schneemann. Contemporary attitudes toward female nudity and heterosexuality have often found themselves at odds with her work because of her sexual politics. Students were sometimes embarrassed at the nudity and ecstatic heterosexuality. Some of them determined that Schneemann was being used as a "sexual object," whereas she valued herself as an "image-maker," an artist in control of her own body as subject. In fact, much of her early work had less to do with feminist concerns than with her highly-developed art-historical knowledge and work as a painter. In the context of her time, Schneemann considered her gestures as liberating acts.

One of the most significant changes that occurred between the mid-seventies era in which I began the work of *PAJ* and my own writing, and the climate of today, is the displacement of critical activity from its organic development out of the experience of art to its institutionalization in academia. Similarly, the lack of interest on the part of many trained in theatre to concern themselves with drama is a great loss to the profession. And the use of theatrical or performance events themselves as a springboard for overarching theories or cultural commentaries has led often to distortions of performance history as well as diminished critical thought. In fact, this trend has produced two theatre cultures. Even though we have all learned a great deal from the new scholarship, certainly many students, artists, and closeted faculty dissidents are tired of the hyperactive theorization and lumpy prose. It is propped up by an outdated view of the publishing industry and marketplace which can no longer support the demands of university degree programs and a faculty promotion system based on academic publication ideals now increasingly forced into trade publication exigencies.

I would like to see graduate programs train more students as archivists and translators as a response to the proliferation of personal historical materials that so many artists and theatres own (especially in view of the influence of the post-war avant-garde), and to counter the scant interest in works in translation by publishers. What is also needed is the kind of books theatre critics and scholars used to write before the turn to theoretical dissertations: namely, histories of theatres and institutions and studies of writers or groups. It is difficult to believe but there is no history of La MaMa or of the Judson Poets' Theatre or The Ontological-Hysteric Theater or any substantial studies of Off-Off Broadway; nor are there any experimental theatre or performance art histories that equal the depth of the traditional theatre history books (however much they are scrutinized now), hardly any biographies of artists outside the mainstream, or monographs of serious authors. With few exceptions, such as the new history of Caffe Cino, they are out of favor, like writing about plays. The absence of such theatre literature is a tremendous loss for the profession that only grows more apparent with the teaching of contemporary performance and drama.

V

I wonder if there exists any longer the freedom to value and to write about a work of art for its own qualities—for the sheer pleasure of it. Even as art is overwhelmed by social realities, critics and artists are beginning to speak more about their spiritual practices, too. Many American artists follow a Buddhist path. Given the spiritual dimension of modernism and the artistic traditions of the ancient, medieval, and Renaissance worlds, we are overdue for a progressive discussion of religion and art to counter the extremes of reactionary cultural views that have generated so much controversy over artworks. Yet, this is a difficult subject for many because there is no sufficiently developed vocabulary of the spiritual in the commentary on contemporary arts. Our more political era has turned away from ideas of "transcendence" and "sincerity" which attach themselves to any discussion of religious and spiritual matters. People are uncomfortable with the idea of religion itself and prefer to speak about spirituality. Understandably, there are the New Age connotations of which many are skeptical. Nevertheless, we cannot ignore so many artists across generations, art forms, and religions who treat spiritual feeling in their work, such as Bill Viola, Meredith Monk, Lee Breuer, Shirin Neshat, Bill T. Jones, Theodora Skipitares, Alison Knowles.

Contemporary music had moved in the direction of creating spiritually expressive composition more than three decades ago. Whether in search of the sublime or in reaction to serial music, many composers working today in the Western tradition (often under the influence of Eastern art or philosophy) have turned toward new forms of sacred music. Among them are Henryk Gorecki, Osvaldo Golijov, Arvo Pärt, Sofia Gubaidulina, Steve Reich, Philip Glass, Wynton Marsalis, John Zorn, John Adams. Similarly, theatre directors such as Peter Sellars and Robert Wilson have staged chamber operas around the lives of saints.

In the world of drama as well, many playwrights, including Maria Irene Fornes, Erik Ehn, Adrienne Kennedy, Tony Kushner, and The Wooster Group have shown an interest in religious subject matter and iconography. Many of their plays are rich in figures of God, Jesus, saints, and angels, and in scenes of heaven and hell. Instead of the sermonizing of much contemporary American drama, liturgical and scriptural styles of speech and prayer, biblical and saints' writings, characterize these plays, which tend toward allegory, epic, and parable. A decade ago I gathered together some of them in an anthology entitled *Plays for the End of the Century*, with the specific intent of calling attention to this largely unacknowledged contemporary tendency.

Even as contemporary life is lived more and more publicly, and with a diminished sense of the private, individuals have also turned inward. Perhaps the dramatic form, which lags behind in its rhythms and has so much competition with increasingly spectacle-oriented experience, can reinvent itself as an exceptional cultural space. Here one might find subtleties of human acts and concentrated speaking and listening, or the long sentences of complex thought, now disappearing from the public realm. Intertwining the moral and the aesthetic, the plays of Wallace Shawn elaborate the collapse of serious-minded culture with such inflections.

Though anonymous "characters" interface on the Internet in transcontinental messaging, the drama is, still, an alternative to the chatrooms of cyberspace. Drama has to do with knowledge, not information; it is built on dialogue, not chatter. Theatre, derived from the Greek word "theatron"—also the root of "theory"—is a place for seeing, in the sense of illumination, enlightenment. (To browse is not to see.) I must admit to being very skeptical of what is called "interactive" or "performative" in this digital age. The performance vocabulary is extended into more and more concepts, like "liveness" and "live presence" and "mediated presence." Borders between sectors of human enterprise and habitation are increasingly blurring, posing a great challenge in understanding the differences between varieties of perceptual experience. The new narratives of language and image and media are scattering about the globe in a rhizomatic frenzy. Too many of them are merely duplicating the shallow values of consumer culture.

Often overlooked in the contemporary culture of speed and noise and exhibition is the role of art as a spiritual discipline, a force of inner necessity that compels the artist to search for truths founded in emotional need. There is a fundamental duality of purpose and expectation in the public perception of art. Viewers are less willing to settle for the contemplative experience and would prefer to consider the artist as an organizer of social reality. But even as they engage in the symbolization of experience, artists are also interested in such matters as solitude, stillness, process, and that place known only to them which Allan Kaprow called a "beautiful privacy," even as they engage in the symbolization of experience. Some acts are a matter of contingency, intuition, and technical problem-solving. And let's not forget the sheer attachment of artists to the object and materiality of their creations. What can this work be? How shall I make it? Where will it take me? The idea of self-alteration through the creation of artworks still continues to influence new generations of artists. So does Gertrude Stein's idea of the play as landscape, which is to say, space as a bountiful field of revelation—a world of spirit. "How a little nature makes religion, how a little religion makes creation," she observed.

These may sound like simple themes, but they are bound to the profound quest that moves the will towards genuine artistic life. What cannot be overstated is the very real conflict between the desire of artists to make work that reflects their attachment to the world, even to making visionary works, at the same time that many of them have abandoned the moral imperative of previous art practice. In our time, aesthetic, formal, religious, social, and moral values are fiercely undermined. What do we value in art any longer? For some, the answer is to consider all life as art, while others speak of the end of art. Which is it that we want more of: life or art? And are the real and virtual simply different names for the same longing?

One of the issues that concerns me now is whether contemporary theatre is becoming too preoccupied with replicating the global crises of society. In other words, has it become too journalistic—simply compassionate and mournful? At the other end of the spectrum is the new theatre of the uncanny, with its fetishization of trauma, pain, and violence that plays out personal demons and biological necessity, not only in solo performance but in the new dramatic literature unfolding. What is needed now are works of the creative spirit that conceptualize not merely document human behavior, works that address public not only personal concerns, works that are more philosophical and poetic discourse than lamentation, even if they must acknowledge the catastrophic imagination.

A performance leaves behind only traces of itself—a photograph, a piece of videotape, fleeting images coursing through the spectator's mind. How little they reveal of time, of images and acts; and what of the voice, the face, the arm. How to comprehend the sense of why and when the art of performance is important in the long view of things. What is performance to being and we to it?

When all is said and done, what remains is the mysteriousness and ravishing heartbreak of a form, valued for its ceremony of presence, even as it occasions absence.

This essay represents an ongoing series of reflections that has evolved over a period of several years, originating as a keynote address, entitled "Performance Contemporary," for the International Theatre Studies Congress "Transformations: Theatre in the Nineties," Free University/Humboldt University, Berlin, November 1998, and continuing in a revised version as a keynote address for the conference, "Towards Tomorrow," at the Center for Performance Research, Aberystwyth, Wales, April 2005. Other modified lectures based on the essay were delivered at Princeton University for the Willard and Margaret Thorp Lecture in American Studies, 2000; Justus Liebig University, Giessen (Germany), 1999; the University of Alcala (Spain), 2004; University of Palermo, University of Calabria, University of Rome III (Italy), 2006; University of Exeter, University of Roehampton (UK), and University of Copenhagen (Denmark), 2007. The earliest version was published as "Nachdenken uber Performancegeschichte," in *Transformationen: Theater der Neunziger Jahre*, Erika Fischer-Lichte, Doris Kolesch, Christel Weiler, eds. (Berlin: Theater der Zeit, 1999). The essay was published for the first time in English in *PAJ: A Journal of Performance and Art*'s 30th anniversary issue, Vol. XXVIII, No. 1 (PAJ 82), January 2006. The final version is published here.

Bodies of Action,
Bodies of Thought:
Performance and Its Critics

Throughout the last decade there has been a notable increase in the attention museums, galleries, and alternative spaces have paid to recent avant-garde movements, particularly happenings and Fluxus, and to individual performance works, while the number of books, essays, and catalogues devoted to the field of performance has swelled even more. There appears to be a full-scale, ongoing attempt to legitimize performance and establish its position within art history, the most recent example of which is the exhibition entitled, *Out of Actions: Between Performance and the Object, 1949-1979*, originating in February 1998 at the Museum of Contemporary Art in Los Angeles and traveling to Europe and Japan.

The catalogue for this exhibit is a highly-illustrated (450 photographs, nearly half of them in color) document representing the current state of contemporary criticism and historical perspective on performance, specifically, "action art." In its intent to create an expansive framework for performance, the catalogue outlines the achievements of its scholarship and the perimeters and longing of the field, exemplified by the inclusion of work from the United States, Europe, Japan, and Latin America, even as it reveals the shortcomings of its discourse: namely, the unexamined assertion of the myth of progress and the limited critical sphere that characterize current performance history.

Paul Schimmel, who organized the exhibit (which I did not attend), opens the catalogue with a long and largely familiar narrative of performance, extending from the post-war period through the seventies. In an obvious allusion to Yves Klein, his essay titled "Leap into the Void" covers chiefly the influence of Pollock, Fontana, Cage, and Shimamoto in their celebration of the act over the object of creation, then moves on to Gutai, *Nouveau Realisme, Arte Povera*, happenings, Fluxus, Viennese Actionism, "performative sculpture" of the sixties, and performance in the seventies. Along the way, he dispels some of the myths surrounding Pollock's supposed spontaneity of composition while acknowledging his inspiration for the Japanese Gutai artists, Klein, and others of the fifties and sixties who learned from him the value of creating a self-image for public consumption. Schimmel challenges Allan Kaprow's influential essay, "The Legacy of Jackson Pollock," in which he asserts that the painter's canvases were "environments," as wishful thinking but, more urgently, he acknowledges Kaprow's development of the "performative environment" between installation and performance. He might also have pointed to the impact of Kaprow's think- ing on the "environmental theatre" of Richard Schechner and the work of his company, The Performance Group. It should be noted that among visual art- ists and their critics, performance history is tactically linked to the history of painting and sculpture—art history—rather than interacting with theatre his- tory. Notwithstanding, already in the opening pages of the catalogue Kaprow emerges as one of the most dynamic of performance thinkers, his ideas cours- ing through the work of the last several decades.

It is Schimmel's contention that the post-war era of art situated itself be- tween the dialectics of creation and destruction and that World War II, the Holocaust, and the atomic bomb left an existentialist legacy that made art- ists more aware of the significance of the individual act. But, since Schimmel doesn't demonstrate how these events are communicated in individual works (the Gutai artists, who speak for themselves, excepted), merely declaring their impact, his politics has an obligatory ring. He also overlooks the strength of American artists' allergic reactions to overt social and intellectual agendas, namely the Marxism, Freudianism, and McCarthyism that informed so much thinking before and after the war. This same turn away from politics was the setting for Susan Sontag's famous essay of the period, "Against Interpretation," and other redefining commentary, such as her "One Culture and the New Sen- sibility." It is also difficult to reconcile Schimmel's reading with the extraordi- nary influence at this time of John Cage, whose writings do not carry strong political content or post-war angst. Nor do Kaprow's early essays on happen- ings envisage them in relation to stated social aims. These artists were against the obvious social or ideological statement, and were more concerned with what Cage called "self-alteration."

What artists, including the latter two, had previously referred to in their writ- ings as "theatre" later came to be called by many names, including "activities," "events," "non-matrixed performance," "non-static art," "actions," "live art," "body art," "solo performance," "performance art," "performance." (In this essay, I myself am forced to use a variety of terms in an attempt to capture the specificity of different occasions, though admittedly shades of meaning are not always easy to demarcate. For example, both the theatre world and the artworld share the word, though not always the same concept or history of, "performance.") Under the banner of the Los Angeles exhibit, many kinds of performance now have been termed "action art." Through this same critical transformation, in the last dozen years, any highlighting of the formal qualities of a work has been overshadowed by the insistence on the social aspect as the significant element in artistic activity, and the artist has been converted into a social activist, as it were.

If the "performative" appears in many guises in this catalogue, whose points of reference are abstract expressionism, minimalism, and conceptual art, it is intriguing that Schimmel designates the category of "performative sculpture" for the sixties to write of Robert Morris and Bruce Nauman, noting in passing the effects of new dance, especially the work of the dancer Simone Forti, on sculpture and the development of minimalism. What is curious is that Schimmel doesn't mention Morris's performances with the Judson dancers Yvonne Rainer or Lucinda Childs or his well-documented *Site* with Carolee Schneemann. The relationship of dance (movement) to performance (action) is surely an area of discussion that awaits greater detail. (Rauschenberg's own work in performance, especially with dancers, was highlighted in his 1997–98 Guggenheim Museum retrospective in a series of videotapes and in the show's catalogue, though it has been by and large omitted from general performance histories.)

Schimmel observes in a brief remark that "Morris literalized in sculpture concepts being explored in the Living Theater [sic], which emphasized the positioning of bodies in space." I wish he had explained this linkage more fully because the absence of theatre history input in the commentaries elaborated in this volume impedes the construction of more encompassing perspectives than these art-conscious narratives, however international they are. For example, the Living Theatre work *Mysteries and Smaller Pieces* (1965), directed by Judith Malina under the inspiration of the "Plague" writings of Artaud and designed by the troupe's co-director Julian Beck, also a painter, was precisely a period example of performance as sculpture. (Some of the most notorious Living Theatre activities were viewed in their time as happenings.) And though they were created in the seventies, not the sixties, Schimmel seems not to be aware of the sculptor Scott Burton's series of "behavior tableaux" (1970–76) performed at the Guggenheim, Whitney Museum, and other sites. (More than twenty years ago Robert Pincus-Witten had written about Burton's work in an essay entitled "Conceptual Performance as Sculpture.") Furthermore, it would be worthwhile to compare the imagery and possible influence of Burton's work on Robert Wilson's *I Was Sitting on My Patio This Guy Appeared I Thought I Was Hallucinating* (1977), a play in which he and Lucinda Childs performed a series of sculptural movements within a minimalist setting; the British artist Bruce McLean also created similar work then which brought together highly-formalized gestures and the rhetoric of minimalism.

Though Schimmel explains in his introduction that this exhibition is not a survey of performance *per se*, and that it is not his intention to explore work by dancers, musicians, playwrights, et al., who have influenced and interacted with the visual arts and performance, nevertheless it is a missed opportunity not to have acknowledged theatre works, especially when they might expand upon performance ideas or illumine new directions in research. (At least since the forties New York avant-garde artists in theatre, dance, and the visual arts have worked together and were inspired by each other's ideas.) One of the unfortunate limitations of the criticism in this volume is the seeming exclusivity of the performance/artworld: though there are quotations or references, for the most part, from social and political theory, philosophy, and psychology writings—all essays—there is scarcely a mention by name of any novel, dance, film, play, or piece of poetry or music. Any exchange between art and theatre critics is practically non-existent, though increasingly theatre critics have been writing about many of the same performers. The result is that two bodies of criticism on many of the same artists and themes, separate and often ignorant of each other, now exist. In my view, no history of performance can ever be complete without incorporating the knowledge of theatre history and criticism, shaped by hundreds of years of intellectual scrutiny and debate. It is long past the time for this acknowledgment in the artworld, whose understanding of performance has generally ranged from hostility to indifference, naïveté to good will.

When Schimmel gets to the seventies, his historical framework begins to seem a bit erratic, unlike the more established grounding of the immediate post-war period, and certainly a misplaced zealousness has put more emphasis on California artists (besides Burden, Fox, McCarthy, Fried, Marioni, et al.) than there needs to be while giving short shrift to New York, a major center of performance activity in the era. Of New York artists, now enjoying a great deal of both critical and gallery attention, he focuses almost entirely on Vito Acconci's body art and Gordon Matta-Clark's "performative installation" work and sculptural performance. Inexplicably, Laurie Anderson is not a part of this chapter, nor are the works of the many feminist artists (perhaps because Kristine Stiles handles them in her closing essay), nor is Dennis Oppenheim or Jack Smith. Smith is the most serious absence from the documentation of New York performance obvious in this catalogue, especially when he has been such a seminal figure since the sixties for so many performers, still evident today in the work of Matthew Barney. Of Europeans, the chapter on the seventies focuses on Gina Pane, Orlan, Marina Abramović, and Rebecca Horn. Decidedly, the view of the seventies highlights the prominence of women in performance, though here and elsewhere it is surprising how little attention is given to Hannah Wilke.

Though I take issue with some of his conclusions, emphases, and omissions, Schimmel has done good work in establishing a reasonable agreed-upon chronology and introducing several of the artists and themes that occur throughout the catalogue, treated from different perspectives by critics in Japan, Europe, and Britain, and also the United States. The contributors from abroad naturally provide more detailed information, which is welcome in the context of the volume, offering a greater sense of immediacy and informed opinion of the culture in question than is apparent to any researcher or infrequent spectator. In fact, one of the issues in performance that has gone unremarked is the fact that so many critics, scholars, and students, here and abroad, are now writing about performances they haven't seen, thus risking through their reliance on contemporary theoretical and social tendencies the distortion of the original work in its historical context. If the best intentions of trying to be inclusive have created a self-consciousness about writing on art beyond the borders of the West, this is only exacerbated further by the genuine challenge of understanding the role of objects or bodies in other cultures.

As if to corroborate that condition, in "Body and Place," his discussion of action art in post-war Japan, Shinichiro Osaki contrasts what he sees as the American emphasis on the optical with the Japanese emphasis on the physical and site-specific in the fifties and sixties. His comprehensive view of Japanese art practice, while uncovering for the American reader more historical contours, also links the artists and their concerns across continents. He is emphatic in noting that the early Gutai artists, unlike their later American counterparts who participated in happenings and Fluxus events, made painting central to their work, thus transforming "action" into form. Unfortunately, Osaki gives short shrift to the Butoh work of Tatsumi Hijikata which was so electrifying in the videotapes shown at the 1994 Guggenheim show, *Japanese Art after*

1945: Scream Against the Sky. And, though Gutai, Hi-Red Center, and other artist groups are now well-known, the work of the avant-garde theatre director Shuji Terayama, who shared similar interests, would have made the Japanese view richer. Lastly, Osaki is reticent on the subject of Yayoi Kusama, whose obsessively sexual work is currently being shown in New York at the Museum of Modern Art and in two additional galleries as pioneering feminist art. He seems genuinely uneasy noting her or any other artist's objects of highly sexualized content.

This is certainly not the case with Austrian critic Hubert Klocker who, in "Gesture and Object: Liberation as Aktion," writes about Viennese Actionism with a real attachment to this uncompromising, aggressive work, with all its imagery of blood, sex, torture, and pain. In his view, the actions of Hermann Nitsch, Otto Mühl, Günter Brus, and Rudolf Schwarzkogler are a reaction to fascism and National Socialism, indeed, to the entire European century of war, genocide, and totalitarianism. Commenting not only on the Actionists but on Joseph Beuys, Valie Export, and others, Klocker is up-front about establishing a European performance tradition different from American developments. Thus, he sees Beuys, Nitsch, and the others, who started their actions in the years 1962–63, as inheritors of the European project of surrealism linked to the unconscious, not the transformed surrealism of American abstract expressionism evident in happenings. Mindful of the post-communist openings to other cultures, Klocker also devotes a section of his essay to the important work of integrating post-Stalinist Russian art into his discussion, especially the Moscow Romantic Conceptualists (one of them, Ilya Kabakov, known in the West for some time) and the group called Collective Action.

One of the most laudable aspects of Klocker's European perspective is to bring Artaud into the discussion of action and the body. He achieves this by restating Artaud's desire to unite thought and action, concept and gesture: in other words, true liberation emerges in transcending the work itself. Oddly though, Klocker doesn't give any extended attention to the influence of Catholicism on the Actionists, perhaps because the spiritual does not fit so easily into the scheme of the social. But it would be fascinating to speculate on the connections among Artaud, the Viennese Actionists, and the lives/actions of saints, particularly since the objects of art are throughout this catalogue frequently referred to as "relics." (Artaud's autobiology should be considered alongside of saints' biographies.) Perhaps the significance of photography—the desire for an image-object—for these artists, which Klocker reiterates, is also part of the same theme. Moreover, Catholicism—the entire subject of religion—and the avant-garde is an unexplored area in contemporary art criticism.

Still, Klocker opens up many new themes in his view of Austrian culture and politics, positioning his subject within the conditions of identity explored by such figures as Wittgenstein, Musil, Kraus, Schiele, Kokoschka, and the literary work of the post-war Wiener Gruppe. In light of this wider tracing and Klocker's own interest in the significance of language, he unaccountably neglects to mention the work in the sixties of the Austrian playwright/novelist Peter Handke, whose *Sprechstücke* ("talking pieces") were considered within the context of happenings and provocational social actions. Similarly, the compelling objects of the artist Franz West of whom Klocker writes, called *"passtück"* (translated as "adapter," it is a sculptural object that when worn takes on an animistic, active character), can also be compared to the work of Polish theatre director Tadeusz Kantor who created "bio-objects," part-human, part-sculpture, albeit more historical in reference, for his own productions.

Klocker, not only here but in previously published essays on the Viennese Actionists, celebrates the "performative" as a revolutionary model for the future of society, grounded in social process (the interaction of action and spectator) and work process (the action of the artist), with a particular interest in the relationship of the act of performance and the art object. Having recently seen several photographs and videotapes of the Viennese Actionists' performances on exhibit at the Baron/Boisanté Gallery in New York, I must admit to finding them fixed in the gestural and rhetorical styles of the sixties, and surprisingly innocent, if at times repulsive. Compared to what is considered acceptable performance activity today, this work seems more playfully anarchic—at least as it pertains to the sexual realm—than abject. Of course, it was.

In the sixties the body was defined as a site of pleasure, and sexual expression was regarded as a liberating force, whereas now the body is viewed as an embattled body politic. Klocker, in his eagerness to carry on the gestalt of the sixties through valorizing the permanent emancipatory desires of action art, overstates his case. Three decades later, it is now unavoidable to address the uneasy questions raised by the Actionists' sexual, psychological, and social actions: how much freedom is enough? (Indeed, both Brus and Mühl have been jailed in the past for their sexual transgressions.) The temptation is to view them largely as utopistic expressions of a very special cultural moment we are not likely to see again, and given the current breakdown of civil society in the West, they are perhaps not the kind of models bearable in the mass cultures already signaling the future. Finally, there is a difference between avant-garde culture and mainstream culture, life and art.

Following the general globalizing tendencies in this catalogue, British critic Guy Brett, in "Life Strategies," brings Latin American artists into the perspective of an international performance history, focusing on the work of artists from Brazil, Argentina, and Chile, such as Lygia Clark, Hélio Oiticica, Lygia Pape, Lea Lublin, Victor Grippo, Marta Minujín, and Roberto Evangelista. He makes the provocative though dubious remark that art in Latin America in the sixties, especially Brazil, had similarities to the Soviet avant-garde in the twenties, but never demonstrates how. Indeed, working backwards from Klocker's insertion into performance history of the post-Stalinist conceptualists, the time is now right for an art historian to tie together the recent new research on the Russian avant-garde of poets, painters, filmmakers, and performers who worked together before the dogma of socialist realism sent everyone opposed to it to their death, the camps, or exile. Meyerhold, for one, actually devised a theory of the body in action, which he called "bio-mechanics."

If Brett believes that the body was particularly central to Brazilian work, also affirming the country's "Afro-Euro-Amerindian culture of the body," he never fully explores his declaration vis-à-vis specific performances. In fact, Brett might have mentioned one of the most well-known theatrical performances in Brazil of the sixties, Victor Garcia's much-acclaimed production of Genet's *The Balcony*, one of this century's great plays about power and performance. In his transcontinentally focused essay, Brett writes about artists working in England, both English (such as Gilbert and George, Stuart Brisley) and immigrants (such as David Medalla, Paul Neagu), asserting that it is time to move away from nationalist myths of art and to consider artists' travel and habitation in other cultures as part of their artistic processes.

Brett raises some substantial philosophical issues about the interplay between the presentation of the self as artist and self-representation as an ordinary person; in other words, the difference between acting a role and being oneself. These are Pirandellian themes that have occupied theatre artists, audiences, and critics for the entire century, and it would be worth the effort to consider them in the context of action art and performance *per se*. Ultimately, what is the difference between the spectator's perception in the theatre and in a gallery, which is to say, the difference between watching an art action or, in the Aristotelian sense, a dramatic action? Or between actions and gestures? Do spectators experience performance art differently from theatre?

There are no studies that address this issue which art critics writing about performance are silent on or oblivious to. Yet, in a near obsession with Duchamp's idea about the viewer completing the work of art (hasn't this always been the case in every art form?), which was never meant in any political sense, they exaggerate the relationship between the action of the artist and its meaning for the viewer as a means of transmitted social reality, as if a work had no other meaningfulness. Brett himself, who sees the issues more in theatre terms than his American art colleagues (he mentions Shakespeare's Globe, muses about "acting"), regards the activity of the performance artist in the role of actor as both a "deconstruction" of and an expansion of the role of "protagonist."

From this vantage point then, performance art ought to be considered the Brechtian mode of our time, and the "action" of the performer equivalent to the Brechtian *Gestus* of the actor. But how does Brecht's model differ in performance art and in theatre? Art critics take for granted, here and elsewhere, that art actions are implicit critiques of mainstream or commercialized culture, but they rarely show how this critique evolves in the actions/gestures themselves. If Artaud, one of the heroic models for action art, contributed to the thinking about the erasure of the body/object in the coming together of thought and gesture, Brecht, in recent years reconstituted in feminist criticism for his understanding of the body as a discourse, demonstrated how the action of a body, and each object in the world, can exemplify social critique as a "performative" (to use a word much in evidence in this volume) element.

Looked at from another perspective of the function of the "sign," that of symbolism, besides Brechtian theory, an area of scholarship unexamined by performance/art historians is the conceptualization of the self in the symbolist era. (Perhaps it has something to do with what I perceive as an anti-literary bias in the histories they construct.) In his book *Symbolist Theatre: The Formation of an Avant-Garde*, Frantisek Deak quite convincingly links many of the *fin-de-siècle* tendencies in conceptual performance (of Mallarmé, Sar Péladan, Jarry, and others) to performance art at this end of the century, especially in his analysis of Péladan's theory of "Kaloprosopia," the art of personality. Similarly, studies of European and Russian cabaret in this period and between the two world wars have much to offer in their research of performance modes.

After a century of avant-garde art in which performance as an activity has been central to its dialogue, and when performance as a concept has come to be one of the organizing frames of any understanding of society, not to integrate the research of theatre into that of performance (and visual) art for the creation of a comprehensive, dynamic performance history is to turn one's back on performance knowledge itself. Theatre with its attention to text and image, performance with its time and space concerns; theatre with its ethos of representation and attention to form, and performance with its action and process orientation, are opposite sides of the Janus-faced currency of exchange we call social process.

The hefty *Out of Actions* catalogue closes with a one hundred-page essay, "Uncorrupted Joy," in which Kristine Stiles both sums up the post-war period of art actions and their objects and proclaims them a visionary guide to the future. She is literally all over the map, in a series of titled sections highlighting specific cultural moments, whether choosing artists (American, German, French, Israeli, Romanian, Polish), groups or movements (happenings, Situationists, AKTUAL), events (the Destruction in Art Symposium, Festivals of Free Expression), or themes (art criticism, feminist performance, the split self, ecology, biology, technology). She uses this technique of juxtaposition to elaborate her views on the art action as an intersection of the aesthetic and the social: action art joins performance and political activism in public life.

Her essay, generous in its compelling sense of conviction, takes as its starting point the very subject of the exhibit: the special quality of relations that exist between actions and the objects they bring into being. She uses the term "commissure" to define the way that objects unite the viewer and the originary action, understood in her terms as signs of an artist's commitment to communicate with them. What Stiles is really striving for in her essay is an ethics of performance values.

Stiles's emphasis on the processes of communication among artist, object, and spectator is noteworthy because so much writing on performance has focused on the act or task at hand, not the viewer or the object. She writes, "Action art and action objects teach us to remember the value of the individual subject who creates objects—both in the narrow sense of the artist as producer and in the much larger sense of elevating human subjects over objects—as the highest value." Not only does she reinforce performance art's original goal to escape the commodification of the artworld, and her own belief that it initially grew from the need to assert the primacy of the human subject over the inanimate object, but her approach works to counter Walter Benjamin's much-quoted observations in "The Work of Art in the Age of Mechanical Reproduction."

Stiles writes as if she wants to return the "aura" to the object and exalt the subjectivity of the artist. Over and over again she celebrates the "relics" and "artifactuality" of art actions. (To some extent, I wonder if her view and the general tendency in the catalogue itself aren't symptomatic of the difficulty art critics have in giving up the art object and accepting the essential ephemerality of performance as a form.) In a similar vein, she calls for re-establishing the significance of artists' own writings and biographies, which a decade or more of theory has pushed to the background. At one level, her essay re-establishes the myth of the artist and the privilege of artistic endeavor.

Though her writing reflects the theoretical underpinnings of contemporary criticism and its positions, especially on psychoanalysis, social theory, feminism, and race, Stiles appears much more committed to art and artists than theory. Still, she magnifies the obvious activity of reception in the interchange of art action, object, and viewer; perception has always been important in the experience of theatre, dance, music, and literature. Why should we assume, for example, that a book one reads has less value than a sculptural object in a performance? If visual artists alter the meaning and use of objects (Stiles brings them into consideration largely as elements of material culture) to reimagine the world, don't writers do the same with words?

And, if in Stiles's essay as elsewhere in this volume, Michael Fried's controversial "Art and Objecthood" enters into the discussion for its dismissal of the subject-object process minimal art suggests through its theatricality, which he disparages, Stiles herself doesn't engage the subject of theatre. Theatre as a form has always been preoccupied with communication—the social process—between the action dramatized in performance space and the perception of the viewer in public, cultural space. It seems as if art critics are just beginning to understand the role of the audience in performance. Again, what are the substantive differences between visual reality and theatrical reality, the different conditions of representation and the real, presence and imagination, drama and action?

In fact, Stiles overlooks the opportunity to explore these issues more extensively and within a comparative frame in her own affirmation of the dramatic impact of a performer such as Raphael Ortiz enacting a traumatic past (his work later would influence Arthur Janov's *The Primal Scream*) and the self-abnegating, culturally dissociative work of John Duncan and Paul McCarthy. In this daring, new area of research which Stiles has pursued here and in other forums, particularly in her work on Gustav Metzger's "Auto-Destructive Art" manifestoes and the Destruction in Art Symposium he organized in London in 1966, and in her previous writings on Romania, she moves the study of performance genres into unsettling directions, dangerous because performances by their nature occur in real, not fictional, time. Stiles makes the startling statement: "The performative language of trauma—what I consider a sculptural language—includes visualizing dissociation through spatial and temporal drift."

Another section of the essay, under the heading "We, Multiples," focuses on the psychic turmoil that generates split selves and multiple personae, especially in art about race or gender. In several instances, Stiles validates such performances for their ability to confront difficult emotional truths which are acted out for others. But is it a form of catharsis?—she doesn't explore the psychosocial/theatrical issue and the blurred boundaries of self and role. Noticeably, here and throughout the volume, the postmodern ironies of the eighties have now given way to the return of authenticity.

Commendably, Stiles stays fairly clear in her writing of the all-too-familiar positions in recent criticism. For example, Carolee Schneemann, now written about in many books on performance, is often straitjacketed by contemporary feminist criticism. Rightly, Stiles points out that her values, particularly in an early work like *Eye Body*, had less to do with feminist concerns than with painting and assemblage processes. In today's critical climate, it is easy to ignore the fact that all women who perform, and their work as understood in different historical eras, cannot easily be subsumed under one heading. (Schneemann is an interesting case since, unlike much feminist performance, her work does not invoke victimhood and it revels in heterosexual expression.)

Stiles is for the most part discriminating in her discussions of different uses of the body and of photography, whose importance in disseminating images of action art, like Klocker, she underlines. And, if most of the attention in Europe has focused on the western half of the continent, she draws the work of artists in Poland, the former Yugoslavia, and Czechoslovakia into performance history, though the work of the Hungarian collective, Squat Theatre, who eventually went into exile in the United States and whose clandestine works in Budapest in the seventies engaged the same international issues of performance and visual art, is not mentioned among the Eastern Europeans.

Stiles's passionate essay is very much a recovery project, turning performance history, with its manifestations of the pleasure and pain of the body and its encounter with the spectator, into an affirmation of human history: the power of being human subjects together. (Recent performance studies have turned toward "masochism"; in 1995, the New York gallery space Exit Art mounted a highly successful exhibit of performance photographs under the title "Endurance.") Staking out a revisionist position, she disregards the conventional avant-garde mode of viewing performance artists as perpetrators of subversive, transgressive acts, instead taking the more positive approach of seeing artists, whom she calls "aesthetic cosmonauts," as integrated into and leading the culture-making process.

The last pages of her essay focus on artists she considers creators of the "new cosmologies of human experience," centering around their themes of nature/culture, metaphysics, biology, technology: Al Hansen and his project of consciousness as process, the environmental performance sculpture of Bonnie Sherk, Gideon Gechtman's documentation of history/memory, Stelarc's post-biological body. And the "uncorrupted joy" of which Stiles writes? It is her fervent embrace of what she deems the life-affirming action of art and the ever-expanding realities envisioned by action artists. By its end, the essay has taken on the qualities of a manifesto.

So much of the commentary here and elsewhere has to be taken on faith, which means that there is more dogma than criticism, more rationalization and promotion than analysis. Though there is much to be admired in the editorial reach of the *Out of Actions* catalogue, it is now necessary to go beyond synthesis, summary, and support toward a deeper evaluation of the essential issues still circulating around performance and the writing about it. This is due in part, no doubt, to its much fought-for status as a field of scholarship, albeit within an art history that has paid scant attention to performance, still in its early stages. Writing about performance art is in need of more critical inquiry and critique of the kind that informs other arts, namely literature, film, theatre, and painting.

Instead, even though there are a few decades of commentary on it (if largely description, documentation, and chronology), performance is still propelled by an advocacy style of writing which has no discernible critical or comparative methodology—no stable, definable critical vocabulary. One never learns why one art action is more important than another, or how one differs from another, or whether one example of an artist's work has greater purpose than any other by the same artist. Negative commentary is virtually non-existent on any aesthetic terms, reserved only for the most extreme or controversial acts. Writing about video and installations reflects many of the same problems.

If the earlier writings on performance—by writers such as RoseLee Goldberg, Gregory Battcock, Michael Kirby, Adrian Henri, Willoughby Sharp—focus on the formal qualities of a work, now several years later the critical enterprise in transforming "performance art" into "action art" has shifted the emphasis to the social significance of performance as a contribution to culture. But I find highly problematic one of the central assumptions of the catalogue: that performance or action art in its attention to process leads *a priori* to an advanced notion of participatory democracy and progressive social vision. On the one hand, critics seem to have extended the Duchampian aesthetic of the interplay between artwork and viewer to the realm of the political; on the other, they ignore the will to performance in fascism and in mainstream culture.

Unlike other art forms whose criticism can be read for pure pleasure while embodying a sense of the critical terms manifest in any given work, the art criticism which has developed around performance is encased in the singular expression of the critic and the solo, often narcissistic, action of the artist who, finally, is not creating a world, but only an event, as it were. This kind of criticism discourages the casual opportunity to read critically and make one's own judgment, nor does the work open up to an exploration of significance outside its own point of reference. Lacking any dialectical framework, a reader or viewer faced with these conditions is hard put to establish any independent criteria of judgment. Furthermore, an art form that often too easily trades critical rigor for the face-value acceptance of artists' statements of intentionality and personal documentation, and one that is overly dependent on museum catalogues (increasingly promotional and trendy) as a basis of discussion, cannot go very far in convincing its audience of the value of performance—or action—art.

Even with all the theoretical apparatus and socially-aware references that nowadays accompany writings on performance, the discussion of individual performances remains largely impressionistic. No informed or coherent history of the performing body or of the object in performance is available, though the body is now at the center of writing about performance and other fashionable topics. Today, after half a century of performance (indeed, an entire century if the historical avant-garde is included), I cannot call to mind a single essay by an art critic that approaches, in analytical intensity or in pure graceful statement, the level of distinguished writing about the actor's or dancer's body or the use of objects on a stage that exists in the performing arts. For all its good intentions, art criticism on performance lacks poetry and sustained philosophical purpose.

As a field of inquiry performance is especially frustrating because it leaves behind only photographs, objects, videos. How inadequate they are as documentation. It is near impossible to understand the relation of a photograph to the meaning of a work's life in time and space. A few published or exhibited photographs of a single performance are usually what is left to mark its place in history. And many of the critics writing about the performance will not have seen it live. It remains to be seen how the history of the performing body will evolve, and what role the photograph will play in this process.

This essay was originally published as a review of *Out of Actions: Between Performance and the Object, 1949-1979*, Russell Ferguson, ed. (London and New York: Thames and Hudson, 1998) in *PAJ: A Journal of Performance and Art*, Vol. XXI, No. 1 (PAJ 61), January 1999.

The Wooster Group:
A Dictionary of Ideas

Anthology

The Wooster Group brings together the intertextual, the intercultural, and the intermedial in a new definition of the *liber mundi*. This theatre chooses all species of texts from the cultural heritage, then stages their dissemination in new spaces and environments, generating a multiplicity of narratives and images.

This is the legacy of John Cage's "library" of sounds and of Rauschenberg's mixed-media works. As an aesthetic strategy it takes for granted that in using the archives of art and culture as a database the issue is not one of ownership, but of distribution. Viewed in another light, the deterritorialization process of this kind of theatre, if extended into the world of cyberspace, changes the very nature of the way we think of art and authorship, composition and interpretation, and the notion of boundaries between art forms, art and everyday life, one culture and another, the created and the ready-made. This approach highlights process—the artwork and the *work* of art.

It is more and more apparent that the post-war American avant-garde model, based on the cutting up, quoting, redistribution, and recontextualization of the world archive of accumulated texts, images, and sounds prefigured the digital mode of perceiving space and time and meaning. This is the new design of information.

Books

Inside *House/Lights* is Gertrude Stein's *Dr. Faustus Lights the Lights*, inside *Nayatt School* is T. S. Eliot's *The Cocktail Party*, inside *Point Judith* is Eugene O'Neill's *Long Day's Journey into Night* and Jim Strahs's *The Rig*; Thornton Wilder's *Our Town* is the center of *Route 1 and 9 (The Last Act)*; *The Crucible* shapes *L.S.D.*; *Brace Up!* stages Chekhov's *Three Sisters* and fragments of *Brace Up!* itself appear in *Fish Story*. Then there are the films, the paintings, the songs, the dances, the television shows. All of them fragments—replacing, restructuring, recreating, pushing the frame. The text of *Frank Dell's Temptation of Saint Antony* includes a long compilation of writings and other media: the Flaubert classic, Lafcadio Hearn's "Argument" which prefaced his early translation of the French text, material by Lenny Bruce who was sometimes known as Frank Dell, books on magic and spiritualism, original writing by Jim Strahs (the Group's in-house playwright), and scenes based on Ingmar Bergman's film *The Magician*. The frantic voice of Dell at the end of the text explodes, "the the books in the library the the they run they play they see radical things."

Foucault characterized Flaubert's work as "the book of books," a fanciful library of books that can be "taken up, fragmented, displaced, combined, distanced by dreamy thought.... " It is this French tradition, and the later English-language examples of Joyce and Pound and Burroughs, that are the antecedents for The Wooster Group's textual and rhetorical styles. Even as it breaks open and reconstitutes literary material, The Wooster Group staging still exudes a modernist belief in the significance of art as a "language" within a work.

Books read, books open, books turned inside out, texts cut apart, turned upside down; books on the floor, words spilling underfoot. The trilogy, the epilogue, parts one and two, parentheses, exclamation point, a work-in-progress. Pull a quote from here, take that paragraph, take out the whole section, cut the play apart, redo it, retranslate, show it on video, record it, perform it live, do it all at once. Collage is the aesthetic strategy at play.

This is texture rather than text; theatre "pieces," precisely. A dramaturgy of the dispersed text. The Wooster Group are not beloved readers. They are browsers who skim the pages of books, randomly collected. They like the sound of words rather than their meaning. They are more interested in passages than in writing. This is the contemporary style of reading—scattered, naive, non-linear. Texts that can be interrupted. A book that can be opened to any page.

As group autobiographies ("lives of the performers"), the productions reflect a collective intelligence, duplicated on the literary level by the anthology-like scripts that are staged. The most Pirandellian of performers, The Wooster Group is always in search of an author.

Conversation Between Elizabeth LeCompte and Richard Foreman

RF: I want to use language to escape language.

EL: Yeah, but I've already escaped language.

RF: Well, I feel trapped.

EL: It's not that I feel trapped. I find it *is* a trap, that I have to constantly move around. But language to me is like what for a child the color red is. I don't have any association of its power.... I don't look to it for anything but entertainment.

RF: I feel ruled by it. I look at language as if it were a kind of Ping-Pong game in which there are a lot of little balls hitting things and going off in strange trajectories and you're dominated, your life is ruled by the fact that these things are accidentally hitting this way, that way, that way. And I want to figure out the scheme of that so I can be clear of it.

EL: And that's what you write about.

RF: You could make the case that this perverse historical period we're in produces serious art only if it's perverse. And I'd like to think that I am forced into what I know is a perverse strategy by the times. I'd like to think that in happier, healthier times maybe I wouldn't even be an artist.

EL: You've said that a lot to me, but I haven't really understood it til recently. I've had this feeling of not being an artist. I don't know what it means to me.... Maybe it's age. I've had a vision of just doing landscape architecture. It has to do with figuring out how to replant the earth the way it was. Returning it. You know, some obsessive thing like that. Returning it to the way it might have been naturally.

RF: Practically every moment I'm conscious, I have the urge to say, "Wait a minute—This life that is passing through me, I want to be more jewel-like." What I mean is that I don't want things coming in and passing through my head the way they are doing now. I want there to be other surfaces inside me that they bounce off of—like light bounces around inside a jewel. So a new structure is made by that bouncing around. And that's why I have to write, to evoke that, to turn myself over to that imagined "thing."

EL: The closest I come to that is landscape architecture. I want to organize space. I can't think unless I'm organizing space. Now obviously I've thought, "Oh, I'll go outside." I realize now, that's a big change. I'd no longer be an artist. I'd be somebody organizing landscape.... But it's the same, yours with words, mine with space.

RF: I don't see the difference between doing that and what I think other contemporary artists do. Just messing around with materials until you find what turns you on, what gives you a thrill.

EL: Yes, but I always have in the back of my mind these people who will be sitting and watching. And I know when I'm messing around and I don't care that they're there—and I know when I'm messing around and I do care.

RF: I've always thought, perversely again, that my moral task in life was to dare to show more and more of the messing around that just turned me on. Without caring what the response is.

EL: Oh, yes. Me, too.

RF: I do care. But that's a failure on my part.

EL: That's right, yes. And I've always felt that way, too.

("Directors Talk About Their Art,"
Village Voice, August 10-16, 1994)

Dramaturgy

The Wooster Group incorporates different technologies—writing, drawing, audiotape, video, film, telephone, radio, record player, computer—into theatrical form. Built on the transformation of the fragment into an anthology, this is a new conception of *dramaturgy*, not merely a play or text, and more than drama. If The Wooster Group is a theatre that looks like it only cares about its image, it is just as interested in rhetoric.

The differentiation and inner dialogue of speech styles and performance languages (live and mediatized) is at the heart of its dramaturgical process. Dialogue is shifted from the relationships of the performers to the relations between theatrical elements. Often, a play-within-a-play or a game structure acts as interlocutor. In *Dr. Faustus Lights the Lights*, on-stage "characters" in Stein's play have their speeches punctuated by a computer-generated sound score of "quacks" and "bings" and "blips." The MacinTalk voice demonstrates its potential as yet another audio track to add to the many forms of production constituting the narrative tracks of a Wooster Group work. (The script as Powerbook.) At the same time it situates within the new media the tradition of sound poetry that includes Stein.

Ecologies of Place

Wooster Group pieces are rooted in the articulation of different kinds of performance space. In their evolving ecology of theatre, the kinds of spaces most used are:

Indoors:
House
Tent
Hotel room (usually Miami)

Outdoors:
Sea
Backyard
Highway (The Wooster Group has developed its own version of the "road play")

Media spaces:
Film
Video
Phonograph
Tape player
Photograph
Computer

LeCompte, a visual artist, starts with the construction of space as a way of conceiving design as structure. Her project is aligned with the American avant-garde tendency to regard space as a field of revelation (social, political, or spiritual). *Three Places in Rhode Island*, and those locations which refer to Maine, outline emotional geographies that are played out in theatre works elaborating abstract versions of the performers' actions.

The tension between nature and culture in the works is paralleled in the relationship between inside and outside (or between three-dimensional design and video). Sometimes, the performers need to get outside the live event and find freedom in filmic space. The contrast between different spaces offers a key to the individual works. Another space of freedom is the hotel room to which a theatre troupe is escaping, at times functioning as a place of sexual license or fantasy. Increasingly, the touring company in the hotel room performs the general condition of Wooster Group life on the road. The frequent shifting of locations mirrors their working process, which pulls texts and images from here and there, traveling through but never inhabiting them. The incessant production of imagery and text is a variation on the idea of construction in their built environments.

A single text or site is too confining and claustrophobic for The Wooster Group. Putting more and more complication into it, by way of other texts and other media, points to a way out of it. They don't want their pieces to end and so they rehearse and rehearse and divide them into parts, then make them into trilogies, and carry along objects and costumes, music and leftover texts, putting them into the same house, turned this way and that. They build and rebuild the house that is not a home in a struggle with the elusive sense of place. And when moving becomes unbearable, they create an afterimage of the landscape they left behind or the echo of voices in it.

Figures of Speech

The Wooster Group actors are "figures of speech" more than "characters." Their plenitude of discourses is manifested in modes of direct address, dialogue, monologue, sermon; the interview, the letter, the lecture-demo and talk show; drama, non-fiction and novelistic writing; computer-generated sound and digitally-altered voices. They are *lazzi* for the contemporary theatre. (The performer's mask/face/image duplicates the techniques of layering and texturing that characterize other aspects of the staging.) Dramatic classics, religious, scientific, literary, and instructional texts are referred to indiscriminately, even interrogated. The production of affects is more important than representation.

The forms of speech employed by the performers are drawn from many sources: conceptual performance, vaudeville, soap opera, film acting and psychological drama, cabaret, musical comedy, melodrama, television, rehearsal as performance. Varieties of speech style and performance style overwhelm narrative in productions whose tension grows out of the juxtaposition of talking and reading, live performance and mediated presence, and competing forms of media. The Wooster Group takes to heart the idea of theatrical production and reproduction, offering both the performance and its documentation within the same event. A live performer may interact with others in real-time, on film or on pre-recorded video, or the voice may be separated from the body. At times the same scene is enacted in two different media, film and live performance (*Hamlet*) or live performance as a re-enactment of another live performance

(*Poor Theatre*). Some speeches are heard on tape or telephone or records or computer. A live actor and an actor on video converse in real-time (*Brace Up!*). In one sense, this is a post-actors' theatre in which the live performance situation forces performers to confront images and recordings of themselves in an ongoing analysis of the nature of "presence."

In *Route 1 and 9* a romantic scene between the young couple in Wilder's *Our Town*, which serves as a point of departure for the piece, is performed on TV monitors by the actors. What is notable about the scene, acted in an intense, soap opera style, is its inherent commentary on performance languages. Namely, the distinctions between stage speech and video speech and between acting and performing. The highly-charged expressive language of Wilder challenges the medium of television. It is simply too intimate and full of emotion for the flatness of the video screen. If *Route 1 and 9* recreates and mocks the educational approach of Clifton Fadiman's fifties' lecture on *Our Town*—indeed, the clichés of arts education itself—nevertheless, The Wooster Group, here and elsewhere, substitutes its own kind of "lesson" in the production.

For L.S.D. the TV screens prompted new modes of experience, according to filmmaker Ken Kobland, a long-time collaborator with the company:

> "We wanted the television to stand as a kind of wallpaper … I've often thought of it as a kind of basso continuo, a continuous undercurrent that's drawing you in but that you can easily escape from. I'm constantly drawn into the sheer beauty of the live images against the flatness and depthlessness of the long table. It's as if the televisions were holes through which you could look out into the world."
>
> (DAVID SAVRAN, BREAKING THE RULES, 1988)

Ground

LeCompte uses the floor as an active element of performance space, treating surface like a canvas. The stage picture is always framed and the borders of the space defined, but the desire to extend the event outside the frame reveals itself in the shifting ground of the set design. The performer's body is the figure in the ground, moving between portrait and landscape, private and public self.

The ground is always shifting beneath the feet of the performers, which is why dance defines their movement, not walking. Dance is often used to animate the sense of place, or simply to kill time or speed up a scene, whether in the house music of *Route 1 and 9* or the eccentric dance of *Brace Up!* or the mock ballet of *Dr. Faustus Lights the Lights*. And, not surprisingly, since reading texts or watching fellow performers from the edge of the stage has so prominent a role in the productions, the typical Wooster Group performer is seated, automatically creating a special relationship with performance space.

In *Sakonnet Point*, *Nayatt School*, and *Route 1 and 9*, reality is diagrammatic—marked out on the ground. Electrical chords trailing the TV monitors in *Brace Up!* form tracks along the floor. In *The Hairy Ape* sound travels upwards from the lower depths, the floor tilts, the performers disperse in rows, only their upper bodies visible. In *North Atlantic* the ship heaves. In *Poor Theatre* there is the scene of rubbing the floor, and in the film in the Coda of Part 1 Max Ernst is shown rubbing pencil on paper. The documentary is re-enacted by Sheena See with LeCompte's voice. Rubbing is a metaphor for The Wooster Group's relationship to all kinds of material and artworks and it is articulated in three different ways: visual (image sources), literary ("found" texts), theatrical (acting styles).

House

In the house there is a table: a sculptural element. A site for reading, playing records, sitting chatting, examining the body, writing, telling stories, drinking. From this place setting all narratives begin. But The Wooster Group will have none of the domestic realism of American drama. Their beloved house remodels the old box set and the ordered cosmos visible through the open houses of Renaissance painting. Children are often at home.

The house splits apart and fractures, like the texts performed inside it, spatially duplicating the literary structure through the use of multiple platform levels, corridors, steps, scale, depth. With each new work the design of raw space moves toward architecture. Production to production, there is the tripling of perspective: textual material presented in several media, the same set/house turned to different angles, the intermixing of live and mediated performance. Wooster Group staging practices, from their grounding in the environmental theatre of The Performance Group, extended the "rough cuts" concept of Gordon Matta-Clark's deconstructed houses into performance space, bringing theatre design closer to installation art and away from Schechnerian ritual.

Jim Clayburgh: "The ground plan for *Rumstick Road* became the ground plan for *Nayatt School*, only reversed in the space and lowered. Then the house finally fell apart to a skeletal structure on legs at the end of *Point Judith* and moved from wood to tin. The *Route 1 and 9* house—built of tin studs and tin two-by-fours—was the same one built at the end of *Point Judith*. It's a constant evolution of the same ground plan, with just a transfer to another space or the change of an angle. Even when I designed *L.S.D.*, the ground plans of all the other shows were on the stage as my reference for working it out."

(Tish Dace, "Plywood and Electronics," Theatre Crafts,
February 1984)

The house no longer appears in *Dr. Faustus* and *To You, the Birdie! (Phèdre)*. Ron Vawter, Paul Schmidt, and Spalding Gray have died. Third-generation performers from different countries and continents now make up the theatrical family, open to "adoption," as it were.

Image

a. Body, text, image, sound, environment are denied the feeling of wholeness—it's the fragment, the angle of perception, that matters. The tension in a performance is manifested in the anxiety of the audience searching for an image of the whole (text; house).

b. The image of the stigmata in *Flaubert Dreams of Travel But His Mother's Illness Prevents It* (the film in *Frank Dell's Temptation of St. Antony*), refers to a wound (martyrdom), aestheticizing the inner life of The Wooster Group.

c. On *Brace Up!*: "In Chekhov's time a samovar was as ordinary an item of domestic life as a television is today." (Paul Schmidt, introduction to his translation of *Three Sisters*.)

d. Simulation as theatrical strategy, or, how the 1964 film of Richard Burton's *Hamlet* on Broadway enters The Wooster Group's *Hamlet* production:

"So the first thing we did was to go into that film and re-edit it so they were always stopping at a line break—in the sections that are verse—and not stopping in the middle. So I would take the film in Final Cut and if there was a pause where I didn't like it I would just cut it out with the video attached and move it somewhere I thought there needed to be a pause. So now we use that video which has all these jumps in it which gives us a physicality which is a little bit strange and removed … So that was the first alteration we made to the source movie. And then Liz decided, 'Well, we'll project it on a huge tapestry in the back, which will be a moving image of the old black and white film with Richard Burton.' And so we started to erase some of those figures who were being replaced by the actors on stage.

"But that's very tedious work; it turns out we had to get a team of specialists to come in—we called them Erasers. They would just sit at the computer all day taking the figures out. You have to go find whatever background they're standing in front of from another shot and place it in front of where their body is. And you just see the ghost of their figure moving across the stage. And then they have other effects to obscure the original from time to time just so there's some relationship there. And it turns the movie into the ghost of something that's gone or decaying."

("SCOTT SHEPHERD, ACTOR," GOTHAMIST,
MARCH 2007)

Just the High Points: Willem Dafoe Says a Few Words About *L.S.D.*

"The more I perform, the more my relationship to the audience becomes totally abstract. Different performers, actors, need different things. For example, Spalding [Gray] loves an audience. He really feels them out there. I don't. It's a totally internal thing. Even when I have a character, I'm always curious to see how I *read*, what people think I am, who I am, and then you lay the action on top of that so you're confronting yourself in these circumstances. It's open-ended. I'm not presenting anything: I'm feeling my way through. If you were acting something, if you were very conscious of acting a character, somewhere you would close it down, you'd present it. You'd finish it. In this stuff, you never know.

"The way I get off in the performances is when I hit those moments of real pleasure and real clarity and an understanding about myself in relationship to the structure. It is work, it is an exercise of me behaving a certain way for two hours, and it can become meditative."

(PHILIP AUSLANDER, "TASK AND VISION,"
THE DRAMA REVIEW, SUMMER 1985)

Kate (Valk on The Found Object)

"First Liz asked me to make a copy of a satin dress that had been worn in *Three Places in Rhode Island*. When it was finished, she tried the dress on Willem but liked it better on Matthew, who wore it as 'the family dog' in *Long Day's Journey into Night*. A lot of the costumes worn in *Long Day's Journey* were taken from earlier parts of the trilogy and used in a different way. Willem wore a purple dress around his neck that Libby had worn in *Nayatt School*. Ron wears the same striped shirt as Jamie did in *The Cocktail Party* section of *Nayatt*. Liz had me sew gold furniture trim on a lot of the costumes. She had me make a black silk lampshade for the standing lamp in the *Long Day's Journey* house. It had the same shape and was constructed like the Red Tent from the Trilogy."

(ANNOTATED TEXT OF *POINT JUDITH*, ZONE,
Spring/Summer 1981)

"I was working as a seamstress when I got out of school, so I just offered myself to Liz. She said, Well, what can you do? And I said, I can sew. So I started making things for her. I was very lucky. At first, this was what it was: a place to go every day, and to make things. It wasn't primarily as an actress. I never really felt like an actress. I was always very much wanting to run away from my psychology."

(DAVID SALLE AND SARAH FRENCH, "KATE VALK,"
BOMB, SUMMER 2007)

LeCompte and Video/Performance

The visual artist Joan Jonas appears as a performer in the role of Celia Coplestone in *The Cocktail Party* scenes of *Nayatt School* and as Masha in *Brace Up!*. More significantly, she has another performance history underlining her presence with The Wooster Group: Jonas's early performances featured many of the techniques that would become media strategies of this theatre. In her video performance, entitled *Organic Honey's Visual Telepathy/Organic Honey's Vertical Roll* (1972), audience members could watch various versions of it on tape on multiple monitors. The process of image-making was a part of the performance, duplicating and altering the information of the performance as it was being performed.

Another contemporary antecedent to this way of working is Carolee Schneemann's performance/installation *Upto and Including Her Limits* (1973). During the performance one of her own films was shown on a double screen projection; audiotapes documenting real life situations were played; three to six monitors showed moments of the performance in a replay or as they occurred. There was a continuous projection of slides relating to the work and to Schneemann's early paintings and collages. A reading area in another space away from the performance included Schneemann's notes, posters from past works, business and artistic correspondence. She was seen live, on tape, on film, and heard on audiotape. The so-called "deconstruction" mode of LeCompte's style derives from film and video editing and collage, which is a spatial rather than a literary impulse.

Medicine/Mania

Doctor, priest, teacher, author—they are variations on the dreaded authority figure at the center of the productions. The fear of death and of loss of control is played out in the refusal of closure, of meaning, and, ultimately, of accountability for the work.

The characters in the productions exhibit a fear of succumbing to irrational forces that masquerades as chaos. Extremities of their behavior show up in a hysterical, manic speed of delivery weirdly at odds with the "cool" surface look of the world they inhabit. The works are full of paranoia, anxiety, rage, and a notable absence of decorum that co-exists with the acknowledgment of sin and a functioning moral order. Pleasure is not so much an expression of joy as an act of transgression, bordering on the pornographic.

Dance is an essential activity for the company, not only to relieve the dramatic tension but also to cover over the lack of resolution of cultural problems. The "social dances" performed create a sphere of freedom, bracketed off from the world, carnivalesque in spirit.

Non-acting and Acting: Spalding Gray Analyzes Himself as a Performer

"Could I stop acting, and what was it I actually did when I acted?" Spalding Gray asks. "Was I, in fact, acting all the time, and was my acting in the theatre the surface showing of that? Was my theatre acting a confession of the constant state of feeling my life as an act? What was the reality of myself on the other side of that 'act'? ... I began to use all these questions as a sort of creative energy source from which to work. These identity questions became a foundation for more personal work.

"The perception of acting as being a 'lie' became, in itself, a kind of dramatic conflict, a tension, the old protagonist-antagonist theatre construct. The conflict between acting (active interpretation) and non-acting (just doing the actions) created a new thesis, a new 'act.' The separation I had experienced in theatre previous to this was transformed into a kind of gestalt. It was closer to the bone. It was a dialectic between my life and theatre rather than between role and text. The 'figure' became myself in the theatre and the 'ground' was the contingency of everyday time out of which this timeless, and therefore 'saved,' figure grew.

"This is not to say a new 'gap' was not emerging. Now there was the new space between the timeless, poetic me (the me in quotes, the self as poem) and the real-time self in the world (the time-bound, mortal self; the self as prose). The ongoing 'play' became a play about theatrical transcendence.

"It was, for me, a grand play between love and death. Love became the act of giving myself away to the work and to our audience. This act was always played off the great wall of prosaic time, the massive flatness of it all, the indistinguishable 'thing-in-itself.' This was the not-self or the place of death in life. The figure became the individual creation and the ground was the allness-of-it-all from which this figure grew. The play was the movement in and out of those two realities.

"This was the new 'play' which I found more interesting, and certainly more immediate, because it was going on all the time. I only had to stop it, and look at it, and any number of theatre situations would present themselves. It was learning how to make frames, to frame the mass of reality. I saw this act as composition. I thought of myself as performer/composer because this interplay from which this set of actions grew did not necessarily take the form of text but more often took the form of a conglomerate of images, sounds, colors, and movement. I did not choose to work this way. I found it to be the only way I could work."

(SPALDING GRAY, "ABOUT *THREE PLACES IN RHODE ISLAND*," *THE DRAMA REVIEW*, MARCH 1979)

Lee Breuer of Mabou Mines once said that Spalding Gray had the third great acting idea of the century. He went beyond Stanislavskian psychology that joined the actor and character, and Brechtian technique that separated the actor from the role, to use his own life as material for conceptual performance.

On Working as a Dramaturg

Norman Frisch: "Although one may pretend that one is attempting to stage some fragment of a text—or even an entire play by O'Neill or Chekhov—what is actually being staged in a Wooster production is the life of the rehearsal room. So the material—that life—that one is staging is being manifested in the very moment one is staging it. It is never static. It is never really knowable. The nature of it is rarely, if ever, agreed upon by the players involved. So the dramaturg, in projecting some order or pattern onto all these fluid, disparate, multi-dimensional elements, takes on a difficult role in interpreting the very private impulses and gestures of one's colleagues. You may think you're making an observation about Masha, or Jones, or Tituba, but if the lines between performer and performance have been intentionally blurred, your observations may be taken quite personally."

Marianne Weems: "I think, too, that as a dramaturg with The Wooster Group, you quickly discover that there's no 'outside' vantage point from which to view the piece. It's like a physics experiment where your mere presence affects the atoms as they interact—you're part of the process, and so you're implicated in the dramaturgy. There's no point in stolidly maintaining a scholarly approach."

(SUSAN JONAS, GEOFFREY S. PROEHL, MICHAEL LUPU, EDS., *DRAMATURGY IN AMERICA*, 1996)

Pedagogy (Subversive)

The Wooster Group reveals a gnostic project: to foment doubt and confusion through the performance, quotation, and collision of images, texts, and styles, thwarting habitual responses to complex ideas. The goal is not the acquisition of knowledge as a civilizing activity or foundation of cultural and social values, but exactly its opposite: the decentering of the human being and the destabilizing of knowledge and beliefs. In its own way, *Route 1 and 9*, through the lessons of *Our Town* recreated from an *Encyclopedia Britannica* educational film analyzing Wilder's play, undermines the conventional notion of the "humanities."

The teaching play—or anti-teaching play—has a long history in modern theatre, especially in the varied pedagogical scenes of eighteenth-century and nineteenth-century drama by the likes of Lenz and Büchner. Closer to our own time, Peter Handke reinvented this form in his "speak-in" plays and Heiner Müller mocked the pedagogical authority of German drama by reconceiving Brecht's *Lehrstücke* in his own re-education plays, which articulate post-Stalinist views of Marxism.

In contemporary American drama, Richard Foreman has most directly taken up traditions of the teaching play as a formal device. Besides the Brechtian model, one of his influences was the artist Jack Smith, who pioneered a mode of performance in the sixties—and prevalent in the performance art of the next decade—in which he used autobiographical fragments, slides, and collections of texts, in a lecture-demonstration format. But a fascinating aspect of Smith's work was the way he incorporated an aesthetics of "failure" as part of the performance. His equipment was constantly breaking down; he would stop and reset or redo a section of his performance (albeit in unrehearsed asides), or give technical instructions. His bizarre staging of *Ghosts* in the late-seventies is one of the earliest examples of "deconstruction" in the American avant-garde theatre.

The Wooster Group retains this way of working that confounds real-time and theatrical time, stylizing it in the frequent onstage interplay between technicians and performers that highlights changes, glitches, revisions, and restagings of the kind occurring in *Frank Dell's Temptation of Saint Antony*. LeCompte, in fact, likes to make aspects of a performance seem unvirtuosic and beset by mistakes. This is a visual arts attitude toward performance, anathema to most theatre. Paul Schmidt, who translated *Three Sisters*, which forms the basis of *Brace Up!*, and acted the part of Dr. Chebutykin—another Wooster Group medical man dispensing advice—made several interventions in that production. He would correct a line reading or pronunciation of a word, summarize a scene that is unstaged, describe the mental state of characters, or discuss the meaning of a speech. The translator then became a "character" in the production, offering an ongoing critical perspective.

LeCompte descends from a tradition of subversive- or anti-pedagogy that began with a critique of the Enlightenment. In her theatre, she undermines the role of art as the articulation of moral values or as a statement of "truths" about the human condition. Refusing the role of director as critic because she is more interested in amplifying modes of perception than in any singular meaning, she plays with the very notion of "interpretation." In their own way, however, in the pedagogical forms of the "lesson," "examination of text," and "rules" that wind their way through the productions, The Wooster Group has been educating audiences in a new understanding of theatrical experience joined to mediated experience that is closer to reality than the realistic theatrical style inherently criticized. Exposing multiple forms of cultural production to embrace the canons of high art and the sentimental kitsch of popular culture, the works extend the legacy of the dark side of the Theatre of the Ridiculous by pointing to the impact of imagery on the American psyche.

What energizes this pedagogical mode is not the wisdom of books. Rather, it is the manner in which texts and tropes are catalogued in The Wooster Group's own library and treated in its satirical dictionary of received ideas. Their works are satyr plays to be set alongside the classics of the dramatic repertoire. This ethos is well-suited to the classics because of their sense of order and control: the productions are, in effect, the bringing to order of disruptive realities—a profoundly classicist project. (LeCompte's formalism is a variety of classicism.)

Questions I've Asked Myself Over the Years

- How much of the work is sheer problem-solving and willful complication of the narrative and how much a serious deliberation on the material?
- Why does this theatre company still need to rebel against authority, whether in the form of the text, or through the themes of education, medicine, and religion, at this stage of life?

- What is the sincere nature of spiritual inquiry in the works?
- Is the incorporation of an afterimage an aesthetic strategy or a form of narcissism?
- Is the work of the theatre overpoliticized by critics in order to legitimize it as theoretical subject matter?
- How much detective work will it take to figure out their references? Can they all be known? Should they?
- Where does the difference between critique and reference situate itself in the productions?

Religion

One of the great themes of The Wooster Group is spiritual crisis. *Rumstick Road*, the first major company production, explored the agon of matter and spirit that was dramatized in the Christian Science beliefs of Spalding Gray's mother, whose suicide was the work's emotional heart. In *Nayatt School*, the use of *The Cocktail Party* as intertext highlighted the anguished Protestantism of Celia Coplestone. And *Point Judith*, the epilogue to *Three Places in Rhode Island*, revisited the Catholicism of *Long Day's Journey*, featuring Ken Kobland's film with nuns. *To You, the Birdie! (Phèdre)* ends with a search for redemption. As a matter of course, the complex maneuvers of The Wooster Group raise religious and moral issues, just as they challenge legal, scientific, intellectual, and medical authority and values.

When Frank Dell asks, "Can matter be part of God?" one has to wonder if this is Ron Vawter's own voice crying out in the wilderness. If The Wooster Group pieces can be understood at the level of autobiography, this work is a particularly soulful commentary by Vawter, who, having once studied for the priesthood, acted the role of Frank Dell until he died of AIDS in 1994. In one sense, *Frank Dell's The Temptation of Saint Antony* stages spiritual crisis at the hour of his impending death. The character Sue reads to him: "There are also certain others who linger in Hades, but not unhappily as a rule. I refer to certain young men of a careless, animal, and occasionally, vicious life who die violent deaths ... These poor fellows are suddenly wrenched from their bodies while still they are in the prime of manhood. They are not, in any sense, capable of grasping, for a while, the difference between earth life and the Afterlife."

Subsequently, in *Brace Up!*, as the character Vershinin, Vawter gives one of Chekhov's bittersweet speeches about the "future" in the style of a sermon, directly addressing the audience. "In two or three hundred years, well in a thousand, maybe ... a new and happier life will begin. Of course, we'll never see it, but we are working towards it right now. We work for it, we suffer for it, we create it, in fact. And that's the whole point of our existence. That's what happiness is, I think." The translator/doctor, Paul Schmidt, who was also dying of AIDS, discusses its meaning in what can only be described as a scene of tragic irony.

The waywardness of appearance and reality that energizes the work of The Wooster Group is not merely a theatrical conceit but a staging ground for the genuine interest in the performance of the self. It was elaborated initially by Spalding Gray and Ron Vawter, both traditionally trained theatre actors with a propensity for self-reflection. The nature of acting on the stage would evolve as fundamental questions about human actions—the crisis of identity and belief—in the world. They brought a quality of emotion to the productions that is no longer there. Both actors, from the alternating prism of Christian Science's refusal of materiality and Catholicism's word made flesh, inserted the issues of moral struggle and shattered belief systems into the collective Wooster Group mind. Dance, then, could be understood as a form of ecstatic performance.

Speaking Voices

Speech acts, though not in the dialogues of conventional drama, have a substantial impact in The Wooster Group conception of theatre: speech and gesture brought together, but as autonomous acts, often separating gesture and meaning and parts of the body. In *To You, the Birdie! (Phèdre)*, one actor speaks in an electronically modified voice on behalf of another actor, the director communicates from her seat in the audience to the actors through their wireless microphones, the actor's body interacts with a video camera to create an image on stage that is part digital, part live. The strictures of neo-classical drama are parodied by the reading of badminton rules during the production, exactly the sort of in-your-face rebellion this theatre is drawn to. As if to further confound performance styles, videos of Merce Cunningham and Martha Graham dances are being played on off-stage monitors for the performers while the stage events transpire.

(After a performance of *To You, the Birdie! (Phèdre)* I asked Ari Fliakos what it was like as an actor to have the director speaking in his ear while he was performing. He said it was "liberating." Sometime later he described it as "a way of making the space physically come together." It was "instant feedback [LeCompte: "Beautiful." "Louder." "We'll work on that tomorrow."] that made you feel very supported ... You don't have to think about your own performance. It serves the same purpose as having television monitors running.")

The Wooster Group revels in the rhetorical play of text and image and hearing and sight, as they demonstrate the very process of "articulation." Meaning is less important than the contrapuntal and polyphonic "voices" each aspect of the staging expresses. What matters is the frenzy of presence.

On one level, the theatre experience plays out the competition between the spoken and the visible, the aural and pictorial, the live and digital. The issue of perception was addressed by Gertrude Stein in her 1934 essay, "Plays," as an aspect of emotion. In other words, how do we receive information in the theatre: through seeing or hearing? How do these senses work together? In a Wooster Group production, how does one experience the various performance styles and modes of production, live and mediated?

In *House/Lights*, which brings together Stein's own *Dr. Faustus Lights the Lights* and the grade-B porno film *Olga's House of Shame*, performers wear earpieces in which they hear a recording of the text from the play and the soundtrack from the film that cues their speech. Several video monitors are placed above the audience, in and around the space, and off stage, guiding the performers who are watching them and synchronizing their actions with film or video.

"Your sensation as one in the audience in relation to the play played before you your sensation I say your emotion concerning that play is always either behind or ahead of the play at which you are looking and to which you are listening. So your emotion as a member of the audience is never going on at the same time as the action of the play." Stein's words read like a Wooster Group manifesto.

Temptation of St. Antony, Frank Dell's

The ecology of place is relocated from Flaubert's desert to a hotel room, and the illuminated manuscript is no longer a text but a chrestomathy. Its mystical structure of seven scenes erupts in simultaneous discourses: literary, filmic, video, and audio vocabularies that employ the media technology rhythms of rewind, fast-forward, cut, and freeze frame. The actors in this narrative within narratives, which never comes to an end, are making a film, replaying audio tapes, reading and being read to, performing, and rehearsing a text which is divided into sections, parts, and episodes. It is alternately narrated and dramatized in monologic and dialogic form. The activity is one of cutting and pasting, rewriting, and recontextualizing.

From the start The Wooster Group developed its experimental attitude through the manipulation of textual materials, autobiography/fiction, mediated experience, and the contraventions of writing and speech. What propels the works are competing forms of narrative, allegory, and the critical impulse. In the world of Frank Dell "appearance is the only reality." The intention is not to make anything meaningful, but to empty everything—the body, the word, the object—of meaning. It is not unseemly that its members should take as a point of departure the writing of Flaubert, who had searched for the text that would exalt form over matter, a text emptied of meaning: subjectless.

Fundamentally, the theatre's own aesthetic strategy is constituted by the struggle between form and subject matter, presence and absence, and on the visual level between light and darkness, black and white. For sure, subject *matter* is always problematic in The Wooster Group whose theatrical style moves towards dematerialization, aligning it with the aims of conceptual art. On the level of performance, this tendency is manifested as depersonalization. What Baudelaire said of the Flaubert text—that it represented "his spirit's secret chamber"—might equally describe their relation to the work and to their own interiority. In its extreme aestheticism The Wooster Group enters the realm of the spiritual.

Remarkably, The Wooster Group has improvised around and retained many of Flaubert's essential themes, which, as it happens, have been central to their own work over the years. Not the least of them is the obsession with style. A brief account of such concerns includes the ambiguities of appearance, magical reality, multiple identities, the conflict of science and faith, sexual frenzy, and the interplay of religious crisis, hallucination, and ecstatic experience. There are also the scenes bearing on temptation and depravity, the use of language as obscenity, and the symbology of monsters and witches. Flaubert's great classic, a compendium of different kinds of texts and voices, literary canon and church canon, the profane, sacred, and heretical, is the ideal work for The Wooster Group's own glossolalia.

Urban: New York School, 1970s and After

Color: downtown black
Temperament: ironic, self-involved, hysterical
Mood: subjunctive
Style: conceptual; rhetorical
Legacy: post-Cagean
Mode: documentary, interrogatory
Performer: authenticity (expressive) vs. artificiality (impersonal)
Politics: high/low
Ideal: Nietzschean redemption through art

Vawter's Spirit

He said: "I'm not a practitioner of any organized religion but I have a great many spiritual ambitions although they remain mysterious and invisible to me. I'm searching for the invisible.... I feel that yearning in the audience. That's where I get my fuel. It's unfashionable to speak of these things and also very difficult. And it's taken a few thousand years to pull religion and theatre apart anyway. So now they're separate let's not confuse it with people going to church, because we're not going to church.... I've always felt that the great influences of my life have reinvented, or created, their own sense of spiritualism.... I think audiences have great desires towards the spiritual and all they need is the slightest excuse from the stage to open them up. So, I try to find a place between character and in front of the audience which would trigger spiritual or meditative experiences."

(TIM ETCHELLS, *CERTAIN FRAGMENTS*, 1999)

Wilson and LeCompte

Both visual artists, they create two different approaches to a theatre based on the idea of the archive. Robert Wilson is a symbolist, a seeker of truth and archetypes. His dramaturgy of the dispersed texts of different cultures and continents dwells in the realm of allegory. LeCompte is a materialist, an iconoclast, spreading confusion and skepticism. Her theatre elaborates the critique of the text. His subject is civilization, hers is society.

If Wilson studies the cosmos, LeCompte is interested in hell. Wilson's theatre is one of decorum, The Wooster Group lacks social grace. He loves the dream world, she revels in real-time. Myth, his guide; hers, popular culture. Minimalism is their sculptural inheritance, bands of black and white light.

How they regard media is the dividing line between these two kinds of theatre-making. Its usage creates the distance between the attainment of knowledge and enlightenment (the aim of Wilson) and the multiplication of information and contradiction (the desire of LeCompte).

X

The Wooster Group works in a form—theatre—that is rooted in the process of discovery. There, everything is supposed to move in the direction of becoming visible. But this theatre refuses the option of revelation and instead performs the tension between being known and not being known. The Wooster Group invites you into their house but you are always a stranger, a witness to the inbred eccentricity and suspicion. There is no sense of intimacy, no comfort, no hint of what may occur from one moment to the next. Something reclusive and self-contained, something very private, even secretive about this theatre/family encourages a theatricality of narcissism, reflected, curiously, in recurring images of water and the echo.

"You Must Have a Shoe Fetish ..."

I said to Elizabeth LeCompte one evening. She readily owned up to it. I had just seen Phèdre try on several pairs of shoes. "So do I," I said to her. We didn't speak of it anymore. Sometimes girls just want to have fun.

Zero Degree of Performance

The Wooster Group began its life with the blank sheets of *Sakonnet Point* that flutter all the way through *Point Judith*, like book covers enfolding *Three Places in Rhode Island*. On these bedsheets Spalding Gray writes the narrative of his life; LeCompte stages it. This is the story of a family. The Wooster Group starts on the road to immortality.

Now the blank pages have been refunctioned as the virtual web/badminton net of *To You, the Birdie! (Phèdre)*. Play-within-a-play. Is *Phèdre*'s web a new formal device masquerading as sport or does it signal a coming transparency in the lives of the players and in the rules of their game?

Alas, in *Hamlet* the simulating players have found the perfect instance for The Wooster Group conception of theatrical life: a spectral presence wherein appearance always inclines toward disappearance. Whether to be or not to be.

This essay was first given as a keynote address for a conference entitled, "The Wooster Group and Its Tradition," organized by the Free University, Brussels, May 2002. It was also delivered as a lecture at the Free University, Berlin; Justus Liebig University (Giessen): the Media Festival, Ljubljana, Slovenia; Location One, NYC—all in 2002; the University of California-San Diego, 2003. Subsequently titled "The Wooster Group: A Dictionary of Ideas," the essay was published in *The Wooster Group and Its Traditions*, Johan Callens, ed. (Brussels: Peter Lang, 2005). It was published under the same title in *PAJ: A Journal of Performance and Art*, Vol. XXV, No. 2 (PAJ 74), May 2003. An Italian translation appeared as "Il Wooster Group. Un dizionario di idée," *Biblioteca Teatrale*, "Il Teatro Di Fine Millennio" issue, curated by Valentina Valentini, Nos. 74-76, Apr.-Dec. 2005 (Centro Teatro Ateneo/University of Rome-La Sapienza), Rome: Bulzoni Editore, 2005. The essay has been updated for publication with additional material.

Landscapes of the
Twenty-First Century

The National Theatre of Mannheim hosted the 12th International Schiller Days 2003, expanding the program of guest performances of German and international productions devoted to Friedrich Schiller's work by co-producing the bi-continental (New York-Paris) Compagnie Faim de Siècle's new work, *Schiller by Night/Landscapes*. Within the context of German theatre, which is dominated by high concept productions of the European repertoire by contemporary directors, the invitation by the city of Mannheim, where Schiller's *The Robbers* premiered in 1782, to have the author given a state-of-the-digital-art treatment fits comfortably in the country's ongoing dialogue with the classics. So, rather than being an isolated event, it became part of the history of Schiller stagings in Germany, viewed alongside other productions at the festival, which ranged from the conventional stagings of state theatres, like the Czech Republic's *Parasite* from Brno, to another video/installation/performance, *Playing Schiller*, by the French company from Lyon, Là Hors de.

Schiller by Night/Landscapes reveals all the promise and challenge of large-scale international productions that try to maneuver between the local and the global. Conceived by Ibrahim Quraishi, whose Medea-inspired piece, *Shattered Boxes*, was performed by his company at The Kitchen in New York in 2000, the new work featured at least thirty installation, light and costume designers, performers, sculptors, musicians, and video and computer artists from the U.S., Europe, the Middle East, and Africa. It took place in seventeen different spaces in a building in the Nekrau industrial area on the edge of Mannheim, to which the audience was driven in buses that departed the festival center at 10:00 p.m. From the start, a sense of danger was cultivated as the passengers were given visa applications to fill out and, upon arriving at a dark and unpopulated area, were immediately ushered into the foyer where they were decontaminated, stamped, and otherwise processed. The more than two-and-a-half-hour evening unfolded as a Piranesi-like journey, rather a contemporary link to the medieval mystery play, through landscapes/events that varied in light, sound, smell, color, climate, and emotional tone. Guards or guides lead the way in the controlled, total environments whose many wrapped figures encountered along the way underscored the general feeling of entrapment in a world that mixed real-time and virtual time, live and digitized images, and the vapors of immateriality with physical states of being. While the "landscapes" (which in contemporary theatre seems to be the preferred definition of space for any series of discrete activities) opened up to many scenes of imprisonment, surveillance, interrogation, and abjection, possibilities of communication and transformation were still viable in this panoramic setting.

Not quite a site-specific work but similar to the genre produced in "found" spaces, with antecedents extending back decades into elaborate forms of happenings and "actions" here and in Europe, *Schiller by Night/Landscapes* steadily led the spectators who were divided into smaller groups (not really an "audience" in the public, communal sense of the word, and more like anonymous museumgoers or pedestrians), through a series of rooms of varying size and stimulation to watch and sometimes participate in the events unfolding. These included: confronting a number of cots holding bodies being scanned; entering a grassy landscape of dancers, some caked in mud, and moving around sculpted cloth figures; wading through water on a brick pathway in a cave-like opening where an image of a woman is projected on a wall and heard on tape; being fitted with long coats and surgical masks and wandering around in a lab-like setting; the entire group of spectators gathering finally to watch simultaneous actions and interactions by all the performers in a large open space. Whatever texts exist—live and on tape—in the work are fragments of Heiner Müller's DESPOILED SHORE MEDEAMATERIAL LANDSCAPE WITH ARGONAUTS, Schiller's *William Tell*, Icelandic sagas, and writings by Primo Levi and Bertolt Brecht. But William Tell and Medea are more inspirational dramatic figures drawn from mythical scenes of tyranny than affective presences in the company's scheme of things.

In fact, in its entirety *Schiller by Night/Landscapes* appears to have been constructed on the order of Müller's "synthetic fragment" ideal—bits and pieces of images, texts, and scenes that work as montage or landscape. Here and elsewhere, the late German author serves as an artistic mentor for Quraishi, who similarly loves this ambiguous territory between myth and history, though how they impact landscape in this piece, as place or concept, is not easily discernible. More to the point, he seems to have grasped Müller's genius in bringing together surrealism and cyberculture as a path to experimentation for his own theatre. It has been interesting to observe how prominent a role Müller has in international political theatre work I've seen in recent years, e.g., in the Argentine group, El Periférico de Objectos, and Italy's Societas Raffaello Sanzio. Though for Germans his reputation is not quite rehabilitated enough so soon after the fall of the Berlin Wall, in other countries Müller is one of the few contemporary dramatists whose texts are quoted or staged by younger artists engaging issues of war, revolution, utopia, and terrorism. His writing points to many technical possibilities in the shaping of literary/dramatic texts for contemporary theatre. It goes beyond mere sampling and collage to a feeling for text that extends all the way backwards through the last century to Karl Kraus's *Last Days of Mankind,* with its quotations from advertising, newspapers, everyday conversation, religious, scientific, and literary allusions, providing an anthropological link to any audience. Müller serves up a poetic language in a politically-disturbing contemporary context.

Quraishi, like many theatre directors who are not writers, has trouble sustaining a textual framework. When I referred above to the "promise" and "problems" of international work on this scale what I meant is that it is, literally, all over the place in text and image. It is everywhere and nowhere, talkative and speechless at the same time, controlled and decentered. Texts simply become throwaway material, even when they have the gravitas of Müller, Brecht, Schiller, Levi, and the Icelandic sagas. To what purpose? This situation is not unique to Quraishi, whose task is made more challenging because he is trying to create a media-oriented mythopoetic theatre which may, in fact, be a contradiction in terms. To his credit, he has avoided wallowing in the detritus of popular culture. Nevertheless, the development of a radical new dramaturgical vision remains one of the basic necessities for the future of contemporary performance. Quraishi is largely working in a post-Wilsonian vein and, like many young directors who create highly visual theatre, he organizes a large number of performers in architectural settings which elaborate a dialogue between nature and culture and ancient and contemporary worlds. No other influential theatre director besides Wilson—including Brook, Kantor, Grotowski, Stein, Mnouchkine, Barba—has created a style that is sustained across continents in the work of younger artists. Similarly, visual artists who in recent decades moved into performance have left behind no discernible performance vocabulary, only art concepts or ways of working with materials.

For some years it has been apparent that the only real ongoing international theatrical vocabulary for new performance and opera has been derived from Wilson's way of working with time/space/text/movement, though The

Wooster Group has been hugely influential here and in Europe for those theatres who are more interested in media, rhetoric, and the actor. There are many
reasons for this historical development, two of them being the accessibility
of Wilson's aesthetic for non-actors and its adaptibility to any setting or era.
However, his style is too refined and politically non-specific for the kind of
work Quraishi does, which is closer to Reza Abdoh, who had worked through
and past the American avant-garde styles of his predecessors. Quraishi's attempt to bring together theatre and the visual arts (including sculpture, video,
installation), the live and mediated image, and a working collective gathered
from several countries, is an ambitious endeavor that necessarily depends on
a new globalized performing arts economy to exist. The international festival
circuit and multi-country sponsorship reflect that condition.

One of the oddities of this and other large assemblies of performers and
artists is the seeming hodge-podge of performance styles and techniques that
are transported from their home countries and traditions. On a basic level of
communication, which is a *raison d'etre* of any political piece, it is still essential
to shape the abundance of performance energy into a coherent experience. One
of the dichotomies of a multilevel, cross-media work whose sense of perspective is dispersed throughout so many spaces, is that it attempts to be both theatre (whose audience members engage a work on the level of group reflection)
and visual art (whose viewers create narratives from their singular experience).
In this perspective, that Wilson's style has become the default contemporary
performance mode for artists who want to do performance (but not exactly
theatre) while seeming to be more involved with visual arts, is understandable.
What this move means for the experience of the "theatrical" in the future can
only be speculated upon, but events point to its gradual disappearance in the
collusion of performance and media.

I went twice to this performance because I wanted to see what it would be
like to experience the same images beyond an initial viewing. Generally speaking, the first experience of any image is the most striking and almost never
repeats the element of surprise or disturbance or pleasure. That feeling proved
true for this event. The impact of imagery in the theatre is always something to
consider seriously. How is it experienced? How complex can it be? Is its power
attached to the body of the performer? To the text? What makes a theatrical image compelling or moving? How long does the feeling last? This kind of
an event lends itself to exploring how an image in an immersive environment
might differ from one in a fixed performance space, but perhaps there should be

a moratorium on the belief that spectators are less passive in an interactive environment than if they were sitting down watching a play. Works that instigate thought present the most active engagement, however they are made. If new forms of performance substitute overstimulation for intimacy and movement for the continuous regard, the evolution of spectatorship will certainly acquire new characteristics. How does performance knowledge differ in its varied manifestations? A complicated, anxious work such as *Schiller by Night/Landscapes* has its heart in the right place, but risks being too much and yet not enough for our desperate times. So deeply rooted in new media, it now has to compete with the viewer's understanding of the world that has been shaped by media. To separate the two for the purposes of argument: Does performance know something that technology doesn't?

This essay was originally published as a review of Compagnie Faim de Siècle's *Schiller by Night/Landscapes* in *PAJ: A Journal of Performance and Art*, Vol. XXVI, No. 1 (PAJ 76), January 2004.

Performance History

O ne of the characteristics of this decade is not only the proliferating twentieth, twenty-fifth, or fiftieth anniversary celebrations of an American theatre organization or group of artists but a revisiting of performance history, most notably in the recent commemorative exhibitions and events marking the thirty-year span of Fluxus. Now, in timely fashion, the landmark 1965 "Happenings" issue of *TDR* (then the *Tulane Drama Review*) has formed the basis of a larger anthology, *Happenings and Other Acts*, edited by Mariellen R. Sandford, the current associate editor of *TDR*, to which two-hundred pages of historical material has been added to expand the performance knowledge of this era. The special theme journal centered on happenings, Fluxus, new dance, poetry and music events, and popular entertainments, with artists such as John Cage, Ann Halprin, Yvonne Rainer, Robert Morris, Allan Kaprow, Dick Higgins, Jackson Mac Low, Paul Sills, Claes Oldenburg, Robert Ashley, and Ken Dewey contributing writings or interviews. The historical and critical analysis was elaborated by Michael Kirby and Richard Schechner, who put together the *TDR* issue, to which essays of Darko Suvin and Günter Berghaus have now been added.

In the post-war period the term "theatre" was used to describe "events" or "actions," "performance" not yet having become the catch-all phrase for live art. In his 1965 essays, "The New Theatre," the introduction to the *TDR* volume, and "Happenings," which opened his influential anthology of the same name and appears now in the new book, Kirby offered foundational texts which methodically laid out the vocabulary of the American avant-garde. He traced its roots from the European movements of dada, futurism, Bauhaus, and surrealism, and in such singular figures as Schwitters and Artaud, on into American painting, sculpture, poetry, film, and dance, eventually drawing together Europe, America, and Japan (whose Gutai group preceded happenings artists here). Through an empirical, critical approach, which is usual in the early identification of any vanguard art, Kirby outlined the nature and formal elements of contemporary performance, the predilection for chance and information structures, the difference in attitudes of time and space from conventional theatre and drama. In a lineage that has since been corroborated by history, Kirby placed John Cage, whose still challenging, three-decades-old interview appears in the volume, as the source of the new aesthetics, a fact which Allan Kaprow was to dispute in a letter to the editor (included here) after the publication of the "Happenings" issue, claiming that Kirby overemphasized both Cage and New York in his writings, while also disregarding the force of Rauschenberg and Pollock.

The terminology that has had the most long-lasting impact is Kirby's definition of "non-matrixed" performance, which he used to distinguish happenings from the style of acting required by dramatic conventions of illusion, character, and audience identification. Over the decades the "matrix" idea has been an ongoing reference point in the writings on performance by art historians and critics, while it has dropped out of theatre criticism. In my view, that development confirms the richer tradition of theatre scholarship which has been able to extend the critical vocabulary for contemporary work, and the inability of the artworld to evolve a larger view of performance. What remains important in Kirby's strategy is his linking of the visual arts and theatre in the development of a comprehensive performance history, which is even more necessary at the end of the twentieth century, now that performance has become so essential to any understanding of contemporary life. Within art history, happenings have grown in significance due to their position in the century-long move from collage to action painting, assemblage, environments, and later to conceptual art, body art, and site-specific work. Today, in the transforming ecology of performance, happenings can be seen as the antecedent of increasingly prevalent installations.

Indeed the list of contributors to *Happenings and Other Acts* only serves to demonstrate how intertwined and various were the worlds of performance, art, and writing, and how collective much of the work in the fifties and sixties was, in contrast to the solo emphasis in the eighties and nineties. Similarly, there was a pronounced absence of ideology and psychoanalysis, and more of an interest in process, materials, modes of perception, task, and structure. A reading of Higgins or Oldenburg or Morris or Dewey on their performances, or of the dialogue on dance between Rainer and Halprin, makes clear that though there were many ways to conceive performance, the understanding of space and the nature of spectatorship were major preoccupations of this generation of artists, whether articulated as minimalist cool or as the heat of intermingled bodies of performers and audiences.

What is also striking is how knowledgeable the then-young artists were in terms of art-historical consciousness, and how important historical grounding was to them; they knew what traditions they were working in, what they were reacting against and moving toward. Their collaborations existed within a community of shared values that emphasized the experimental nature of work, and formal and aesthetic issues over political ones (except for the Vietnam period), which their writings and other historical documentation confirm. Memory of the spectacular experimental energy of the arts in the fifties and sixties, and extending into the seventies, has led to a real disenchantment with the artistic quality of contemporary work by those who are familiar with the creativity of the post-war decades.

As Sandford points out in the preface to the volume, one of her intentions is to address the under-representation of women in the early "Happenings" issue. Though the exclusion of Carolee Schneemann's own work comes immediately to mind, in truth, there were only a handful of women, such as Alison Knowles (already noted in the original volume), Charlotte Moorman, Mieko Shiomi, Shigeko Kubota, Yayoi Kusama, Yoko Ono (still oddly absent from the new anthology), besides dancers or performers who on the whole left no substantial body of writings about their work, closely identified with happenings or Fluxus pieces. Still, of dancer-choreographers, Meredith Monk or Simone Forti might also have been represented in the earlier or new publication; of video performance, the work of Joan Jonas; of music, Pauline Olivieros. Putting aside the issue of the representation of women, it is also fair to ask why, of men, Jack Smith, now recognized as a seminal figure of this period, does not appear in the new anthology, nor the futuristic dancer-critic Kenneth King.

What is remarkable, though, is the number of artists featured in the 1965 *TDR* issue still highly visible today, at home and abroad. As I write these notes, within a range of weeks, in SoHo there have been current exhibitions of Oldenburg, Whitman, Morris, Schneemann; and publications of Halprin, Higgins, a theatre production of Schechner, a new film of Rainer. A recent volume of collected writings, *Essays on The Blurring of Art and Life*, by Allan Kaprow, has shown him to be a major thinker in the performance/artworld in the post-war period—always insightful, witty, risk-taking. He knows how to write about formal structures, different kinds of materials, and the nature of seeing, in essays that are art-smart yet moving toward social thought, pushing the boundaries of public space, spectatorship, action. Schneemann's recent retrospective of her paintings, constructions, drawings, photographs, videos, installations, and lecture tapes, at the New Museum of Contemporary Art, highlighted her ferocious mind and pioneering feminist research and art. *Happenings and Other*

Acts has added her famous happening, *Meat Joy*, and the anti-war piece, *Snows*. Schneemann's personal, poetic writings, as opposite as could be from the discrete, cool Kaprow—the two demonstrate the artworld's critical polarities of expression and impersonality—mark her, along with Kaprow, as one of the most provocative artist-critics of her generation.

In her earlier fights against censorship of thought, and through the influence of Artaud, Schneemann has historical links to the Frenchman Jean-Jacques Lebel, whose essay "On the Necessity of Violation" was written against the background of the 1968 social upheavals in France. The inclusion of this essay in the book, in addition to the choice of those by Suvin and Berghaus and the Schneemann material, since they do not appear in the 1965 volume, seem to reflect Sandford's attempts to give her subject a more social and political frame, in keeping with the current direction of performance history. Lebel brought together Freud, Hegel, and echoes of Breton's last writings on myth and surrealism to address issues of taboo and repression. His psychosexual manifesto leads in a direct line to the poststructuralist thinking of Baudrillard, Foucault, Deleuze and Guattari, whereas the Americans were influenced by Norman O. Brown and R. D. Laing. No American artist identified with happenings and its offshoots wrote such political diatribes, though Julian Beck of The Living Theatre, then active in Paris with Lebel, amassed a considerable body of anarchist writings.

Seen in another light, today's perspective on the body is far removed from the sixties' attitude which regarded it as a site of ecstasy, whereas now much of the performance writing links the body to death, disease, and repression, viewing it wholly as a site of contestation. Likewise, in their quest for all forms of liberation, artists in this period did not orient their work or rhetoric around inclusive heterosexual or homosexual worldviews, while today much of the writing about the body and social oppression is derived from feminist theory shaped by lesbianism, and queer theory shaped by gay thought.

Apropos of French philosophy, in his "Reflections on Happenings" Darko Suvin measures the new performance against Rousseau's thought in the longing for a back-to-nature dream that would transform urban space into a realm of innocence. This appears to him as a debased Rousseauist ideal because it doesn't physically change society, and excludes most of society except the petit-bourgeois intelligentsia privileged enough to appreciate the wonders wrought by new perceptual awareness. Elsewhere, in his suggestive though not always explicit essay, Suvin links happenings to the European modern drama of Brecht, Pirandello, and the expressionists, and to the genres of allegory and mystery play.

In his own attempt to integrate European perspectives into an American narrative, Berghaus synthesizes information that is by now well-worn art history, largely taking historical documentation at face value. Unfortunately, he doesn't create a larger frame or relate his subject to relevant theatre examples, such as The Living Theatre or Peter Handke, whose early *Sprechstücke* were viewed as happenings. Quite correctly, he highlights the more political stance of British and European pop and happenings artists, the political work of Joseph Beuys and Wolf Vostell, in contrast to the strain of Duchamp, and *informel* attitudes in the conceptual work of Yves Klein and Piero Manzoni. Inexplicably, in writing of the Europeans, he leaves out the visionary Polish artist Tadeusz Kantor, who straddled the worlds of visual arts and theatre.

Considering the Europeans as closer to the originary impulses of dada, Berghaus stresses the revolutionary potential of avant-garde performance, its scandals and anti-social elements, in fact, closing with a section on Viennese Actionism, one of the most radical and disturbing moments of performance history, when Hermann Nitsch, Otto Mühl, Gunter Brus, and Rudolf Schwarzkogler created a violently ritualistic, sado-masochistic, and narcissistic form of expressionism that exaggerated aspects of Austrian artistic tradition and Catholicism. Berghaus notes especially as "one of the most spectacular political Happenings," the Viennese Actionists' notorious *Art and Revolution* event at the University of Vienna, in 1968. The self-mutilation, drinking of urine, vomiting, smearing of the body with feces, whippings, masturbation, declamations against the state, family, and democracy that went on, accompanied finally by the singing of the Austrian national anthem, perverse as it may seem, was not uncommon behavior, of one form or another, in counterculture gatherings of the sixties: the police arrested the performers and they were jailed or given community service.

What at one time was a *de rigueur* form of social revolt now seems revolting, which only emphasizes how difficult it is to write about performance outside of its historical context, or rather that performance doesn't necessarily transcend its own age. Likewise, the then-frequent charge of "fascism" against all forms of authority seems self-dramatizing against what we now know of twentieth-century history. Given the freeing up of social mores and regulations in so many aspects of human life in the decades since the sixties, one can only ask now: How far can the social contract expand before it collapses? What are the limits of freedom and utopian desire? In the context of the eventual co-optation of any radical gesture in democratic, capitalist societies and, in the latter case, Austria's history in recent decades and its swing to the right, how can one believe the claims of those who speak of such marginal activities as performance acts as if they had any real bearing on the direction of society, in the long view of things?

Surely, there is some suspension of disbelief going on in the extravagant claims for social intervention and subversion performance now generates among many academic critics and the artists who follow their theories. The continuous assault on the distinctions between art and life may have outlived its credibility in the world we inhabit now. A study of happenings and what came after forces one to question the current widespread attitude toward performance as a means of personal and social fulfillment, which has come to replace its value as art.

The appearance of *Happenings and Other Acts* is timely and significant, not only for making available essential historical documents, but as an antidote to the largely unreadable writing and ill-informed glorification of all manner of "performance" and "performativity" now flooding books and journals, and written mostly by academics who have no connection whatsoever with actual art practice or artists, or any discernible feeling for artistic process. Michael Kirby, who died in March 1997, was a unique historian and critic in that he lived and worked among artists in a center of arts activity, New York, and at the same time held an academic position. He not only wrote about art and artists but spoke the language of art. His death (and that of the founder of *TDR*, Robert Corrigan, a few years before him) marks the sad beginning of the end of this generation of art-centered critic/educators who took for granted the organic relationship to their subject.

Sometime during the course of writing this commentary, I attended a Saturday afternoon symposium on art and media at the Guggenheim Museum. After presentations on their work by Laurie Anderson, Gary Hill, and others, there were questions from the audience. One woman, who perhaps had read a little too much of Donna Haraway, asked the panelists to address the issue of technology blah blah blah woman blah identity blah blah. An obvious art professor, who most likely had wandered uptown from the College Art Association meeting that week, tried to explain what she meant when the panelists seemed perplexed, adding his own commodification jargon of blah blah representation blah blah blah patriarchal blah male masterworks. In a matter of seconds it was apparent that the artists were at somewhat of a loss to respond.

They didn't even understand the language in which the remarks were addressed to them or the "ready-made" phrases in which they were framed. So far has the world of performance come in three decades that most "innocent" artists now live separate lives from those academics who, wizened by years of theoryspeak, are conditioned to regard every action as quivering with political significance and every work of art supercharged by revolutionary potential. There was a time when a performance just happened.

This essay was originally published as a review of *Happenings and Other Acts*, Mariellen R. Sandford, ed., in *Performing Arts Journal*, Vol. XIX, No. 2 (PAJ 56), May 1997.

Hymns of Repetition

How appropriate that in the fiftieth year since the death of Gertrude Stein and centenary year of Virgil Thomson's birth, their landmark opera collaboration, *Four Saints in Three Acts*, the hit of the 1934 theatre season, should be staged in New York City for whose avant-garde artists and audiences it has meant so much over the decades. Robert Wilson, his work extending this modernist legacy that began to flourish in America at Black Mountain and in post-war arts experiments, directed and designed the new production. It had opened earlier in the year at the Houston Grand Opera before being seen this summer as part of the Lincoln Center Festival 96.

Wilson's staging pays homage to the original production, a collaboration that included John Houseman, Florine Stettheimer, Frederick Ashton, and Maurice Grosser, in very subtle ways, such as the emphasis on the hand gestures of the singers and the costuming of one of them in a broad-rimmed hat that looks like a halo. The original production had more in common with the raw, hand-made look of post-Ubu avant-garde performances between the wars and entertainments in Parisian nightclubs. Wilson brings an elegant, luxurious style and a century of modern-art knowledge to his understanding of Stein, who has been a major influence on his own way of putting together words and sounds as poetic text. But more strikingly, in the author's eloquent designation of a play as a landscape. The use of supertitles for the New York production prompts an unwitting ironic comment on their relationship as artists whose work plays text against image. How does what you see relate to what you hear? Stein wondered in her essay "Plays." Here she writes, "In Four Saints I made the Saints the landscape," adding, "A landscape does not move nothing really moves in a landscape but things are there, and I put into the play the things that were there." What more does one need to know?

If the *Four Saints* libretto is Stein's most complete elaboration of play as landscape, it is also Wilson's most successful realization of her extraordinary concept. Story is never so important as the relations between things, so imagery takes precedence over dramatic action, and the absence of psychology negates memory in favor of the immediate experience of a work. Stein's miracle play, which synchronizes Paris of the twenties and baroque Spain, the writing life and the lives of the saints—art and religious devotion—is no more about St. Theresa than *Einstein on the Beach*, its descendant, is about Albert Einstein. Wilson's treatment of historical figures has always been "Steinian."

What is the "reality" of a work of art? Where does its temporal quality reside? Even in stillness there is the movement of life, and both Wilson and Stein, in disregarding the anecdotal, show how eventful, how full of vibration, the time of a landscape can be when it is filled with people and things. Then, performance space is transformed into a landscape of constant surprise. In Stein's playful manner of writing *Four Saints*, the "plot" is extended as a work-in-progress, always calling attention to itself, turning off in different directions, wondering what to do next, getting others involved with the process of creation. "How many saints can sit around," one of them asks. "How many acts are there in it?"

If Wilson's 1992 Berlin-originated production of Stein's *Dr. Faustus Lights the Lights* was German in its expressionist tendencies and clipped diction of actors for whom English is a foreign language, his *Four Saints* is demonstrably French in its quotation, full of lightheartedness and air. And, if the original production seems to have been more sculptural in its intentions, the new presentation is certainly more painterly. Among the wonders of this production is the reference to landscape painting in the exquisite stage compositions, which, since the purposely less refined big choruses in Wilson's early work, such as *The Life and Times of Joseph Stalin*, now more than two decades later, have evolved into the smooth-flowing choreography of large groups on stage. How lovely to observe the picnic scene which has the saints seated, scattered about the stage floor, while behind them, in an allusion to the *saltimbanque* of modern painting, an acrobat flips across the stage. The scene generates a visible feeling of warmth and sheer rapture in the joy of creativity for its own sake that synchronizes with Stein's ecstatic text.

But even as the staging is full of secular pleasures, there is always present the iconography of religious painting, in the outstretched or upward seeking hands and extended palms of the singers. (The photographs of the Houseman staging may lead one to speculate that the precise gestures of the performers' hands as shown have been a decisive influence on Wilson's preoccupation with the vocabulary of hands in his own work. In fact, in the original production, a dove that appeared on St. Theresa's hand in the opening scene in which she is photographed—an egg-shaped clear balloon is substituted in the new version—suggests that it may be the source for so many of the scenes in his *oeuvre* which feature a black bird on the wrist of a performer.)

How blissful to watch the saints carrying small models of houses—the heavenly mansions of St. Theresa's *Interior Castle*—like their counterparts in Renaissance painting. Perhaps it also inspires the flat side views of a large hand (of God?) that hovers over the saints, and the angel who lingers there, too. Wilson gives full expression to his fascination with scale in the theatre. If the original production had a stuffed lion, now he has huge cutout giraffes that peer out from the wings, an oversized pear and a slinky snake, and sheep that rise up from the ground to fill a luscious blue sky with dreams. Other objects that seem to take on a performing life are the Japanese headrest that St. Theresa I (there are two of them) lies on, large hanging trees (one of them, Wilson's ubiquitous upside-down tree), a crescent moon, a single window-frame, a model house, and wide horizontal bands that form choir pews.

Wilson has shown through his staging and design the deep connection between minimalist style and spiritual style. A little biplane floats across the sky when Sanford Sylvan as St. Ignatius, in his somber baritone, sings so wondrously of pigeons on the grass which, Stein revealed, refers to a vision of the Holy Ghost. Her illuminated text, which celebrates visionary consciousness, the artistic and the saintly, is made up of simple acts of language that trace the rhythm of conversation in the divine pleasure of repeating letters and syllables and sounds outdoors. In the Steinian ecology, language exists everywhere in the landscape, as if all space were semantic, the world a book.

Virgil Thomson, in one of the great meetings of the minds in the American theatre, created an opera that would bring to Stein's work the sound of waltzes, marches, hymns, and children's playsong. John Cage counted at least thirty-eight allusions to nursery rhymes in the score. It drew on nineteenth-century German music and American parlor music—sources from which Scott Joplin had earlier created another kind of syncopation, ragtime—and, in Paris, Les Six. Though Stein had provided the radically innovative libretto for the ninety-minute opera, it was Thomson who, in completing the piano-vocal score by 1928, before Maurice Grosser would devise a scenario for the piece he organized as a series of stage "pictures," shaped Stein's frequently long line of poetry into smaller units. He distributed them among individual singers and chorus, resulting in a structure that omitted very little of her text. He also split St. Theresa into two roles, a soprano and a mezzo-soprano, enhancing the self-conscious attitude of the original. Thomson's setting rather than Grosser's (it is not credited in the program but serves a more inspirational function) is the basis of the Wilson production. How easily Stein's language moves from speech to song, reveling in its inherent musicality. This may be the legacy of Walt Whitman, which also infects the free-spirited approach of Thomson. Dennis Russell Davies, known for his support of non-traditional composers, brings a sense of knowingness to his conducting that always preserves the gentle and leisurely pace of the work.

To the American vernacular style Thomson had added the parts of Compère and Commère, character types drawn from the French music hall already familiar to Parisian audiences from Cocteau's *The Wedding on the Eiffel Tower* (here they are metamorphosed into human phonographs) and the Cocteau-Stravinsky *Oedipus Rex*. Coincidentally, their at times vaudeville-style interludes function in the manner of a "knee-play," one of Wilson's favorite devices, the bracketed sections of movement that act as the "joints" of a production. In *Four Saints* the Compère and Commère, who perform highly-stylized, angular hand movements at expressive moments, take their places at opposite ends of the downstage area, from where they comment on, narrate, and become part of the goings-on. Wilbur Pauley's Compère, whose deep elongated sounds accentuate his long, thin features to bring a good deal of humor to the opera, is costumed in a black half-gorilla suit of the kind one of the actors wore in the 1988 Wilson-David Byrne collaboration *The Forest*.

The costumes, designed by the Italian painter Francesco Clemente, reflect his sensual mix of the abstract and the ritualistic, and his feeling for emotional colors. For the most part, the performers, men and women, wear long ivory-colored hoop dresses of turn-of-century style, but if you look closely in the front of each costume there is a male or female sexual symbol. Clemente created for St. Ignatius a long, floor-length robe covered with bees, and for St. Chavez, another full robe crisscrossed by large arrows and eyes: the two Theresas wear royal blue dresses with a white heart across the bosom. The chorus of saints is fitted in beautiful, earthy tones of green, brown, and terra-cotta, though one of the performers is wearing a Bauhaus-style costume. A more enigmatic, symbolic presence in *Four Saints* (not in the original libretto) is the "primitive" blue-faced young man, in loin cloth, a white scarf wrapped around his head, and wearing white gloves, who is related to figures in Wilson's productions of Debussy's *Le Martyre de Saint Sébastien*, the *CIVIL warS*, and *The Forest*, and even more provocatively, to the 1934 staging, perhaps an allusion to the contemporary impact of Stravinsky's *Rite of Spring*, seen in Paris twenty-one years earlier.

The figure is an ancient, otherworldly spirit in the opera, a reminder of the relationship of modernism and paganism, modern art and ritual. He first appears in a large constructivist-style light wood boat, then at various times throughout the opera wanders among the singers. But his most glorious rendering is at the intermezzo when, with the sweep of a wand, the color of the cyclorama (much remarked on in Stettheimer's conception) rapidly changes to a spectrum of the rainbow, for brief moments in time the splendor of the Jennifer Tipton/Wilson lighting signaling to the audience the prominence of light in the early modern theatre, as an aspect of modernism's spiritual quest. The color of light is one of the many kinds of ecstasy in this production.

Coming at the end of the century, Wilson's spare but gorgeous staging of the Stein/Thomson classic proposes a new way of looking at Stein, and just as valuably, a splendid sense of how to comprehend artistic traditions. His production is a virtual casebook, embodying histories of imagery and histories of performance style that represent a culmination of modernism, as it were. The real achievement of this new *Four Saints* is the way it frames performance history to elucidate for its audiences the process through which ideas, art, and style are transmitted through artworks. In other words, where do images, objects, figures, and language go? What comes after them? How does it happen? What does it mean to imagine and reimagine "canon," "repertoire," "classic"?

Seeing *Ocean*, the last collaboration of Merce Cunningham and John Cage, before his death in 1992, back to back with the opera as part of the Festival, makes all the more evident the American lines of avant-garde influence. Here in this piece is Cunningham's (he first asked Wilson to collaborate on *Four Saints* more than two decades ago) own special attention to the hands and fingers of the performers (like Martha Graham before him), the dance itself lacking any perspectival focal point, a simultaneity of events replacing narrative. Here is the field of sound celebrated by Cage (he had already set Stein texts to music in the thirties), with one-hundred-and-twelve musicians surrounding the audience who surround the dancers on a circular stage set up in Damrosch Park. Stein gave both artists license "to act as if there is no use in a center." The expansion of perception and performance knowledge is what matters. This was to be a new Enlightenment in the history of performance ideas. It begins in the reality of space: space around the word, space around the sound, space around the performer. Space would act as a field of revelation.

Looking back over the twentieth century, what emerges is a distinctive American style that can be traced from Stein to Cage/Cunningham, then to Wilson, and in music, from Thomson to contemporary composers such as Philip Glass, John Adams, Robert Ashley, Steve Reich, Laurie Anderson, and

Meredith Monk, who continue to search for new, colloquial musical languages. American avant-garde theatre tradition rooted itself in European modernism before becoming absorbed at home in the experiments of the last half-century, the two traditions merging in work whose texts are more poetry than drama, the staging more painterly than anecdotal, the music more speech than symphony, and whose profound spiritual awareness is less dogma than philosophy. The American sublime is a vernacular marvelous.

This essay was originally published as a review of Robert Wilson's production of *Four Saints in Three Acts* in *Performing Arts Journal*, Vol. XVIII, No. 3 (PAJ 54), September 1996.

The Economy of Tenderness

E ver since *Fefu and Her Friends* Maria Irene Fornes has been writing the finest realistic plays in this country. In fact, one could say that *Fefu* and the plays that followed it, such as *The Danube* and now *Mud*, have paved the way for a new language of dramatic realism, and a style of directing it. What Fornes, as writer and director of her work, has done is to strip away the self-conscious objectivity, narrative weight, and behaviorism of the genre to concentrate on the unique subjectivity of characters for whom talking is gestural, a way of being. There is no attempt to tell the whole story of a life, only to distill its essence. Fornes brings a much needed intimacy to drama, and her economy of approach suggests another vision of theatricality, more stylized for its lack of exhibitionism. In this new theatricality, presence—that is, the act of being—is of greatest importance. The theatrical idea of presence is an aspect of social being expressed by character. The approach is that of a documentary starkness profoundly linked to existential phenomenology.

Fornes's work goes to the core of character. Instead of the usual situation in which a character uses dialogue or action to explain what he or she is doing and why, her characters exist in the world by their very act of trying to understand it. In other words, it is the characters themselves who appear to be thinking, not the author having thought.

Mud, which has as its center the act of a woman coming to thought, clarifies this process. Here is a poor rural trio, Fornes's first lower-depths characters, which consists of Mae, Lloyd, and Henry, who lead lives devoid of any sense of play or abandonment; their lives are entirely functional. Each of them exists in varying relations to language—Mae through her desire to read and acquire knowledge realizes that knowledge is the beginning of will and power and personal freedom; Henry, who becomes crippled in an accident during the course of the play, must learn again how to speak; Lloyd, barely past the level of survival beyond base instincts, has no language of communication beyond an informational one. *Mud* is the encounter of the characters in seventeen scenes that are separated by slow blackouts of "eight seconds," the story of struggles for power in which Henry usurps Lloyd's place in Mae's bed, and

Lloyd kills Mae when she eventually walks out on Henry and him and their destitute existence. The violence committed in this play is the violence of the inarticulate.

Through the plays of Bond, Kroetz, Fassbinder, Wenzel, Vinaver, plays that outline the contemporary vision of tragedy, a new and different realism stripped bare came into drama in the seventies in Europe. But this refinement of realism, to the extent that it could be called a movement, never happened here, largely because of the heavy input of psychology and speech in American theatre, the scant interest in stylized gesture and emotion, the lack of attention to the nuances of language as a political condition. (Though one could point to such plays as Tavel's *Boy on the Straight-Back Chair*, Shepard's *Action*, Mamet's *Edmond*, Shank's *Sunset/Sunrise* as steps toward an American rethinking of realism, they are only isolated phenomena.) What Fornes has done in her approach to realism over the years, and *Mud* is the most austere example of this style to be produced in the theatre on this side of the Atlantic, is to lift the burden of psychology, declamation, moralism, and sentimentality from the concept of character. She has freed characters from explaining themselves in a way that attempts to suggest interpretations of their actions, and put them in scenes that create a single emotive moment, as precise in what it does not articulate as in what does get said.

She rejects ordinary realism's clichés of thought patterns, how its characters project themselves in society; she rejects its melodramatic self-righteousness. Though her work is purposely presented in a flat space that emphasizes its frontality, and the actors speak in a non-inflected manner, it is not the detached cool of hyper- or super- or photo-realism, but more emotive, filled with content. Gestures, emptied of their excesses, are free to be more resonant. *The Danube* resounds with the unspeakable horror of nuclear death precisely because it is not named.

Mud's scenes seem, radically, to be a comment on what does not occur in performance, as if all the action had happened off stage. Fornes's realism subtracts information, whereas the conventional kind does little more than add it to a scene. She turns realism upside-down by attacking its materialism and in its place emphasizing the interior lives of her characters, not their exterior selves. Hers is not a drama infatuated with things, but the qualities that make a life. Even when Henry buys Mae lipstick and a mirror in which to see herself, the moment is not for her a cosmetic gesture but a recognition of a self in the act of knowing, an objectification of the self.

There is no waste in her productions. Fornes has always had a common sense approach to drama that situates itself in the utter simplicity of her dialogue. She writes sentences, not paragraphs. Her language is a model of direct address, it has the modesty of a writer for whom English is a learned language. She is unique in the way she writes about sexuality, in a tender way that accents sexual feelings, not sex as an event. It is a bitterly sad moment when Henry, his body twisted, his speech thick with pain, begs Mae to make love to him: "I feel the same desires. I feel the same needs. I have not changed." Emotion is unbidden in her plays. Just as language is not wasted, so the actors don't waste movements. Each scene is a strong pictorial unit. Sometimes a scene is only an image, or a few lines of dialogue. Here realism is quotational, theatre in close-up, freeze frame, theatre made by a miniaturist: In *The Danube* an acted scene is replayed in front of the stage by puppets, creating a fierce honorableness in its comment on human action. It is not aggressive in its desire to create a world on a stage invested with moral imperatives, it is interested only in tableaux from a few lives in a particular place and time. Each scene presents a glimpse of imagery that is socially meaningful.

The pictorial aspect of this realism signifies an important change in theatrical attitudes toward space. Whereas traditional realism concerned itself with a confined physicality determined by "setting," the new realism is more open cosmologically, its characters iconic. That is one of the reasons why this emotive, sinewy realism is rooted in expressionist style. (Expressionism keeps realism from becoming melodrama.) Contemporary painting also turned to expressionism, after a period of super-realism, in order to generate an approach to emotion, narration, and content. If styles change according to new perceptions of human form and its socialization, then painting and theatre, arts that must continually revise their opinions of figuration, should follow similar directions in any given period. Today, the exaggerated theatricality in everyday life has brought painting and theatre closer together.

The new realism would be confined by mere setting, which is only informational. It needs to be situated in the wider poetic notion of "space" that has ontological references. In the ecology of theatre, setting is a closed system of motion while space is more aligned to the idea of landscape that influences theatre, not only in writing but in design, as a result of now regarding the stage as "performance space." The very idea of space itself indicates how much the belief that all the world's a stage has been literalized. The concept of theatrical

space alludes to the global repercussions of human action, if only metaphorically. (It is not coincidental that the concept of "performance space" developed
in the same period, the sixties, as the exploration of outer space.)

In recent years Fornes has become such a self-assured director that the
movement in her productions seems nearly effortless, totally inhibiting actorly
artificiality. She doesn't force her actors' bodies on us in an attempt for them
to dominate space. She leaves spaces on the stage unused. She makes the actors appreciate stillness as a theatrical idea, they are considerate toward other
theatrical lives. And Fornes acknowledges the audience by giving them their
own space and time in the productions. In *Mud* the short scenes and blackouts
emphasize this attitude toward reception. They leave room for the audience to
enter for contemplative moments. The authorial voice does not demand power
over the theatrical experience. It is not territorial. There is room for subjectivity,
as a corrective to evasive objectification, on the part of all those involved in the
making and witnessing of the event. *Fefu and Her Friends* is the play that most
literally invites the audience into the playing space—there are five of them to
be exact—and in order to achieve this effect Fornes creates a style of acting that
seems, simply, a way of talking, it is so real.

Fornes has found her own stage language, a method of discourse that unites
play, actor, and space in an organic whole that is always showing how it thinks
even as it allows for fragments of thought, unruly contradictions. One of the
characteristics of Fornes's plays is that they offer characters *in the process of
thought*. Her characters often question received ideas, conventions, the idea of
emotion, even how one engages in thought. "What would be the use of knowing things if they don't serve you, if they don't help you shape your life?" asks
Henry. All thought must be useful to characters and find meaning through life
itself, to allow life its fullest expression. Mae, who is studying reading and arith-
metic, rejoices in the process of acquiring knowledge, even if, as she admits, her
poor memory keeps her from retaining all that she is learning. *Mud* is imbued
with a feminism of the most subtle order, an understanding based on the ruling
idea that a free woman is one who has autonomy of thought. Mae's decision to
leave home and seek a better life coincides with her new knowledge of her self
and a sense that there is a world outside of the self.

On one level, Fornes's plays equate the pleasure of thinking with the measure of being. That so many of her plays—*Dr. Kheal, Tango Palace, Evelyn
Brown*—besides those already mentioned here, to one degree or another deal

with the acquisition of language, alludes to what must surely be one of her consistent interests: the relationship of language to thought and action. The dramatic language is finely honed to exclude excessive qualifiers, adjectives, clauses. Sentences are simple, they exist to communicate, to question. There is a purity to this language of understatement that does not assume anything, and whose dramatic potential rests in the search for meaning in human endeavor. That is why the human voice, as an embodiment of social values, has so significant a place in this kind of writing.

Fornes's work has a warm delicacy and grace that distinguish it from most of what is written today. Apart from her plays there is little loveliness in the theatre. And yet I must stop to include Joseph Chaikin and Meredith Monk in this special group of artists, for they also reflect this "loveliness" of presence. Loveliness?—a humanism that guilelessly breathes great dignity into the human beings they imagine into life, and so propose to reality. Working for more than twenty years in Off Broadway's unheralded spaces, Fornes is an exemplary artist who through her writing and teaching has created a life in the theatre away from the crass hype that attends so many lesser beings. How has she managed that rare accomplishment in this country's theatre—a career? What is admirable about Fornes is that she is one of the last of the real bohemians among the writers who came to prominence in the sixties. She never falsely tuned her voice to the times. She has simply been busy writing, working. If there were a dozen writers in our theatre with Fornes's wisdom and graciousness it would be enough for a country, and yet even one of her is, sometimes, all that is necessary to feel the worth of the enormous effort it takes to live a life in the American theatre.

II

Early in *Abingdon Square* a young woman says to an inquisitive friend, "You have to know how to enter another person's life." In many ways that rule of etiquette has shaped the theatre of Maria Irene Fornes, whose profound theme has always been the conduct of life.

This is particularly true of *Abingdon Square*, in which she creates a universe more Catholic than any of the other worlds of her plays. The teenage Marion marries a loving older man, has an affair with another man, a child with a third, descends into a personal hell, and in the end nurses her husband after his stroke out of a sense of compassion and remembered love. At a time when so much writing about women (and men) celebrates the joys of sexual freedom, Fornes is writing about sin, penance, forgiveness, the power of love. She does not deny her characters the choice and excitement of self-discovery in transgression—in this case, adultery—but concerns herself instead with the repercussions of such liberating acts. *Abingdon Square*, then, is a counter-reformation for our ideological age, in which responsibility for one's actions is regarded as a hindrance to personal fulfillment. Fornes's abiding humanism is in stark contrast to contemporary drama's moral relativism and contingency ploys.

Fornes is an unabashed moralist, which is why her thinking is so suited to the epic style she has been developing as writer and director in recent years, at least since *Fefu and Her Friends*. Epic dramaturgy is rooted in the medieval morality play, which produced a synthesis of theatrical and spiritual style. If Brecht used this form to proselytize for his secular religion of communism, and the expressionists for the rebirth of modern man, Fornes makes it her own to represent the spiritual lives of women—the kinds of choices they make and why.

In her recent production of *Abingdon Square* at the San Diego Repertory Theatre she has brought all of these strands together in a staging of more clarity and evocativeness than the original production of the play in 1987, at the American Place Theatre in New York. The play itself has been considerably revised since a workshop at the Seattle Repertory Theatre in 1984 and Fornes's own 1988 staging at the Studio Arena Theatre in Buffalo. In San Diego it was performed on alternate nights in English and in Spanish.

Stylistically, *Abingdon Square* is a journey play, but more important, another kind of *Lehrstück*, or learning play. Enlightenment must be spiritual, not merely the absorption of received ideas. Knowledge is understood in the Platonic sense, as absolute beauty, virtue. Fornes's moral tale is strengthened by its distance from contemporary life and values and its elaboration over a ten-year period in the World War I era. It exudes a willful circumspection and sense of refinement.

In such a universe a person must know his or her worth. Marion looks to Dante for instruction. She keeps a diary to chronicle "things that are imagined." Learning—the book, the diary, the act of writing—holds a special place in the work of Fornes, for knowledge struggled over is a form of empowerment, a way of mastering one's life, a guide to value, the cultivation of worldliness. A manuscript must be of the illuminated kind, revelatory. (Kroetz develops this same theme in *Through the Leaves*, also using the epic form.) One of Fornes's preoccupations in her work is the evolution of a higher, transcendent knowledge from sexual knowledge. The body is a body of knowledge.

Fornes takes a very ascetic approach to life. It is important to live in a state of grace and to save your soul, for there is a sense of heroism in the admission of shame. Her asceticism accepts the dualism of body and soul. Nothing must be extraneous, merely decorative, self-destructive. The good life is measured in terms of accountability, purity of heart, transformation through work and study. Chekhov had that code of ethics; his thought moved along the same bourgeois lines of self-improvement. The comedy of characters who fail to achieve this gracefulness, therefore, is never one of mockery or the grotesque. It is that of manners—humors—as when the dour husband Juster reads a long, suggestive passage about pollination from an E.A. Bowles garden book in a brief scene after Marion and a cousin gossip with "sinful" delight about a *ménage à trois* they've heard of. How do the three of them make love? Fornes's laughter sometimes comes in threes instead of the usual comic pairs. One of her early plays she called *The Successful Life of 3*.

More than any of her other works, *Abingdon Square* develops rhetorically through a prayer-like formality. Sentences are simple, short, unequivocating: very few contractions are used. There is genuine communication, not diversionary chitchat. Characters tend to understand themselves and reflect on their behavior, traits reinforced by the liberal use of the pronoun "I" in strong, declarative sentences. At times the language is confessional, transcendent. In this way, the quality of voice is given primacy in the writing: it is the link to God. There is a certain sacredness attributed to the word because it expresses self-knowledge, which in Fornes's hierarchy of values is esteemed as a gift. The upper-class Marion shares this intuition, as well as the innate qualities of goodness and charity, with her earlier embodiment, the dirt-poor Mae of *Mud*.

Fornes's lessons evolve in a precisely defined horizontal space that emphasizes stations of a life. The lack of depth in the stage privileges the portrait, the still life of tableau, as an object of contemplation, accenting the iconic nature of the scenes. There are thirty-one of them, usually brief, some only visual, others in monologue, separated from one another by a blackout. The sense of miniaturization also enhances the dimension of scale, making the events on stage at times more dramatic. Every element of the staging moves toward a meditative rhythm, space to breathe between scenes, darkness and stillness to welcome thought. The stage space and the auditorium forge a single architectural unit.

The (didactic) pictorial frame, reflecting Forness's early life as a painter, is well-suited to the epic construction of the play. Doorways, windows, walls, glass panes serve to emphasize the sense of the frame. In one important scene—a frame within a frame—part of the center back wall gives way to reveal an alcove wherein Marion is practicing the mortification of the flesh, as it were, shaking, arms stretched heavenward, in a trance-like recitation of "Purgatorio" from *The Divine Comedy*. A concerned old aunt finds her and in the final moment of the scene lays her body over the conscience-stricken Marion, evoking the Pietà-like resonance of religious painting. Forness's space is theological.

If this drama is positioned between heaven and hell, light and dark are its poetic counterparts. Before her marriage to the much older Juster, Marion re-joices, "In this house light comes through the windows as if it delights in enter-ing. I feel the same." Toward the end of the play, when both husband and wife are at the brink of madness, Juster will say, "Paper would burn if it were held up to her glance. When I reached the door I saw her back reflected in the glass. She was so still that there was no life in her." The issue of enlightenment, which is so central to the work, is played out in the chiaroscuro effects of the staging. One can feel the sensuous interplay of light and emotion in the visual style that characterizes Forness's directorial intelligence.

Besides emphasizing the pictorial, the San Diego staging, for all its quietude, was more operatic than the original. The highly emotional, taut quality of the writing, its subject matter of love, and the stylization of movements shaped the melodic line of the production. Scenes were played in many different musical moods, at times hymnal, on occasion ragtime, then nocturne, or adagio. Rich-ard Strauss's *Four Last Songs*, a touch of Vivaldi, or an aria from Purcell's *Dido and Aeneas* used between some of the scenes heightened their musical quality, transforming the work's epic nature by provoking at times a wonderful humor-ous tension between melodrama and expressionism. The human, high drama was then subtly contrasted to the indifferent life of plants on the stage and of trees growing in the garden, glimpsed through the parlor doors leading outside, and through which Marion and her lover initially reveled in their illicit affair, now turned from farce to tragedy. If more and more directors here and abroad are becoming attracted to opera and music theatre, this is a rare instance of the operatic informing dramaturgy in ways that point to new possibilities of rhyth-mic experimentation within the epic vocabulary. Melodrama is a natural incli-nation in the highly emotional space of passion and its repression that defines opera because it addresses, to a great degree, heroism. In fact, the triumph of passion over negotiation (the latter the subject of contemporary life) is perhaps what is making artists and audiences turn now in increasing numbers to opera. The beauty of the soul *in extremis* is desperately needed on our stage, ridden with role models instead of heroes, opinion in place of knowledge.

So is the imperative to create a greater place with artists of mature vision. It is one of the scandals of the American theatre, obsessed as it is with "development," whether of the playwright or funding sources or subscribers (and the parallels between the real estate industry and the theatre are notoriously striking in their attitude toward preservation), that at the age of sixty-two, after three decades of a richly committed life in the theatre, Fornes is still working on the margins. Most of the theatres she works in, like the San Diego Repertory Theatre, which offered a home to this remarkable production, survive on the edge of bankruptcy. When *Abingdon Square* was produced recently in London, it went from the fringe to the National Theatre.

At her age, and with such a long record of distinguished achievement entirely within the medium of theatre, a fully elaborated directorial style, and a grand reputation as a teacher, Fornes should be given all that the American theatre has to offer in terms of resources—choice of actors, technicians, designers, access to larger audiences, longer runs. Imagine what other artists might learn from Fornes. Imagine how her own work might grow under new artistic conditions. Yet, her work has never appeared on the main stage of any of the major theatres that pride themselves on providing an alternative to the commercial exigencies of Broadway—the Vivian Beaumont, the Guthrie, the Mark Taper Forum, Arena Stage, the American Repertory Theatre, the Public Theater, among countless others. At the center of theatre's exclusionary practice and arrested development is the absence of the mature dramatic voice.

For too long the American theatre system has ruthlessly infantilized artists and audiences by coddling "new" playwrights and directors, falsely setting up generation gaps where instead we should be able to see theatre artists develop in relation to one another, generation to generation. An art form must carry on an internal dialogue with its own history, and the successive histories of artists and audiences, to honor cultural memory in any meaningful way. The American theatre obscures the profound relationship between art and society at every turn. No space is created for American writers as they mature.

The American theatre has never found a way to integrate its avant-garde artists into the larger world of theatre as Europe did, by giving them a place in their major institutions after they've proved their worth, nor even the way that the film, literary, and art establishments/industries have done here. In theatre the avant-garde spirit is made perpetual outcast. This dilemma increases as artists age, because they cannot constantly, to recall Lillian Hellman's good phrase, cut their conscience to fit each year's fashion, slavishly following the new hype of funding sources, theatre publicists and boards, trendy "isms." Are you now or have you ever been an (avant-garde art) ist? The real twist in the theatre scene is not that it pandered to the masses but that it pandered to the funding sources and their shifting "priorities." Both conservatives and progressives, the right and left/liberal, have corrupted the funding process at the most base level. Art has become a branch of journalism or the social sciences, and critical discourse mere publicity. Only the true artists of the theatre can resist the grant hustle, the hype. They risk marginalization, obscurity, censure, unemployment. But then, being an artist is not a rights issue.

Fornes was in San Diego with her one-hundred-year-old mother Carmen, her frequent companion during theatrical engagements in this country and abroad. I hope that Fornes herself lives to be one hundred, still moving from place to place, bringing her work to the world without any trace of bitterness, simply considering herself lucky to be working in our economy of planned obsolescence of people and things, and that she may be fortunate in old age to have her own fellow travelers, if, that is, the light of our most courageous theatre artists has not been snuffed out by the shades of official culture already appearing on the horizon of the twenty-first century.

III

If spiritual sorrow is a quality of her moral universe, the physical reality of the body is at the center of its drama. In most of the plays Maria Irene Fornes has written in the past two decades, illness and pain are everyday certitudes. Think of Julia with her open wound in *Fefu and Her Friends*, *Mud*'s hapless Henry and Lloyd, the mysteriously ill characters from *The Danube*, and the husband who suffers a stroke in *Abingdon Square*. Perhaps all along and all the while she has filigreed her work in delicate shades and with the economy of tenderness, Fornes, for whom a character's acquisition of knowledge is so insistent an ideal, has been imagining a language of pain. Her dramatic bodies act as epistemological sites, transformed by sexual experience, emotional expression, intellectual pursuit, or, symbolizing goodness, spiritual imbalance, evil. The individual body is never disconnected from the world but is a measure of its social biology.

More than any of her plays *Enter THE NIGHT* most completely attends to the perception of illness: AIDS, it is. But this play rejects the familiar comforts of social drama, even departing from convention and propriety in one piercing, long speech to expose the psychological process through which contemporary theatre turns plays about illness into a genre, prophesying a future in which theatre's subject matter is dictated by the illnesses most suffered by audience members, and funded willingly by pharmaceutical laboratories. Fornes's own drama is never cast with victims.

The disarming trio of the play, the nurse Tressa, her married friend Paula (she has heart trouble) who owns a farm, and Jack, a stage manager whose lover has died of AIDS, in the uninhibited bonds of a long friendship, dramatize different kinds of love and fantasy. Their unexpected cross-dressing and crossing of cultures elaborate the mysteries of spirit and flesh, race and gender, performance and fashion in scenes that are alternately innocent or psychosexually provocative, but surprisingly touching.

If the quoting of film dialogue and talk of actors and acting is a long-standing feature of Fornes's oeuvre, dating to the early plays *The Successful Life of 3* and *Molly's Dream*, in *Enter THE NIGHT* the performance situations are more emotionally charged, even allegorical in part. Fornes uses two films to highlight its themes: D.W. Griffith's 1920 silent *Broken Blossoms* and Frank Capra's *Lost Horizon* from 1937. The second act of the play opens with a cross-dressed enactment of the scene from *Broken Blossoms* in which the male character Huang (the Richard Barthelmess role, now played by Tressa), who has come to the aid of the young girl (Lillian Gish's role, now played by Jack) cruelly beaten by her father, with great care wraps her in an embroidered gown, crowns her with flowers, makes up her face, and places her softly in the bed in his room. Though they are never shown in the play itself, Griffith's actual film titles explain that Huang has left China to bring the message of the Buddha to the "barbarous Anglo-Saxons." He is the only civilizing force in the girl's wretched life.

The Oriental robe, slippers, box jacket, and pants that Tressa wears in this scene and earlier in the play have a strange attraction for her. The clothes make her feel like an Asian man: in her body, in her voice, in her face, in her feet. When she dresses like a Western man it is only for fun, whereas the Asian man in her clothes existential calm in the becoming suit of androgyny. Paula admires Tressa as a "lovely" man. Jack is soothed by seeing her dressed like this, and grows nervous if she wears women's clothes when they are together. But why? When for the first time Paula comes upon Jack and Tressa, cross-gendered, performing the last few minutes of their "act," which she recognizes immediately as a scene from *Broken Blossoms*, she is given a glimpse of their very private erotic world. The two who had made love one night long ago now caress each other in the silent signs of art, their ritualized behavior evolved into another form of lovemaking.

Tressa's cross-dressing is not mere play, but a state of mind inscribed in the most fervent gestures. Neither is it a subversive act: it is private, not social. It has no consciousness of a society beyond itself. Her performance, which comforts Jack and poeticizes her own passion for him, is more a reflection of Fornes's linkage of spirituality and sexuality, an ontological rather than a sociological condition. Elsewhere, in the more playful setting of *Fefu and Her Friends*, where the character Emma speaks of the "divine registry" of sexual performance and a heaven peopled with "divine lovers," the key to the kingdom is unequivocal: "If your faith is not entirely in it, if you just perform as an obligation and you don't feel the most profound devotion, if your spirit, your heart, and your flesh is not religiously devoted to it, you are condemned." Sexual feeling is a kind of spiritual agency, an exquisite radiance.

Fornes's characters, who always seem to be acting out scenes, reading, reciting, and listening to music—in general, demonstrating her love of the variousness of performance styles and rhetorical forms—know how to talk to each other and to share deeply felt emotions, often shocking in their combination of private revelation and guilessness. Heartbreak and humor generate the syncopated rhythms of the plays, making them seem remarkably light for all their soulful temper. The characters don't judge or psychologize: among friends, there is only acceptance. In dramatic worlds that value human discourse and the knowledge gained from reading, conversation quickly develops into an exchange of questions and answers, books sometimes becoming metatexts, at other times, conversation flowing like the genre of philosophical dialogue. What is important is that one understands the arts of conversation and seduction, for the measure of a person's worth is the choice of words, the quality of voice, the generosity of spirit, the will to an erotic sublime. And when performance acts are used to explore hidden mindfields, there are subtle lessons between the lines on passion and intimacy, on faith, hope, and charity, on the significance of theatrical gesture as the tragicomic reality of human behavior. Fornes transforms drama into a spiritual anthropology.

If *Broken Blossoms* amplifies the dramatic narrative at the level of the personal, *Lost Horizon* carries it to a cultural plane. Fornes, whose own writing at times has the simple ardor and open-heartedness of a medieval nun, and not less an inclination toward instruction to compel the human drama, has intuited a metaphysical language in the manuals of piety that inspire these films, bestowing on them the pure yearning of folk art, or, considered in another perspective, the structure of myth. Her work is inbued with strong religious feeling, in its concern for the condition of the human soul and the moral issues attached to any contemplation of righteousness or redemption. When Jack, who is somewhat of a male version of *Fefu*'s Julia, experiences a dark night of the soul in his nightmarish depiction of gang sex that can also be thought of as a mortification of the flesh, with much the same largesse that Chekhov would give the gift of consolation in the form of a beautiful image to one of his own grieving characters, in the closing scene of the play, Fornes has the women, now grouped with Jack in a Pietà image, recite with him moving passages from *Lost Horizon*. The three friends, in their sympathy of love and shared cultural memory, for their vision of the future marvelous turn to Shangri-La, a mythical abode in the mountains of Tibet that is the home of the High Lama, a more than two-hundred-year-old Catholic priest who founded this world of quietude and perfection, where neither sickness or stress nor death rules. There is no irony, but rather a pre-political innocence, in Fornes's use of the film as pure escapist fantasy.

While the world outside spirals toward disaster in its orgy of destruction (Capra made the film as the Nazis prepared to tear apart European culture), the High Lama has been preserving its books, music, and other riches of the mind, so they can be rediscovered one day as a heritage of humankind, the "fragrance of history." His sermon on the mountain, only a fragment of which is quoted in the play, tells of a coming era when the meek shall inherit the earth and humanity weather its great storm. The filmic narrative is never revealed in the play, and neither is the film shown, but at its closing, as the High Lama's actual voice from the film is heard rhapsodizing on his dream of regeneration and tranquility, the live voices join with his, their chorus echoing as if in prayer.

The three souls are brought together in a devout expression of healing and mercy. This is the true meaning of grace, always circulating in the world of Fornes, in the Augustinian sense it has come down through the ages. Or perhaps it is the glorious recompense of moral gravity sustained by charm. In her melody of virtue, the act of kindness has the most exquisite tone, reaffirming the transcendent power of art to bring spiritual renewal with the surrender to metaphor.

The first section of this essay was originally published as "The Real Life of Maria Irene Fornes" in *Performing Arts Journal*, Vol. VIII, No. 1 (PAJ 22), 1984. The second section was originally published under the title "The State of Grace: Maria Irene Fornes at Sixty-Two" in *Performing Arts Journal*, Vol. XIV, No. 2 (PAJ 41), May 1992 and as "The Aging Playwright and the American Theatre," *Village Voice*, June 1992. The third section is an expanded version of a portion of my introduction to *Plays for the End of the Century*, Bonnie Marranca, ed. (Baltimore: Johns Hopkins University Press, 1996). The essay was published in its final form in *The Theatre of Maria Irene Fornes*, Marc Robinson, ed. (Baltimore: Johns Hopkins University Press, 1999) and now appears in this volume.

The Solace of Chocolate Squares:
Thinking about Wallace Shawn

For more than three decades a self-effacing, small, bemused guy who always looked middle-aged has been a regular presence in Hollywood movies that range from *Manhattan*, *All That Jazz*, *The Bostonians*, *Clueless* to *The Princess Bride*, *Toy Story*, and *The Incredibles*, and in popular television shows as well, including *Murphy Brown*, *Taxi*, and *Star Trek*. All the while the greater part of his audience has been unaware that this same actor is also the author of some of the most perceptive dramas of American life being written for the contemporary theatre. Dramatic works such as *The Fever* and *The Designated Mourner* get behind the facade of the extravagant nineties to offer a devastating portrait of an affluent and complacent society isolated from the world's tragedies by its self-involvement and lack of political understanding.

Shawn had already started on his critique of ideologies in the controversial Reagan-era play *Aunt Dan and Lemon*, which challenged liberal equivocation by offering an eccentric right-wing female character who is enamored of Henry Kissinger as a man of action. Now, with the catastrophe of September 11 and world terrorism shaping political discourse, his commentaries on society gain an even sharper focus. The 2004 revival of the play in New York suggested a new global, historical setting in the context of the Bush presidency and Iraq invasion, and alongside the timely documentary by Errol Morris, *The Fog of War*, which details through the eyes of former Secretary of Defense, Robert McNamara, the U.S. policy that led to Vietnam.

Another war in another foreign country is the setting for *The Fever*. The text unfolds in several parable-like stories that are strung together as narrative, collapsing time and space, dream and reality in the ninety-minute monologue of its protagonist (played by Shawn), a guilt-ridden man shivering in a hotel room in a poverty-stricken country. In his mind, one moment he is at home in a comfortable, urbane setting (obviously, New York) and the next he is experiencing the terror of civil war. Reflecting on his childhood and adolescence he describes in novelistic detail the objects of his world—and himself, as a kind of gift, lovingly wrapped by his parents. He recalls the wonderful meals and

94

smart conversation on books and theatre that he enjoys with educated friends. He looks at his privileged life from the inside out, his own nauseated body now reflecting the heartache of the social organism. In the process of self-examination, "performance" has a particular function, in that the author uses the technique of role-reversal to inhabit another skin and imagine himself as a victim of torture. His own life of ease, growing up as the son of William Shawn, the influential, long-time editor of *The New Yorker*, sets his play in a theatrical frame that collapses boundaries between autobiography and fiction.

The kinds of questions *The Fever* poses are simple but profound. What is my life about? How does the world work? In an ongoing dissection of the meaning of conventional phrases, he asks: What does it mean to be "decent"? What does it mean to be "deserving"? What does it mean to "make" money? If he wonders how one can pursue beauty and pleasure in the face of a brutal world, Shawn still clings to the belief that life is worth celebrating. The critic Stanley Kauffmann, writing about *The Fever* in *Salmagundi* in 1998, observed that Dostoevsky's *Notes from the Underground* "seems to haunt the play" in its author's hyperconscious reflections.

What is so fascinating about Shawn is the way in which he develops an ethics of performance as a throughline in the works. His dictionary of phrases, of which there are many entries, offers among them the notion that life and art are to be judged by standards of performance. In *The Fever*, the narrator laments the impotence of art when measured against social action. Ever the self-critical intellectual, he reads his life like a book. "My feelings! My thoughts! The incredible history of my feelings and thoughts could fill up a dozen leather-bound books. But the story of my life—my behavior, my actions—that's a slim volume." He constantly questions himself as a performer in the human drama. "I could perfectly well put an end to the whole elaborate performance," he says. It is not always certain if Shawn is merely acting out a character—e.g., narrator, male voice, speaker—or if he is playing himself in a kind of psychodrama. The autobiographical elements seem very close to home. *The Fever* finds him ill in his hotel room and fantasizing himself into a state of siege; he passes through stages of fear, anxiety, anger, self-loathing, and insight, trying to reconcile his love of pleasure and coddled childhood with the injustices of the world around him. At the same time, he understands whose labor it is that keeps him in this comfortable state. His leftward leanings are confused further by the knowledge that he is now living in a post-1989 world celebrating the defeat of communism.

Before being produced at the Public Theater, *The Fever* was not performed in theatres, but in private New York City apartments, highlighting its need for intimate engagement. The author contends that it was originally written to be performed for groups of ten or twelve. A note at the end of the published version of the play suggests than men and women and different generations could perform it. That would certainly give force to its power of collective myth. Conceptually, the play points to the problematic relationship of art and institutionalized theatergoing, and to the ineffectuality of theatre as an agent of social and political change. Operating on a subtler level, performing *The Fever* in domestic spaces only underscores the fragile safety of such a place in times of political turmoil. This perception unfolds in the living rooms of the very social class under scrutiny, upper-middle-class urban liberals and intellectuals, in the process revealing the anxiety lurking beneath comfortable surfaces, as if at any moment the entitlements might disappear.

The 2007 production of *The Fever* at the Acorn Theatre in New York, in which Shawn replayed his role, emphasized the non-hierarchical nature of the work by allowing the audience to mingle with him on the set over a glass of champagne before the show started, then briefly after it ended. Shawn also added a prologue that acknowledged the shared sense of being in the theatre, where, he explained, people go to watch people pretend to be other people. If one of his most constant themes is the idea of home, and, especially, being at home, Shawn quickly turned the play into anything but a comfort zone for his visitors. In the post-September 11 world characterized by extremes of war and poverty, *The Fever*'s themes strike even closer to home, jarring contemporary audiences. No longer are the reference points the "revolutionary" or "guerrilla" or "Marxism," which gave the original version a pronounced Latin American inflection. Now "terrorist" has entered the narrator's consciousness, making the play more global in its scope.

In the six years that separate *The Fever* and *The Designated Mourner*, Shawn sharpened his insights into the complexities of personal lives and public acts, distilling them with a sense of dramatic mastery in a genre he has made uniquely his own, and implicating the audience in its cultural reach, as if they were part of the same community. That is not hard to do with an educated New York audience who can easily recognize the frame of reference in the plays. Yet, *communitas* as an ideal is under scrutiny in Shawn's theatre.

The Designated Mourner evolves a portrait of a highly educated class destroyed by a new political regime. There is the husband Jack, his wife Judy, originally played by Shawn's long-time companion, the writer Deborah Eisenberg, and Judy's father Howard, a poet, acted by Larry Pine who has worked often with the author. Shawn himself took the part of Jack, a middle-aged man alternately self-mocking and devastatingly honest, and, by his own estimation, a "rat," an "asshole," mere "bric-a-brac" instead of a self.

In the opening scene, Jack sits at a table eating a piece of cake, and, by way of introduction, describes himself as "the designated mourner" to whom the task of grieving for something lost has fallen. He is the survivor of a proud community—emblematic of a certain idea of culture—that once existed. As if to light a ritual fire commemorating it, from his table he sets the burning pastry wrapper afloat into the air to ignite the drama. This is only one of the food rituals in the play, which is a description of that world, that loss, and the role that Jack plays in it.

His world of rarified intelligence and discriminating artistic experience is torn apart by revolution. First a rock is thrown through a window. Then there is the gradual rise of authoritarian factions and demonstrations in the street, destroying the once well-appointed surroundings through random acts of violence and lawlessness. The curiously disaffected characters seem powerless to comprehend or counteract them. It is as if they expected that the chaos would one day overtake them or that perhaps they could share the same political ground as the underclass in revolt. This is one way Shawn's subtle drama demonstrates both the level of naïveté and the fearfulness beneath the veneer of gracious living. Death squads, arrests, and increased privation devalue the artistic and political culture of the world whose demise Jack comes to endorse, illuminating the unbearable sorrow of its inhabitants.

What is compelling in Shawn's technique is the way he uses the life-as-performance aspect of his characters to challenge the lack of action in the plays. The "drama" of both *The Designated Mourner* and *The Fever* derives from orality: they are spoken in direct address, forging an emotional link to the audience, through stories being told. Since they are narrated rather than dramatized, the drama happens in the mind of the audience, encouraged by the craftiness of a master storyteller. Dramatic "action" is simply absent from the performance space—it's not there. What is emphasized instead is the process of thought articulated in the long sentences Shawn likes to write (and to speak to an audience). The feeling is more of the voice than of text.

A work in two parts, and in the New York production, staged in two different settings (or, perhaps "installation" is a better description of place), *The*

Designated Mourner was located inside a haunting urban ruin that long ago had been a men's club a few floors above an abandoned restaurant, in lower Manhattan's financial district, near Wall Street. The room that provided the setting of the play's entire first section revealed once luxurious features that were now despoiled by peeling gray walls and crumbling ceiling blocks. The actors were a few feet from an audience limited to thirty persons, in an attempt, it would seem, to reach out to audience members individually, rather than as an undifferentiated mass. They were so close you could sense the textures of the fabrics of their clothes, more Bendel's than Bloomingdale's: Jack's open knit sweater and shiny black, gold, and red-striped scarf, Judy's wide-flowing pants and long kimono-style jacket, Howard's elegant dressing gown. Their very proximity denied the possibility of complacency while also blurring the distinctions between theatrical reality and social reality. The primacy of the voice assumed the intimacy of conversation. André Gregory, who directed the production, placed the characters in a small area dominated by Howard's bed, continuing his long-time interest in environments and "found" spaces and intimate actor-audience relationships, as well as his association with Shawn.

That *The Designated Mourner* is so effective in its dramatic style has to do with the sense an audience has of struggling with the brutality of fact in such a closed space. There is a certain truth in acts of speech that are very much in the moment, unraveling the process of thought, and unencumbered by needless activity. Besides, a studied familiarity was generated by Shawn's casual encounter with the audience members beforehand, evincing the same sense of detached bemusement that he brought to the portrayal of Jack.

Jack not only does most of the talking but he is openly contemptuous of the overly refined intellectuals whose combination of irony, detachment, and idealism he chronicles and unmasks. His own devolution from highbrow to lowbrow is classified in terms of food and entertainments. The very rejection of the rules of taste upheld by his intellectual class clears the way for this transformation. "I was quite fed up with the search for perfection," Jack admits. Paralleling his disintegrating marriage is the total collapse of the cultivated social milieu the seemingly charmed characters inhabit.

Why is it that some people are made to eat dirt while others feast on the songs of Schubert?—his wife wonders. This politics of culture is at the heart of *The Designated Mourner*. In the play, which takes as its purview the varieties of cannibalism, it is observed that the officials of the regime now consolidating power eat in "new restaurants with new styles of cooking." When friends and acquaintances of Jack and Judy are murdered, their heads fall forward on a dinner plate. Even Howard, his writings now suspect, succumbs to the new etiquette. Jack's response is a prayer that goes like this, "Let me learn how to repose in the quiet shade of a nice square of chocolate ...."

For the second section of the play the audience is shifted to another floor of the abandoned downtown building, a former squash court, ascended by way of a dingy staircase after crossing through spacious, dilapidated rooms. If Part One is framed as a portrait, surely Part Two is a still life. Now, Jack and Judy sit at opposite ends of a nondescript couch, nearly motionless, and only a few feet from the somber audience. It is as if they are revealing their life stories to a silent gathering, Jack in the present and Judy in the past, as memory and history. The narrative continues in the claustrophobic dirtiness of a sickly green room lit only by fluorescent light, Howard a phantasmic witness by the closed door near its entrance. In a form of controlled terror mimicking languor, and intoned like a long descriptive passage in a novel, the abject Judy gives an account of the last dinner party that Howard prepared for friends, ending with their arrest. By this time, everyone in the room is exhausted by the drama's unyielding pace of psychological terror restrained only by a reflexive decorum.

In writing about the play several years ago in an earlier version of this essay, I observed, "The companionship of an isolated small group in such forlorn surroundings lends a queasy feeling to the event, like being among the few survivors of a disaster that has occurred outside. The allegorical subtlety of the circumstances suggests that this situation could be more real than might be imagined." The catastrophic events that were to transpire the following year in this very same part of New York City where the play was staged makes even more haunting the echoes of its despair.

The shabby space reminded me of the woeful apartment house design of a 1999 production shown at the Volksbühne, in the former East Berlin, where the Swiss director Christoph Marthaler staged his post-Soviet *Three Sisters*. Indeed *The Designated Mourner* has a *post*-Chekhovian quality, with its sense of an ending, and ceaselessly talking/writing/reading characters who dwell in the world of sensation. Fixated on words and objects and alternating between poetry and trivia, they talk past each other in fragments. Chekhov is an emotional point of reference for Shawn and Gregory, whose film *Vanya on 42nd St* was also set in an empty building in disrepair, the New Amsterdam Theatre on Times Square, presaging the choice of site for this play. (Larry Pine played Astrov in the film. He also appears with Shawn in Woody Allen's *Melinda and Melinda*.) Not coincidentally, in the film, too, the actors sit around a table, reading aloud scenes from *Vanya* rather than acting them. The shadow of Chekhov always wanders in Shawn's liminal dramas. Gregory, who in no small measure over many years has helped to craft an artistic vision that supports one of the most fruitful collaborations in the world of New York performance, emphasizes the fluidity of realities in the starkness and uninflected speech and the absence of touch that define his staging of *The Designated Mourner*. Only rarely do characters speak to each other, their spectral presence sufficient unto itself. For the most part, they look directly at the audience or beyond it, yet not making genuine eye contact.

More than two-and-a-half decades ago, Maria Irene Fornes's highly-praised *Fefu and Her Friends* had been performed in five different environments in which audience members shared theatrical space—"rooms" of a house—with the actors. The performance style was cinematic, intimate, and seemingly "natural" though under her direction Fornes's actors spoke to each other and not to the audience; they dramatized events rather than simply recalling them. In the intervening years, this kind of acting in close-up has become familiar in performance art and varieties of solo performance, especially as autobiography has come increasingly to dominate such forms. The lines between fiction and creative prose, which Shawn straddles, increasingly fade in favor of the portrait. So it is not surprising that storytelling takes the place of dramatic action in his work. Even the page layout of the published text replicates the style of fiction more so than drama.

Shawn and Gregory themselves offered one of the best examples of the privateness of dramatic form extended into film in *My Dinner with André*, which they co-authored and acted in, and Louis Malle directed. It took place—where else?—in a restaurant whose rituals of eating and talking provide such a joyous meeting between old friends. Here the raconteur Gregory does almost all of the talking, regaling a perplexed Shawn with stories of his spiritual journeys around the world in search of self, in particular his days and nights in the woods with the Polish director Jerzy Grotowski. In their talk of books, plays, parties, love, philosophy, and the use and abuse of words, both Shawn and Gregory lament the poor state of theatre and the alienation of people from the ordinary perception of reality. It had been produced as a play first in London where major theatres have always been more hospitable to Shawn than those at home. In fact, *The Designated Mourner*, which also premiered in London, is available in a film based on the 1996 Royal National Theatre production, directed by David Hare, with Mike Nichols, Miranda Richardson, and David de Keyser as the hapless trio. In it the characters are seated at a table throughout the entire piece, adopting the format of *My Dinner with André*, if less extravagantly. Shawn's work, like that of Marguerite Duras, lends itself to the transposition of the same text in both theatre and film (and, in her case, the novel), because of its reliance on the discreet narrator. Vanessa Redgrave is featured as the solo voice in the new HBO-film version of *The Fever*.

By Shawn's own admission, he is thankful enough to get up in the morning and have a good cup of coffee and *The New York Times* at hand. The esoteric view of two men having dinner in a restaurant struck a nerve in American audiences to go beyond being a cult film. Here were two men really talking to each other, one voice brushing against the other. Though *My Dinner with André* may be his most-known work, in actuality, discussions of food, mealtime scenes, and the social whirl of city life are almost always present in Shawn's plays. They grow out of his point-of-view and experience as an urban intellectual, a New Yorker. Shawn came to maturity as a dramatist in the eighties and nineties when money, status objects, celebrity, and high living would increasingly dominate the columns of newspapers hyping American affluence. Being cosmopolitan and at the same time a writer of moral tales for an immoral age, he focused on class as subject matter for the plays. He began to address the unequal distribution of wealth and resources in an ongoing social critique centering on the entitlements of class he was born into.

In *The Fever*, Shawn attempts to conflate the local and the global: "The cup of coffee contains the history of the peasants who picked the beans, how some of them fainted in the heat of the sun, some were beaten, some were kicked." This economic situation is perfectly acceptable to the conservative Aunt Dan, devilishly played by Linda Hunt in the original production at the Public Theater, who explains to Lemon, "We all know there are countries in this world that are not ideal. They're poor. They're imperfect. Their governments are corrupt. Their water is polluted. But the people in some of these countries are very happy—they have their own farms, they have their own political parties, their own newspaper, their own lives that they're leading quietly day by day. And in a lot of these countries the leaders have always been friendly to us, and we've been friendly to them and helped them and supported them." One of Shawn's essential themes is the eaters and the eaten: His strength is that he can speak from both sides of the social spectrum. For their complicity in the status quo he implicates the educated, the wealthy, the powerful, the fashionable, and those in the university and in government.

If *The Fever* confronts the apprehensiveness of privileged individuals, this theme explodes in *The Designated Mourner*, for here is a play about class, style, taste—fashion, really. Characters' likes and dislikes, their politics, are based on the choice of clothes, food, art, and ideas, in a manner that calls to mind the masterful *Operetta* of Witold Gombrowicz. "So, who here can say what the difference is between poetry and prose?" Judy asks, in a rare address to the audience. Howard belittles Jack's favorite foods—soup, mashed potatoes, ice cream. Jack applauds the boldness of Howard's decision to dress in blues and greens, and to learn about the Sumerians, but not the Assyrians. For such people, politics is also a matter of taste, in the sense that Hannah Arendt understood it: taste as expressed in ideas. None of the political views of the encroaching powers are ever explained. Instead someone remarks on the "unattractive figurines in the sculpture garden" and the new government's withdrawal of free concerts. The revolution is as much cultural as political, and, it is revealed, the generation taking over seems to be twenty-something.

Jack is of the old school, formerly an admirer of English literature. Excessively attentive to the expressions people habitually use, he questions the accepted sense of words, like "memories" or such euphemisms as, "I'm fine, really." In his plays Shawn loves to analyze the conventional meaning of words to demonstrate how language usage distorts reality. For him, the debasement of language is not only a function of the deceptions of society, it also signals the fall of a human being from culture—the descent from grace, to be more precise. Not surprisingly, central to his later plays is the activity of classification as an entrée into the minds of intellectuals. How do they think?

Describing an evening in the theatre, Jack is compelled to point out his distaste for the grammatical forms chosen by the playwright. When in *The Fever*, the narrator mentions a production of *The Cherry Orchard*, it has to do with a friend's criticism of the acting in a certain production. The use and abuse of style is manifest in everything. In such dramatic worlds, life and art are judged by performance standards. In that sense, *The Designated Mourner* is a play that takes performance—how one conducts a life—as its subject. So, what is elaborated in the larger scope of the narrative is Jack's discovery of the impossibility of arriving at self-definition. This work of exacting formal intelligence is shaped as a dramaturgy of interrogation: Can one exist as an authentic self in a society that favors dissemblance? What are the parameters of individual responsibility?

Similarly, it is the question André Gregory puts unstintingly to himself in *My Dinner with André*. "I thought I was living my life, but in fact I haven't been a human being. I've been a performer. I haven't been living. I've been acting. I've acted the role of the father. I've acted the role of the husband. I've acted the role of the friend. I've acted the role of the writer or director or whatever." The perspective that Gregory outlines is noteworthy because it is in direct opposition to the understanding of performance celebrated today. In other words, he draws a distinction between being a person and being a performer. This nuanced detail reflects his belief in "authenticity," now called into question by the contemporary sense of performance, which regards acting-out as a means of self-invention, empowerment. Shawn also frames his perspective on the performance vs. life question in the same Pirandellian terms: the ontological rather than the sociopolitical. The Shawn/Gregory view is moral whereas the more widespread celebrity-influenced approach is amoral, outlining a generational divide in both American culture and theatrical thought.

Notwithstanding, new directions in theatre have influenced our view of performance acts in the years between *My Dinner with André*, with its sixties ethos, and *The Designated Mourner*, which grows out of a particular kind of theatre culture of the last two-and-a-half decades. The more contemporary trends mingle performance art, fiction, and autobiography. Gregory is one of the few directors who has emerged from the experimental theatre of the sixties to continually reinvent the theatrical experience and break through to a more eclectic audience without, apparently, compromising his personal and artistic goals. As for Shawn's own contribution to performance, it is very different from that of the recently deceased solo performer Spalding Gray, for example, in that it is more social. From his own table settings Gray observed everyday life in a style that is equal parts comedy of manners and existential anguish, working in the gap between Gray the character and Gray the person. Both men, however, used the conversational mode to question their happiness in the world, though Shawn is more self-consciously literary in his texts. The ongoing confusion of person and persona attaches itself to Shawn even though, unlike Gray, he speaks through other characters rather than exposing himself in the way that Gray did. (An exception, of course, is Shawn as himself in *My Dinner with André*.) Paradoxically, he is in effect always being Shawn and the anti-Shawn critiquing values derived from the social drama of his upbringing in New York's literary circles. In the final analysis, however, Shawn's personal search, like Gray's, esteems authentic selfhood over dissemblance, even as its achievement seems elusive.

It is somewhat ironic that *The Designated Mourner* opened in New York in the same year—2000—that *The New Yorker* celebrated its seventy-fifth anniversary. The intellectual milieu of the magazine's readership, with its cultural assumptions and catalogue of contemporary mores, a world Shawn's father helped to shape, is, subliminally, the subject of scrutiny here. At the time the play opened there had been an ongoing commentary about the decline of "high" culture in America. The failure to make it to the bestseller list of then-new novels by Bellow, Updike, and Roth was pointed out as an example of the loss of a national readership for serious fiction. Four years earlier Susan Sontag had written a *New York Times Magazine* article, "The Decay of Cinema," lamenting the absence of an art film audience. Almost monthly there were news features on the sparse young audiences for classical music in major concert halls. The decline of theatre continued as a perennial topic. Controversies about the Great Books and revisions of the canon had by now preoccupied a few generations of scholars and intellectuals. To sum up the end-of-century view of culture's decline and fall Jacques Barzun published his history of the modern world, *From Dawn to Decadence: 500 Years of Western Cultural Life, 1500 to the Present*, which judges our age as one of lapsed intellectual and moral rigor and creative failure. The events of September 11 led a number of voices in the culture to declare the irrelevance of the academic field of cultural studies.

In its probing conscience, Shawn's work contributes to the current dialogue on values and taste—culture and kitsch—which attaches itself to the contemporary view of society as spectacle. Circulating in the work is the cultural dilemma of intellectuals of his baby-boomer generation, probably the last one educated in the masterworks tradition that demonstrates not only a genuine attachment to great literary works, painting, art cinema, and serious music, but a simultaneous embrace of popular culture and entertainments. The lack of differentiation between kinds of artistic experiences, and the oppressive glamour of art and literary worlds, coupled with the sense that society lacks a center of gravity, has brought about a revulsion towards the shallowness of contemporary cultural expression and the complicity of intellectuals in its creation.

Echoing Shawn's pronounced critique of liberalism, the left, and the cultural elite, playwrights Mac Wellman, Charles L. Mee, and John Guare have exposed similar class and cultural issues to satirize current attitudes, the latter's

Six Degrees of Separation being the most well-known of such plays. Each of the authors uses a deliberately quotational language doting on brand names and the "found" language of everyday speech, sprinkled with the received ideas of politics and pop psychology. No longer the playful writing of Theatre of the Ridiculous dramatists who employed similar strategies in the era of pop art, some of the most insightful plays written now articulate a darker underside of speech as mythology belying the emblems of class.

The Designated Mourner offers a devastating view of the all-consuming search for stimulation and the limitations of aestheticism, when ungrounded in a social contract. At the same time, the play allows that a life lived in the pleasure of the senses and cultivation of the self *is* seductive. Writing in *The New Yorker* in 2000, John Lahr, one of Shawn's long-time admirers, pronounced the work "among our generation's few great plays."

When none of his friends are left to mourn, Jack declares that he is the last person alive to even remember who John Donne is. The educated world of his is gone. One can't help but ask, What is the role of the intellectual—of art—in the new world whose ruthless, tasteless coming into being Jack bears witness to? From among the moral arguments the play puts forth, the audience is free to swing between the cultural hypocrisies of the old way of life and the limitless choices of the new one. How is anyone to distinguish between varieties of barbarism or vulgarity? His peer group murdered, Jack feels free to acknowledge, "I've always been a lowbrow at heart." He now eats the food he didn't dare previously to declare he liked. He goes to new restaurants and develops different tastes. Mostly, he stuffs himself with cake. He writes a sex column for the newspaper and enjoys looking at naked girls in magazines. In a diary he calls "Experiments in Privacy," Jack records his current activities, namely, urinating in his bathtub on a book of poetry and then defecating on it. His anti-Enlightenment project now complete, he has become postmodern. Surely, Jack is one of the most devastating portraits of intellectual slumming that exists in contemporary drama.

Even Judy's death, which he learns of while looking at photographs of a "new approach to executions" in the morning paper, leaves him unmoved. The pornography of violence is now transposed as visual style, affectless in its repetitiveness. At last absolved of the search for selfhood—no longer the figure of a man but of a ghost—and having exchanged language for imagery, art for entertainment, and emotion for irony in his hierarchy of experiences, Jack describes himself sitting on a park bench, reveling in the evening breeze. Asocial, his slippage from the civilized world complete, he is folded back into nature as pure instinct. Is this truly his end or will he be reborn in the transforming power of new figures of speech?

In many ways, *The Designated Mourner* is a very New York play that reflects life as it is lived in an affluent milieu like Manhattan. Here museum-going is a new form of shopping, and food has overtaken politics and real estate as the topic of choice. That the play features so many food allusions and metaphors—besides unfolding atop the remains of a former restaurant—is not merely to suggest a commentary on the preoccupations of contemporary urban life. The table, the meal, as recurring motifs in Shawn's work from early on, is the ubiquitous *mise-en-scène* of our age of spiritual hunger and the obesity of entitlement.

That the dinner table is a realm of private, unguarded speech may also help to explain why, in the allusion to home and family, it came to take a prominent place in the autobiographies of solo performance. Talking to an audience is a way of making more personal the domestic drama. If food and culture, eating and storytelling, are deeply linked in the worldview of Shawn, it is because his great theme is the nature of appetite. It encompasses the gastronomic, cultural, literary, sexual, political, economic.

What sets Shawn apart from most of his contemporaries is his passion for ideas and commitment to a set of values that knowingly links the moral, the political, and the aesthetic. He chooses to pursue meaning rather than abandon himself to irony or cynicism. While he is writing about the death of culture and, by extension, the death of theatre, at the same time he has created one of the few examples of the sustained dramatic voice and compelling study of character that has virtually disappeared from the American stage. Unlike most contemporary art, *The Designated Mourner* does not derive from popular culture masquerading as sociological insight, which makes it satisfyingly adult as a means of expression. Its own roots are in literary culture and philosophical argument. Likewise, *Aunt Dan and Lemon* is disturbing precisely because it openly airs right-wing views and a social Darwinism that the liberal view in the play cannot defeat by good intentions. Who is to take responsibility for making ordinary people feel safe? In what sense can one speak of morality with regard to violence and war? How ironic that the asocial Lemon has an eating disorder.

The Fever and *The Designated Mourner*, in their integrity of form and ambition, are plays for a post-dramatic, post-utopian age. They evolve as stories about the world for people who might allow themselves to be changed by them. Now they seem more starkly relevant for a country that has lost its grounding in the world, a good portion of its citizens obsessed with performing for each other. Whether by coincidence or design, a gentle breeze is given to the bereft mourners in both plays, as a gesture of their author's grace and compassion. The sweet wind, a little tap on the face that brushes the cheek's surface with joy and the fleeting air of freedom, carries with it the possibility of redemption for these disconsolate souls who are not quite prepared for the angel of history, blown this way and that in the great gust of events still unfolding.

This essay was first published under the title "The Solace of Chocolate Squares: Wallace Shawn in Mourning" in *PAJ: A Journal of Performance and Art*, Vol. XXII, No. 3 (PAJ 66), September 2000. An expanded version was published in *Codifying the National Self: Spectators, Actors and the American Dramatic Text*, Barbara Ozieblo and Maria Dolores Narbona-Carrion, eds. (Brussels: Peter Lang, 2006). An early version was delivered as a lecture at Muhlenberg College, Center for Ethics and Leadership/ Theatre Department, October, 2001 as "Table of Contents"; a keynote address for the "Acting America" conference at the University of Malaga, Spain 2004; and as a lecture entitled, "Wallace Shawn and the Politics of Culture," at the University of Richmond, Virginia, April 2007. The final version of the essay is published here.

The Theatre of Food

When I hear the word "market," I think food, not stocks. I've always loved food and growing up in an Italian family I took good home cooking for granted. It was several years before I realized that most Americans had been eating canned and processed food or TV dinners, while at home I was being nurtured on flavorful soups, spaghetti (before it became known as pasta), olive oil, fresh salads, dark green vegetables, and home-made pies and cookies. Both parents cooked and there always was—still is—plenty of good food available day or night.

Working on *A Slice of Life* unloosed in me a flood of memories and images dealing with food. I can still recall my father driving me mornings to the bus stop for high school as I sat in the station wagon with a dish of peppers and eggs on my lap. I was frequently late for school but would never think of skipping breakfast. My father has always talked about his Neapolitan mother's cooking and the twenty-five loaves of bread and delicious pizza she made each week for a family of seven. And my mother, who opens nearly every conversation with a rundown of what meals she's prepared for the day, has now started to make the fried celery dish her own mother, an immigrant from Calabria, used to include every Thanksgiving until her death, in 1970. That's how long I have been talking about it. I can still remember the flavor of my grandmother's sauce, the color, and the way it looked in her dishes, which I now own. Surely, this is the stirring of "taste memory."

My food world was characterized by family drives in the evening to our favorite childhood stops for ice cream or lemon ice, hot dogs, root beer, and White Castle hamburgers. After-school treats with friends included, not all on the same day, I might add, Ring Dings and Tastykake, Mexican hats, red licorice, peanut butter cups, Hershey fudgecicles, and cherry Cokes. When I later worked in a donut shop for a few months the best part of it was bringing home the leftovers after an all-night shift. My college roommate and I took over the kitchen in an A & W drive-in for a summer where we spent nights cooking and stuffing ourselves—in the days before any one was afraid of meat or fat—on California burgers, onion rings, French fries, and chili dogs. I remember the afternoon I had to work lunch hour alone and customer after customer ordered more hamburgers than I could manage on the grill. As they grew smaller and smaller I, half-panicked, half-convulsed with laughter at the shrinking burgers, imagined myself in a Lucy Ricardo routine. But did anybody notice that what was slapped between squishy buns and smothered in garnishings was no bigger than a fifty cent piece? Probably not—it still tasted swell.

These images always remained only a memory away, but if food be for thought, my own path to a book of food writings took many circuitous turns before settling down to the topic at hand. After years of writing about theatre and editing *PAJ* my interests branched out in the late eighties, inspired by my living part of the year in the Hudson Valley. Once I had begun growing my own flowers and vegetables, it was not long before I decided to work on a gardening book. The result was *American Garden Writing*. Soon I took up another project, *A Hudson Valley Reader*, which collected several hundred years of writings by people who had lived in or traveled through the region. Now, my interests were becoming intertwined like a beautiful but uncontrollable ground cover. The "extracurricular" activities eventually influenced me to write a series of essays about what I called the "ecologies of theatre." There came to be no separation between my theatre work and the life I experienced in nature.

It was only a matter of time before a food book would suggest itself. From the start I had planned to organize a volume of writings which would include authors not known for writing about food. Even so, I was overjoyed to discover through my research an abundant choice of material, fascinating and sometimes little-known texts by novelists, poets, critics, and journalists who are already celebrated figures in the literary world and whose work has helped to shape contemporary cultural life. Their contributions to my book, along with those of professional food writers who explore the deeper meanings of food in societies everywhere, demonstrate how much the writing life is rooted in the rituals of the everyday world, interfacing the private and the public, the local and the international. For a writer any subject can be the starting point for imaginative reflection on simple human acts that has a way of becoming the most profound commentary on culture, history, or art. If the best food writing has the psychological and intellectual range of literature, what is also true is that writers bring the same literary inventiveness of the novel or poem to the casual essay and memoir.

For *A Slice of Life* I gathered together a collection of individual pieces that accent the "writing" aspect of food writing, in its many personal and cultural inflections. Most of the individual contributions take the form of the personal essay that is usually created out of a writer's need to explore a special theme or simply to loll about in a meadow of paragraphs that exist for the pure pleasure of it. Putting thoughts to paper to see where they go. Chewing on sentences encrusted in memory. This is where the story of food begins.

For me, the world of food—its politics, customs, and aesthetics—started to unfold in a wider narrative as I began my travels through Europe. My first experience was as a college student living with a Danish family, in 1969, when I spent a semester at the University of Copenhagen. Here I was exposed to an entirely different cuisine—one based on butter, meat, cream, beer—that, historically, was set in opposition to the preference for olive oil, vegetables, bread, and wine in the Mediterranean diet, beginning with the defeat of the Romans by the "barbaric" tribes of the North in the medieval era. Returning many times since then I've been able personally to observe—and to taste—the gradual but steady intrusion, first of Mediterranean, then of Asian cuisines, into the Nordic countries and across the European continent, olive oil and butter accommodating each other like the increasingly heterogeneous cultures of each country.

It was the great Dane, Isak Dinesen, who understood the sensual pleasure of food, creating in her story "Babette's Feast," a charming reflection on the true meaning of grace at the dinner table. But there is another morsel from the Dinesen biography that is even more luscious, the passage in her memoir, *Out of Africa*, in which she describes how her Kikuyu servant Kamante named dishes after certain events of the day, like "the sauce of the lightning that struck the tree." Here, in one phrase, nature and culture were brought together in a fascinating poetics of the pre-literate mind.

Anthropology has become a strong current in contemporary food writing which is now often indistinguishable from travel writing. Likewise, cookbooks representing diverse ethnic cuisines appear regularly, even though they seem to share the same cultural ambitions. Take my word for it, few of them approach the literary charm of M. F. K. Fisher or Alice B. Toklas. Still, it is no longer enough simply to write a cookery book with recipes: they must come with anecdotes and family histories and photographs. This is an intriguing development over the last decade that is duplicated in the general public's interest in genres such as biography, the memoir, and documentary.

Where previously one could track the dreamworld of contemporary culture in film types such as journalists, investment bankers, or artists, now chefs—the latest celebrity species—are featured increasingly as characters in films centered in restaurants. A short list of them includes *Dinner Rush, Eat Drink Man*

Woman, Big Night, Tortilla Soup, Who's Killing the Great Chefs of Europe?, Mostly Martha. Chef characters are written into current television advertising scenarios, too. The proliferating cookbooks and cable food shows, and expanded coverage in newspapers and magazines, when added to the popularity of cooking classes and designer cookware, all hype the new food culture. In SoHo, my Manhattan neighborhood, through the big glass windows of its restaurants, those dining out are simultaneously looking and being looked at, in a new form of cultural spectacle. As a fanciful gesture super chef Daniel Boulud has even named a chocolate dessert after the opera singer Renée Fleming—"the diva Renée." If performance is the condition to which American culture seems increasingly to aspire, then it is no surprise to watch unfold in the variousness of its repertoire the new theatre of food.

The cost of a glass of wine and a dish of pasta in most New York restaurants has become, well, gastronomical, even as all too many weight-conscious diners leave their meals unfinished. Everywhere in urban cultures those with money to spare can afford to drink designer bottles of water all day or buy only organic food or obsess over the raw and the cooked, to salt or not to salt. The restless complexity of the diverse economies of gourmandism is insinuating itself into social life. Still, if nationwide, better-stocked supermarkets and an improved restaurant culture have transformed American eating habits, I am always surprised by the number of clerks at the checkout counters who don't know the names of ordinary fruits and vegetables.

American affluence and global tourism, accompanying the travels of food across borders, offer to our tables a luxuriant way of dining. The return to the bourgeois idea of the comfortable "home" is reinforced in the culture by a growing emphasis on design, though the leisurely family meal itself is largely out of fashion. And what of the idea of the "natural"? It changes in every era, like the idea of the natural actor. Americans like the pretense of *the natural* as if the complexity of stylization would contaminate the supposed order of their world. The same holds true of the disdain of the formal garden and preference for the untamed in nature, even as social life is more and more regulated.

What does all this eating and talk of food mean to our society? I can't help thinking that contemporary expressions of appetite have as much to do with spiritual hunger as self-gratification. The experience at table offers one of the few realms of privacy and intimacy in a culture of increasingly vulgarized public obsessions. It honors speech, direct communication—the face-to-face, not interface. Sharing a meal is a hands-on experience, not a virtual reality.

There are weekly declarations that the American public is growing more obese at the same time that many others refuse to eat or engage in other varieties of self-denial as equally compelling statements of self. Seeds, like birds and plants, are increasingly endangered, threatening the genetic diversity of our food supply. The Seed Savers Exchange in Iowa has been a growing force in the preservation of heirloom vegetable seeds, a project abandoned by the Department of Agriculture which favors the monoculture practices of big corporations that now control our food production and distribution.

Famine is worsening in the poorest countries of the world even as the rich have more and more of the world's food products at their disposal, in or out of season, and, especially in America, in larger and larger portions. Fast food accelerates abroad while, simultaneously, the Slow Food movement, started by the Italian Carlo Petrini to protect artisanal, regional foods, and culinary traditions from the onslaught of regulation and conformity, is gaining ground as a political force in the European community, impressed by his ideal of "eco-gastronomy." In Europe the outcry over genetically-modified food is loud and strong—they do not allow it on the continent except for animals—whereas in this country Americans don't seem to be bothered by the biogenetically engineered products already sitting on store shelves. The bowl of fruit is no longer a still life. It has an ethics of production.

Food products are now subject to the same criticism as contemporary art: they are becoming less and less distinctive in order to travel more easily on the international market. As the varieties of consumption took on new meanings in cultural life over the decades, so did the use of food in the culture and in the artworld. It is not my aim to outline a history of food in art, though that would make a fascinating topic. A cursory glance over the entire last century of art practice reveals that food has been a part of the making of modernity. One of the most influential early narratives of the lives of modern artists, Roger Shattuck's study *The Banquet Years*, begins with a detailed account of Rousseau's wild dinner party in Paris in 1908, which Gertrude Stein, Alice B. Toklas, Picasso, Braque, Apollinaire, and several of their friends attended, setting the tone for an entire era.

Marinetti, who wrote the earliest avant-garde manifestoes of the new century, brought the spirit of futurism to reimagining Italian cuisine as well as painting, poetry, performance, toys, cities, clothing, politics. With great flair, he declared himself against pasta and celebrated more chewable foods, such as rice. He promoted modern kinds of utensils and ultra-violet lamps to give food more intensity in cooking. With his blessings the Holy Palate Restaurant opened in Turin in 1931, featuring the unique if outlandish futurist cuisine. One of the favorite dishes of Marinetti, "Equator+North Pole," created by the painter and stage designer Enrico Prampolini, featured a sea of poached egg yolks in the center of which was a cone of whipped egg whites full of orange pieces looking like the sun. The peak of the cone was strewn with black truffles shaped like airplanes.

Avant-garde artists between the wars, particularly the dadaists and surrealists, celebrated many big public events. One of them, the Dada Festival in 1920, so enraged Parisian audiences that they threw vegetables and steaks at the performers. Tristan Tzara's *Vaseline Symphony* elicited a hail of eggs. Isn't it interesting that the public has always thrown food at actors or singers they disapprove of? Tomatoes seem to be one of the choice spoilers, which may have something to do with its history as a dreaded poison in addition to the splattering effect that makes an instant action painting on the body of its victim. It still seems to be going on. Philip Glass remarked in a 2002 issue of *Time Out* that during a performance of *Dance*, his collaboration with Sol LeWitt and Lucinda Childs a dozen years earlier at the Brooklyn Academy of Music, "On one evening someone ran down the aisle and began throwing tomatoes at us." BAM was the site of another notorious instance of audience food-throwing at the stage during the run of the Kathy Acker/Richard Foreman/David Salle theatre production of *The Birth of the Poet*. The BAM audiences of 1985 who came to the theatre expecting to be fed a certain kind of warmed-over avant-garde performance were enraged by the new "postmodern taste."

In the post-war era pop art acted as both a critique of consumerism and a celebration of it: in Andy Warhol's soup cans and Coke bottles, Claes Oldenburg's food sculptures, and the kitchens of James Rosenquist and Roy Lichtenstein. At the same time, happenings often included food, one of the weekend celebrations of this new performance form even calling itself the YAM Festival. Kaprow had his *Apple Shrine* and his *Eat* environments. Coincidentally or not, the landmark Experiments in Art and Technology evenings had EAT as its acronym. Lucinda Childs's Judson solo, *Carnation*, was a dance with kitchen utensils used as objects of humor and a touch of scorn.

And who can forget Carolee Schneemann's infamous sixties piece, *Meat Joy*—would anyone use that title today?—with its celebratory sausages and chickens entangled around writhing, painted bodies on the Judson Church floor. Exhibited as part of her *Interior Scroll* documentation is an artefact smeared with beet juice and coffee. In the same period, the Austrian artist Hermann Nitsch was performing Catholic rituals in which the blood of slaughtered animals was poured over the performers. The ritualistic tendencies then had nothing to do with comments on consumerism, but rather with the profound influence of the theatre of Artaud.

All the while, John Cage was busy picking his mushrooms and cooking for friends, sometimes upsetting their stomachs with a mis-identified specimen. In the late seventies he came to my apartment to tape an interview with Richard Kostelanetz and Richard Foreman for one of the early *PAJ* issues. I remember he wouldn't touch any of the snacks I had prepared, or even the water. He had an attaché case filled with his own macrobiotic supplies. I wonder if Cage's silence isn't really a field of rice.

Let me tell you about the time, a few years after his death, that John Cage appeared to me in the form of three mushrooms curved around the base of a dead pine tree. It happened in the mid-nineties when I was at the Rockefeller Conference Center in Bellagio, on Lake Como, working on my book, *Ecologies of Theatre*. One afternoon I was returning from a pavilion in the woods where I had been reading Cage's writings as research for an essay on him, eventually titled "The Mus/ecology of John Cage." Walking along one of the trails, I spied the mushrooms. When I arrived back at the villa and told everyone at dinner of the vision, they took it in their stride—most of the guests were artists or writers and were used to this kind of thing, I suppose. Betye Saar, who happened to be there as a visiting artist at the same time, sprang into action and took some photographs of me in front of the tree with the mushrooms. When the book got done, I chose one of Cage's *Wild Edible Drawings*, made of berries and flowers and roots, for the cover.

Cage once wrote an entire essay, "Where Are We Eating? and What Are We Eating?" about his experiences traveling and dining while on tour with the Merce Cunningham Dance Company that was based on variations of a theme by Alison Knowles. She is one of the Fluxus artists most known for her attachment to food in the work process, especially beans. Knowles also likes to make salads for large groups from time to time, often involving them in the event. One of the well-known pieces from the Fluxus canon is her *Identical Lunch*, which consists of a score for ordering and eating a tuna fish sandwich.

Several Fluxus artists have used food in their work. I like the idea of Geoff Hendricks's "Mashed Potato Clouds" for the 1969 New Year's Flux-Feast at the Cinematheque in SoHo. Ben Vawter gave *Flux Mystery Food* performances and

Daniel Spoerri prepared *31 Meal Variations* for various artist friends as well as writing books on food. Not long ago I found his Greek Island diary and cookbook, *Mythology and Meatballs*, in a used book shop. Fluxus artists around the world continue to make banquets such an essential part of their activities.

As the visual arts moved more toward performance and the autobiographical, it was not surprising that the home, with its regulation of family life and domestic space, would become central to any narrative. The development of body art pushed artists into deeper psychological realms. Especially for women, food—as seduction, punishment, instrument of will, taboo—would take on special significance. Examples of the use of food in performance are everywhere: Rachel Rosenthal's food obsessions, Martha Rosler's semiotics of the kitchen, Adrian Piper's fasting and Eleanor Antin's dieting, the Kipper Kids's food ceremonies, the celebratory dining events of Suzanne Lacy, Paul McCarthy's surreal foodscapes, Hannah Wilke's wise-cracking gum, the chocolate victimhood of Karen Finley, Linda Montano's holy anorexia.

Montano, in fact, was way ahead of everyone in editing a special section on "Food and Art" in a 1981 issue of *High Performance*. It featured interviews with many influential performance artists and documentation of works dealing with food. They range from Bonnie Sherk's feeding-time in a San Francisco zoo to Barbara Smith's psychological dramas and Les Levine's wall drawings made of jam, and even an *American I Ching Apple Pie* by Carolee Schneemann. It was to be another eighteen years before food became so prominent a subject in a periodical devoted to performance, namely the 1999 issue of the British publication *Performance Research*, entitled "On Cooking."

Today, the visual arts increasingly incorporate food as image or object, opening up economic, sexual, and social themes that build on earlier feminist critiques of the role of women and the more playful images of consumer culture. For years Rikvit Tiravanija has been serving Thai meals to international audiences in his installations to go. William Pope. L, in addition to his infamous eating of the *Wall Street Journal*, has also painted a U.S. map of peanut butter and another of hot dogs. But, few works of contemporary art have been so outspoken as Judy Chicago's installation *The Dinner Party*, which has now found a permanent home at the Brooklyn Museum. A triangular banquet table with place settings and ceramic floor text that document the women throughout history who were and were not invited to the table, it uses the form of the dinner party to explore women's historical role in domestic and cultural space. Another kind of feminist art statement is posed by Janine Antoni, whose large chocolate sculpture in the shape of a cube, entitled *Gnaw*, has been featured in the food journal *Gastronomica*. Her bite marks are visible as gestures towards art history and her own relation to food. Chocolate, the floating signifier of the world, is a beloved ingredient in contemporary art.

Vic Muniz, the Brazilian artist who now lives in Brooklyn, created a series of *Pictures in Chocolate*. He uses Bosco, the chocolate syrup familiar from childhood, to depict a Freud in Bosco, a Charlton Heston as Moses in Bosco. To me, the most moving pictures are the *Sugar Children* series in which Muniz sprinkled sugar over the photographs of children of sugar plantation laborers, then photographed them. The twice-removed image acts as a commentary on the geopolitics of production and consumption as well as on the political economy of identity. His photographs offer a visual equivalent to the kinds of sociopolitical histories of sugar, salt, spices, and cod that have been written recently, exploring the patterns of trade, migration, tourism, geography, and local politics that determine food production and distribution.

If the potato has also been the subject of a new food history, its more striking manifestation comes in the form of the Irish Hunger Memorial, a work of public art that was unveiled in Manhattan's Battery Park City in the summer of 2002. An installation the size of a quarter-acre facing the Statue of Liberty, it recreates an abandoned Irish cottage, fallow potato fields, and stone walls, also including native Irish plants in the site. But, the memorial goes beyond the remembrance of the Irish potato famine to underline the immensity of world hunger in displayed texts that accompany it.

As the idea of history is expanded and reshaped in our time, situating previously marginal subjects in a contemporary context, it acknowledges more varied realms of human experience. Each new food history uncovers more secrets of the human race. Even casual examples of food writing by their very nature act as forms of narrative. To dine is a kind of performance where, from our place "setting," we exchange stories, debate ideas, and reveal our dreams, the unspoken settling temporarily in the silence between servings. Not surprisingly, many of the influential plays in the world repertoire take place in the kitchen or dining room. Here huge psychological dramas are served forth and characters devour one another or set themselves free in forked sentences. A certain brand of boiled-over British play of the late fifties, perfected by Arnold Wesker and John Osborne and known as "kitchen sink realism," showed that all was not well in the family. Of course, Bertolt Brecht had already made the connection between theatre and eating when he disparaged the conventional stage as a "culinary theatre," as if the consumption of stale ideas during a performance were a form of bourgeois gluttony.

What is a dinner plate but a field of narrative that tosses back all kinds of images between adverbs, especially one's own? How full of meaning is the word "helpings" in the syntax of dining. For better or worse the dinner table is the center of the world, the family meal the source of the drama of the self. It is worth noting that the current renewed interest in storytelling and the anecdotal in various art forms—literary, visual, filmic—parallels the ascendancy of restaurant culture. A meal becomes an event through the addition of good conversation that has more often than not less to do with the food consumed than with the quality of companionship articulated. Even more so, the act of eating accompanied by a discussion of how the food was prepared, how it tastes—some cultures excel at this—is an instance of immense pleasure. Yet, everyone, at one time or another, has experienced the difficulty of swallowing angry words. The dinner table is one of the great settings of heartbreak.

In the best of circumstances, through the experience of food we make culture and contribute to the civilizing process, taking the measure of human activity in random acts of speech. Is it any wonder that the notion of "taste" describes both food and aesthetic judgment, and that "palate" can mean both the roof of the mouth—what an image!—and the savor of the intellect?

All the more remarkable to learn of the profound meaning of food in extreme situations, such as a cookbook put together in a concentration camp or the American soldier in a Japanese prison who made his abject compatriot a birthday cake of rice, bananas, palm sugar, and limes. The Arctic explorer Ernest Shackleton's account of his starving men on Elephant Island notes that one of the books the men had on board the abandoned ship was a cookbook from which they read out recipes each night as they waited to be rescued, discussing them in detail, even suggesting improvements. Their diaries reveal a craving for carbohydrates. A world away, one of the most fascinating customs is the Thai funeral cookbook composed of recipes and anecdotes by a person before his or her death to be given to mourners at the funeral.

I have had occasion to travel abroad a great deal, having lived for at least several months at a time in Denmark, Italy, England, and Germany. One of my happiest trips was the spring, some years ago, when I was invited by Alitalia on a press junket to Umbria for what I imagined would be a theatregoing blitz, topped off by the Spoleto Festival. But, as it happened, the Europeans who joined our American group turned out to be food writers. We saw very little theatre but ate our way through the best restaurants in Umbria where I lost count of how many were named "La buca di San Francesco," as if a little plenary indulgence never hurt anyone. Only years later did I realize that this was a foreshadowing of my own divigations from theatre. More recently, I was settled in Berlin for the better part of a year, the starting point for visits on the continent as far east as Warsaw and as far south as Seville, each offering their own characteristic topographies on the dinner plate.

Bringing back special foods from abroad is one of the great pleasures of travel. Right now I have in my pantry a salami from the Marco Polo airport in Venice, pimentón from Madrid, a tube of Swedish salmon paste, sardines and a can of olive oil from Barcelona, porcini mushrooms from Bellagio, pumpkin oil from Graz, and a package of figs stuffed with walnuts and candied fruits that I just carried home from Cosenza. But do you know what I've learned? None of these foods tastes the same in New York. Something is always missing. It has to do with the color of sunlight or the design of a window frame or birdsong—what one might call the *mise-en-scène* of a meal. Everything is different, starting with the pronunciation of vowels. Taste is both an activity and an engagement of the senses. It requires the attentiveness of one's entire being.

If favorite foods transported home don't seem the same when we return, neither do familiar foods from home taste the same in another country. Sometimes appetite mocks the traveler who has forgotten the cultural relativity of taste in distractions of the exotic. I recall the time Gautam and I were walking down the street in Kathmandu and saw a sign that read, "Pizza." After several weeks on the Indian subcontinent, we couldn't resist. We walked up a narrow staircase and ordered one. We could almost taste it as we climbed the stairs. What arrived was round and doughy but the resemblance to pizza stopped there. When one's heart is set on a certain food, craving overwhelms probability.

That truth was brought home to me again when, two summers ago in Nova Scotia, we stopped by the side of the road to have a picnic lunch with our traveling companions, a couple from Sardinia. The sea and air and sun were glorious. After we had eaten, everyone looked forward to a cup of coffee, even though there was only a jar of the instant kind with us. But not a drop of water was to be had anywhere. Our friends were so desperate that they simply opened the jar and took a deep breath, temporarily satisfying themselves with the aroma of memory. That, I came to understand, is the difference between desire and thirst.

When I realized that I had been returning from recent trips to Europe with notepads of recipes and observations on food, like the special candy in honor of St. Teresa made in Avila, or Modena's *Tortelli di zucca*, the idea of working on a book about food gradually drizzled its way into my thoughts. Being a theatre critic, it occurred to me that reading recipes or writings about food, even listening to others extol the glory of meals enjoyed, is something like reading or hearing about a performance I had missed. It isn't always necessary to experience the event—sometimes it's better not to—because vicarious pleasure has its own deep connection to human experience when imagination takes hold. But, then, what I enjoy most about cooking is stirring as an occasion for letting my thoughts flow with the contents of the pan. And what I value is the exquisite pleasure of the last forkful, not the first.

Food has everything in the world to tell us about the mentalities of an age, its desiring tropes and geographies of taste, its contribution to the life of spectacle. Today, just as we have come to see natural history understood as part of the history of the world, the subject of food is now embraced as a history of humankind.

An early version of this essay was originally prepared as a keynote address for the Food and Art conference at the Maine College of Art, Portland, August 2001. It was subsequently revised and given as "Foodworld," at the National Arts Club, New York, September 2002 and in its original form at Location One, New York, October 2002. A revised version was published as the Preface to my anthology, *A Slice of Life: Contemporary Writers on Food* (New York/London: Overlook Duckworth, 2003). The integrated version is published here for the first time.

Aural
Histories

❑

Performance and Ethics: Questions for the Twenty-First Century
A Conversation with Peter Sellars

Peter Sellars has directed a wide range of works in theatre, opera, television, film, and video, in Europe and in the U.S. He is well-known for his highly original earlier stagings of Mozart's operas *Cosi Fan Tutte*, *The Marriage of Figaro*, and *Don Giovanni*, as well as premieres of John Adams's *Nixon in China*, *The Death of Klinghoffer*, and *El Niño*. His productions have been commissioned by the major opera houses and theatres of Europe, appearing also in many festivals abroad. Among the works he has staged recently are Olivier Messiaen's *St. Francoise d'Assise*, Stravinsky's *The Story of a Soldier*, Paul Hindemith's *Mathis der Maler*, Tan Dun's *Peony Pavilion*. He has also worked with Bill Viola on the twenty-fifth year survey of the video artist's work. Sellars's project *Children of Herakles* was created with the participation of refugees, government officials, writers, and immigrants in several European cities and in Boston. This conversation was taped during the run of *Children of Herakles* at Teatre Lliure as part of Forum Barcelona 2004, in June of that year.

Here we are in Barcelona at the end of your six-week tour of Children of Herakles. *Why don't we talk about your efforts to open up a Greek classic for contemporary audiences?*

Well, for me, one of the most important things about Greek theatre is theatre as part of government, theatre as part of a democracy, theatre as one of the primary cornerstone institutions of democracy. Trying to give citizens both the information they need to vote in a way that has some depth of perception and at the same time has them hear voices they don't normally hear. What moves me so much about Greek theatre is this aspiration towards the care and maintenance part of democracy, which of course is where America is in serious trouble. You can make all the declarations you want, but in fact working democracy is constantly menaced, for example, by money. That's why Euripides is filled with all these speeches against money having the final voice. As we know in America, your ability to enter public space, which has been privatized, is your ability to pay.

One of the most powerful images of Greek theatre is this giant ear carved into the side of a mountain—a listening space. The power of Greek theatre is acoustic. It was about creating architecture in which a single voice reaches the top of the mountain. The Greek masks took the voice and projected it further. And the idea is that you make a structure that has a seat for every citizen. In Greece, democracy is a wonderful thing unless you happen to be a woman, a child, or a foreigner. Those are the people who couldn't vote and had no citizenship. Every Greek play is about women, children, and foreigners. So the idea that you're actually creating this special sound space, listening space, for the voices that are not heard in the senate, for exactly the voices that have been ignored in the corridors of power, as a society you say, wait a minute, unless there is a place we are really hearing them, we don't have a democracy. We have to make a special effort to make sure that these voices are heard and included and recognized.

In European societies under the Soviet Union, theatre functioned the same way, which in some measure is why it has lost its power and impact in society now. In the absence of a diverse media, free press or public spaces, people read the interpretations of the classics, usually reinterpretations, as political commentary.

Exactly. And it became, again, a place where what could not be said anywhere else could finally be said. You're creating the potential of a democratic public space. What is public space?—I think is the biggest question of the twenty-first century. What way can we create and sustain a space where a diversity of voices are present? All of the questions around why we aren't hearing from certain people and from certain parts of the society are really in play about how we shape theatre right now. It's a public space where we are physically the planet. So, this creation of shared spaces across the twenty-first century is the primary motivating factor for me in shaping each of these projects. Who needs to meet, in what ways can they meet, in what ways can we create the platform so that meeting has potential for the future? The first hour of *Children of Herakles* serves several functions. The idea that we begin with testimony, with experience, is a response and reaction to the political climate in Bush's America, but also increasingly in Europe, where ideological voices of pure doctrine are being elevated and trumpeted everywhere.

When the audience participates in the dialogue in the beginning of the evening, do you find that their language is fresher or different, or are they just repeating attitudes in the media? How have audience discussions and reactions differed in each of the cities you've performed the work?

What's very interesting is that a dynamic sets up. They've come to be spectators, they've come to judge, because they're trained to be consumers, and that's their only idea of themselves. Suddenly this first hour disrupts that entirely. You can't say it was good or bad, you can't say, "liked him, hated her." Suddenly your aesthetic judgment is irrelevant because it's not primarily an aesthetic experience. It's not a consumer experience. You're suddenly, as a citizen, engaged in an actual debate. It isn't about your own judgment but about your positionality: where are you in relation to that speaker, where are you in relation to this idea? You suddenly become part of a very dynamic and fluid situation. What's so marvelous is the body language of the audience. They're not anonymous in their seats. The audience begins to recognize itself as a community and begins to hear its own voice and to realize that we are not spectators in the world; we are in fact participants. So that first hour is the transformational period that I find so important in Greek theatre. We forget that Greek theatre was a participatory experience. All of the ceremonies, the dances, the drinking, the drugs was about creating a powerful participatory experience. In each city we have our own dynamic depending on where the show is located and what the context is. As artists, we have to spend as much time creating context as creating the work. In that sense, as much time on who's in the audience as who's on stage. This will be our work in the twenty-first century.

Over the years you've staged several Greek plays. What made you choose Children of Herakles now?

We first started working on the *Children of Herakles* because of Diane Malecki, the woman who has produced all of my work for twenty years. She lives in New York, I live in L.A., three-thousand-miles apart, and we see each other on the road or when I come to New York. We met in Rome, several months after September 11, and she said, "Peter, we have to cancel everything we're doing for the next two years, and do a piece that responds to what's going on in America right now." Norman Frisch had given me this play five years before, and said, "This is a play for you." I read it and was so moved, and I said, yes, I must do this play.

The idea of September 11—when something like that happens, you can either say, who do we not have good relations with, who do we need better relations with, who do we need to deepen our contacts with, who do we need to deepen our conversation with and our understanding, and create more open channels of communication. Or you can say, every foreigner is a potential enemy. A nation that was created by immigrants becoming anti-immigration, I think, is the clinical definition of psychosis. America is attacking its own origins. That is a very deep personal and spiritual crisis for a nation.

Children of Herakles, in fact, is all about how you treat foreigners, how you view the rest of the world: Are you open to the rest of the world or not, and when people come to you in need, can you recognize that need and work with them on their issues so that they get the support they need to go back and bring freedom to their own country? The beautiful thing Euripides does is that he doesn't just say let all the immigrants in. He says, feed them, educate them, and support them in the struggles in their own country because, of course, most of them would rather live in their country. They are coming to you because they're desperate, not because they want to take over your country. That notion of dealing with people's issues, which is what America keeps forgetting, is that all these people are coming to us from all over the world because they can't live in their own country, and because they are asking us to help them deal with their issues so they could live in their country. American foreign policy has been dictated by the business community and by American profits that outstrip the self-determination of entire peoples. That is not a sustainable economy, let alone a stable global political reality.

How has your experience of spending so much time in so many different cultures in Europe, and seeing the U.S. from that point of view, impacted this project?

All of my projects rehearse initially in America. Even if we can't show them in America I have to make them there because they're American. Everyone in the cast is an American, even though they came from many different places. These are Americans dealing with their own future and the issues in their own lives. All of my shows are about that. When I'm invited to work abroad, I always have to say, I can't. I can't direct Italian actors or French actors or Russian actors. I say, no, I can bring to you this thing we're doing with Americans. Theatre has to be based on your childhood, on your shared future, on your shared past, on all these questions of what is shared that you have to ask yourself in your own culture, in your own society.

Now you're performing mostly in festivals so that also creates its own context, doesn't it?

It does. But because we're working with immigrant and refugee communities, that suddenly invades the room in very interesting ways. We have all these refugee families now in the audience, a real dynamic because part of the research to make the project means that we're inviting into the theatre all kinds of people who are normally not going to theatre.

We rehearsed in New York, then we went to Bottrop, in what was the heart of industrial Germany. Now the factories are empty and available for art projects. Gerard Mortier supported us in the Ruhr Triennale. We developed the second half of the rehearsal period with Kurdish refugees, in this little German town where Kurdish refugees are being resettled: Syrian Kurds, Turkish Kurds, Iranian Kurds, and Iraqi Kurds. For the first time all four groups could work on a project together, so we were also creating kind of interesting conversations within the Kurdish communities of Germany. We made a whole project with their kids in the show, and then before the show, parents and family members were speaking, as well as key politicians, dealing with these issues. While the show was going on, the parents and grandparents were downstairs cooking, so at the end of the performance, the audience was invited downstairs—we did it in the foyer of a technical high school, so it was a place where there are lots of kids everyday. Like a town meeting in a local community center. Meanwhile, the guests included Dr. Rita Sussmuth, a German Parliament member and European Parliament member—a conservative—who is responsible for rewriting the immigration legislation in the EU right now. We were doing these performances the week of the German elections, so everything was very charged. Her plane was late, but once the performance had started, she sat at the back and watched the play. At the end of the play she said, I can't speak, I can't speak after that. You saw that all the policies she was so proud of, in the face of that play, had to be questioned. It took me twenty-five minutes to get her to agree to address the audience after the play, and she faced a very fierce group of people.

How did you do this? You come into a community, do your research, meet refugees ...

In each city, we start working with different refugee and immigration organizations, e.g., for the presentation at the American Repertory Theatre in Boston, the Physicians for Human Rights, the International Rescue Committee, a whole range of really interesting organizations that are doing quite heroic work on a daily basis, were part of the project. This is one of the biggest issues about doing Greek drama—can you use the word "heroic" without quotation marks? What would heroic mean? I think heroic does qualify if you have fifteen minutes to collect anything that's important to you and walk five-hundred miles, and start your life from a completely new place, leaving your friends, and everything else behind. The idea that the people we're seeing, who make it to the West—if you can make it from Afghanistan to Amsterdam—are not just the survivors, these are people who are profoundly motivated and who are going to change the world. The biggest issue in the twenty-first century is the empowering of a core of people who are fleeing from their own countries—from whatever dictatorship and whatever war—after, hopefully, getting food, shelter, and educational opportunities in the West to be able to go back and rebuild their own countries.

The main thing is you have to start, as an artist, creating context. The word "immigration" is such a hot-button word and the word "refugee" is a hot-button word. You have to say, wait a minute, what do we mean by that? And so in the first hour of the evening it is really important that a group of people can say OK, let's start from the same place together. We're all coming into the room from very diverse perspectives. We need to first shape a common experience and a common basis for a real discussion. That first hour is also giving us all the same starting place with which we can go forward into the play. We begin working with organizations that are supporting immigrants in each country. Sometimes that's the UN; there are a whole range and many tiers of organizational levels. They begin introducing us to immigrants and refugees and kids. Robert Castro, who is a crucial collaborator on this project, a brilliant young American director—we're really co-creating this project—works with the children all the time. Robert and I are in each city in advance with several visits, meeting and talking with a lot of people, trying to learn what are the main issues in that culture at this moment in history.

They surface across many conversations and a very wide range of people. In each country we ask the theatre or our producers to really get involved. Every night's performance begins with two dinners, which is what the audience doesn't see, and what is for me the most important part of the evening. Sharing food is one of the most basic ways of being human. We have in that first hour prison guards, border guards, immigration judges—a whole range of speakers from the official side who go to work everyday and deal with this, as well as refugees and immigrants themselves. When we went to the American Repertory Theatre Robert Woodruff made this a priority of his new leadership. We did it for twenty-six sold-out performances. We worked in collaboration with the Carr Foundation, the John F. Kennedy School of Government, the Human Rights Center. The speakers ranged from Michael Ignatieff and Doris Meisner, the head of the INS under Clinton, to the chief legal council for the INS as it was being folded into Homeland Security. We had the most amazing range of fifty-six speakers that gave a total picture of the state of immigration and refugee issues in the United States. The audience was hungry for this discussion. That was last year, and then we all said to each other, this is a project that just needs to continue, so this year four more countries.

What are some of the experiences you've had in Europe where the refugee problem is an increasingly dominant political issue?

At the opening night in Vienna, the Minister of Interior for Austria—the man who is the architect of the immigration and deportation strategies of the Austrian government, a right-wing figure at this moment—had dinner privately with four African refugees. That sharing space, before they see the public, is a moment where somebody who spent ten years in a refugee camp in Kenya and is now living on the streets of Vienna is having dinner with the Interior Minister. So the very top of the system is meeting the very bottom of the system. There is, for the first time, direct dialogue.

In France, we were in the theatre that I've performed in for many years, Bobigny, which is in the very suburb that was built for Africans, Chinese, and Arabs. All the kids in the show lived in the neighborhood; meanwhile, the audience was taking the subway to get there. When we were there, it was at the time of the closure of the Sangatte Refugee Center that was the last stop before the Eurostar goes to England. We were able, thanks to the incredibly generous collaboration of Ariane Mnouchkine, who had been doing a lot of work in the Sangatte Refugee Center, to smuggle out several refugee women to come live in Paris for two weeks and speak in our performances. The new French government, with Sarkozy, who was at that time the Interior Minister and re-ally aggressively pursuing deportation, put passport control and immigration inspectors at the subway stop before and after the performances. In the perfor-mances themselves, the Afghani and Iranian women had to speak in a private booth in the basement of the theatre because they couldn't show their faces in public, for fear of arrest. So you had that situation, in the twenty-first century, in a Western democracy, sitting in a room where somebody had to speak to you from a secret location. And I will never forget sitting in that theatre and hearing the voice coming through the speakers of an Afghani woman saying, "We don't want your money, we want your freedom." That was the temperature in Paris.

I can't help but ask, wouldn't your eventual goal be to have some legislation that would change the situation?

Yes, but I think we have to recognize that in art we move at a different pace. Real change is actually transformation. Quick change never lasts; it always cre-ates a backlash, whereas real change is actually moving deeply through people's attitudes across a generation. What we do in theatre—the word "culture"—is about cultivation. You're planting a seed as deeply as you can plant it, so that it will have long-term consequences.

Hannah Arendt had elaborated the idea of theatregoing as citizenship. Herbert Blau had that vision, too. I see you in that tradition.

Of course, yes, absolutely. I'm really picking up on that tradition—profoundly.

Other current examples dealing with the same issues are Ping Chong's Children of War, Immigrants' Theatre Project, *and the* Antigone Project *at the University of Chicago. It's interesting that the revival of this tradition and a return to the classics is a prominent direction in theatre now. Do you feel that?*

Profoundly, profoundly. One thing that's very important is to access a voice that goes beyond the editorial pages of this week's newspapers so that we actu-ally get what the roots of the discussion are. At the same time, this huge histori-cal overview gives us a much bigger arc that invites us to think about the future in a more creative and open way than just simply shifting a few degrees in cur-rent policy. That's why Euripides is always showing you children and old people in play after play. What he's trying to say is, look fifty years back, and look fifty years ahead. Don't just solve the problem for the next ten minutes. He's always trying to extend the historical scope of your understanding of the topic and ask you to take this longer view. A voice from twenty-five-hundred years ago just simply opens up your thinking and response to a topic that usually in the current political debate has been configured in the narrowest possible terms. So the reenergizing of the debate by reimagining the vocabulary of the debate is a very important contribution for artists to make at this time.

You chose a specific translation so you must have had some idea in mind about the language of the text. You're speaking of language now—how does it define your vision of the original?

I needed something that was also going to truly enter the debate at this moment. Ironically, when I do a Greek play I always hire Robert Auletta to rewrite it and to make a new American play out of Sophocles or Aeschylus. In this case, when I found the 1953 University of Chicago edition, by Ralph Gladstone, I was stunned at the language. It gives you this Eisenhower, early-Cold War, hard-edge Americanism that was very useful. The fragmentary nature of it actually sounded like television. Sentences were a little hard to parse, which in fact is how people speak on interview programs. I was very moved and stunned by both the indirection and then the shocking direction of that version. I have not adapted it, significantly.

Has the costuming of the production remained the same wherever it was performed? In particular, one can single out the orange jumpsuit.

I haven't changed it for two years. I have made Guantanamo Bay a big topic of all of my work, for many years. As long as they've been part of the U.S. prison system, I've had orange jumpsuits and shackles in production after production because this is the unseen part of America for most Americans. They do not understand that in courtrooms all over the country, you are brought in front of a judge and jury in shackles and an orange jumpsuit. Those are issues of how American justice works to label people and create prejudice in advance that need to be questioned.

I've made a lot of my productions prison productions. I set Stravinsky's *Rake's Progress* in the Super Max prison in Pelican Bay. In the Venice Biennale last year, I made Kalidasa's *Love Cloud*, that beautiful sixth-century Sanskrit text. It was set in Guantanamo Bay as an image of a Guantanamo prisoner in sensory deprivation imagining the woman he loves who is on the other side of the world and trying to send a message to her.

To go back to the language of Euripides, couldn't we say that Heiner Müller's language is Euripidean and Sarah Kane's, too? They reflect a return to this depth of justice and anger and violence and profoundly deep philosophy ...

Really cutting, breaking under the surface. This play shocks you. Half-way through it becomes the case of a young woman who is giving her life for her cause and for her brothers and for the hope of eventual return and right of return. That image we have all over the world now is of young people offering their lives, furious with the elder leadership—saying, you portrayed us in front of the whole world as victims, for two generations. When are we going to stop being victims, and show the world that we have courage and we have a future and we will take matters in our own hands and we will help ourselves? I will start by giving my life as a young person. That is an act of idealism. Now that's something America can't begin to understand at this moment. Euripides is moving into the heart of that idealism of a young woman who will give her life to see that her brothers have a future.

I want to tie this thought to something else, too. Would you say that your interest in these kinds of figures, about whom one can use the words, "heroism" or "grace"—a figure with a sense of honor who's willing to die, to offer herself up in a sacrificial way—is related to your choice of recent productions, such as the Messiaen opera on St. Francis of Assisi, or John Adams's El Niño, and your work with Bill Viola?

Yes. I would emphasize two things, one of which is the nightmare of the way religion is used as a weapon in American politics, where the public stance of politicians is based on a series of religious gestures that are in total violation of the separation of church and state. I'm appalled at the hijacking of religion or, as Tariq Ali says, the clash of fundamentalisms. What we're dealing with East and West is people using religion in a very exploitative and narrow context for political advantage. I have to go on record as really rejecting that. At the same time, what is missing from our culture is the dimension of the sacred. The entire way in which we're looking at the world is purely as a series of material objects, to be consumed, bought, traded, sold, including people. When you see the despoiling of the planet right now, that world poverty has tripled in our lifetime, the defilement of rivers, of ecosystems, you say, "Is nothing sacred?" That's why for the last ten years I have been working very directly on work of openly spiritual content.

Handel's *Theodora*, *St. Francis*, *El Niño* is a body of work deliberately trying to stage sacred text and asking what in a secular society can we present in a theatre. A theatre is not a mosque, it's not a synagogue, it's not a church, it's not a temple. It's public space. At the same time, every human being has a spiritual life. So what is it that we're not demanding when you walk in these doors? You don't have to be a believer. It's a very important thing in a theatre to speak of spiritual topics and sacred topics, but not simply with believers, and to ask everybody present in some way to acknowledge what the nature of their spiritual life really is. Artists—Michelangelo, or a shaman—have always rendered spirituality in a way that goes beyond doctrine. It is very important that there is a spiritual life that is simply not subject to the hijacking of scholastic theologians. What is that energy?

I've worked with Korean shamans, in different productions of Ligeti's *Le Grand Macabre* or the Stravinsky *Symphony of Psalms*. In *Children of Herakles*, on stage all night you have Ulzhan Baibussynova from Kazakhstan, who is incredible. She comes from one of the oldest shaman families in Central Asia. What you're getting there is a direct line of deep shamanism as the sacred owl feathers on her hat are in fact inviting the spirits to enter the room. You'll see frequently when Ulzhan is performing, her eyes are not wide-open—it's not here I am and this is my ego, but the opposite. The eyes are slightly down like in Buddha sculptures and allowing the voices to come through you. You're allowing the ancestors to speak through you. This idea of theatre is very important. I've invited artists from many different cultures to share those types of experiences in these productions exactly to recognize that there is a larger dimension of spirituality than we're seeing day-to-day in Western culture. Can we begin to open that up? This is possible even when I'm working within Western culture.

As in Messiaen's St. Francis?

There you have Messiaen creating ecstatic things from Hindu culture in the middle of his Catholic opera. That's really a profound and amazing image. And for me the other dimension that's going on in *El Niño* is again testing all of this in experience. Can we actually deal with the nature of our spirituality, not just as theology, but as experience? What is the experience of spiritual life?

When you think about it, Judaism and Buddhism are very prominent in what used to be thought of as avant-garde theatre, which is mostly where the spiritual dimension resides in American theatre. Starting with the Living Theatre, back in the forties, and John Cage. I'm also thinking of Steve Reich's video operas, Meredith Monk ...

Her *Quarry* goes right to the heart.

Then there's Bob Wilson, Richard Foreman who considers himself a closet religious writer, Lee Breuer, Laurie Anderson, Philip Glass—one can go on and on. It's almost like a hidden tradition because no one really speaks of American theatre in this historical sense.

Well, Bonnie, I think your writings actually go in that direction and, for me, it's also the profound tradition of American art, which is transcendentalism. It really has to do with Whitman and ...

Gertrude Stein ...

Gertrude Stein, and Melville. This whole question of spiritual issues, and the articulation of spiritual issues, is the bedrock of democracy and is the basis for equality, not as a rhetorical position but as a spiritual aspiration.

Let me go back a second because this is a fine point. What you're really talking about is an ethics of performance.

Yes, and I'm talking about that in an Emersonian context and I'm talking about that in the context of Cornel West. I'm talking about that in the context of Gandhi, and I'm talking about that in the context of Martin Luther King. In my lifetime the single most important ethics of performance was the March to Selma. When Bernice Johnson Reagon lifts her voice, what is happening to democratic space as it's being created in the streets of Albany, Georgia? The question of the power of that music and those people singing in the vans on the way to prison, and what it means to sing in the presence of those dogs and water cannons—this is ethical performance at the highest level imaginable. The power of the Black church, which, in my view, has actually kept Shakespeare alive, is our direct connection to the Elizabethan theatre. It is the power of the language of the King James Bible as transmuted in the Black church. Keeping the rhythms of Shakespeare alive and rolling and powerful, and the idea of that expressive language being itself an act of liberation. Those are the actual lines to trace in American culture: the profound liberation of white culture by its interaction with black culture. That is where the rhetoric is lifted and transformed to another place. All of those things really come into play and then, of course, obviously in the last generation, the whole Chicano theatre in the fields, César Chávez marches, and Dorothy Day.

I'm thinking of Eric Ehn, too.

Thank you. Exactly. For me, that is the tradition.

Yet, if you pick up most art catalogues, or spend time in academia, there seems to be an avoidance of any notion of authenticity, of transcendence, of the spiritual in favor of a materialist point of view. Even the history of modernism is so spiritually secularized.

Whereas if you look at what Jackson Pollack or Rothko are really working on, it's not secular at all. That's why the courses I teach at UCLA in the Department of World Arts and Cultures are called "Art as social action," which in alternate school terms is "Art as moral action"—big four-hundred-student classes—and two smaller courses are the collaborative intercultural performance seminar called "The Invisible World," which is about spiritual traditions in art-making, and the graduate seminar called "Enlightenment: Theory and Practice," which is focused on first and third-century India and China, tenth- and eleventh-century Persia and the Arab world, and then eighteenth-century Europe. The whole question is one of tracing those moments where illumination and enlightenment are part of the culture. In what way is the culture transformed through a moment of spiritual aspiration and accomplishment which creates a body of art that leaves its mark and creates a culture where these questions can be opened?

How do the students respond? Students are very interested in religion now.

Very powerfully, because nothing else in their experience is treating this subject matter. I think the other thing that we've come through—in one way necessary, in another way now limiting—is the history of critical studies, where intellectuals have set themselves up as critics. That is not really a positionality that has a future. I understand that there is a lot to be critiqued, but now there's a lot to be created.

Critical discourse is getting too pedantic and overly erudite. It's so abstracted. You know, it's like people talking about the destruction of the planet and not knowing the names of plants in their backyard.

And, if I may say, negative in its orientation. At this point, frankly, the world is in need of positive action and forward motion. This whole idea of re-empowering students is to say, wait, wait, wait—don't come in at the end of the process and say what went wrong. Place yourselves at the heart of the process and look forward. The idea of creating momentum and direct empowerment is the most crucial thing for this generation right now.

I have the feeling, though, that even among artists there is the sense that many don't really want to make art but to do culture. We are in the midst of a turn away from art, a denigration of art. You know the distinction I'm drawing?

I do. I actually don't teach in the Theatre department, I teach in the Department of World Arts and Cultures. It's important that those words are in the plural, and that those cultures create art, and create many different arts. This question of the dynamism of interdisciplinary work and the dynamism of the intercultural reality of our lives now really has to be the topic of the twenty-first century. The way culture works is extremely important to liberating art from the art market. Art has defined itself so narrowly in economic terms in America.

More so in visual arts. Theatre is so marginal.

But what theatre you see or don't see has to do with what it costs and who's going to pay for it. So regional theatre looks a certain way because of the economic system that surrounds it. Off Broadway looks a certain way because of the economics of it. What you're looking at over and over again is the economics, instead of anything else. The economics has been the priority of all the people involved in making it, and has been the filter through which it is both created and perceived. To actually liberate these things from economics and ask another set of questions, culture is necessary. You have to say, what does a certain gesture mean or not mean? Theatre only takes its power from its cultural location. It's culturally heroic to say something in a certain place. The same words are cowardly and inadequate in another cultural position. It's actually the play of culture that gives art its power or lack of power, which is a very important valance for artists to be engaged with.

It is also important that the artistic remain uppermost in creating a complex theatre, rather than merely having sociology in a performance space. I'm a little afraid of the danger of the slippage, because I think it's necessary to have really creative imaginative works and not just to represent reality.

One of the most satisfying aspects of *Children of Herakles* is that after the first hour of the evening, where you really have a debate or gathering of people sharing the experiences and testimonies, speaking of what's going on out there right now, and of how their lives were formed through their own experiences as refugees, their own experiences of fleeing for their lives, their own experiences of trying to support their families, in hideous conditions, against adversity, and of course how that shapes their views, then Euripides begins. Suddenly, after about ten minutes of Euripides, you realize why poetry exists. In fact, after this first hour, which is interesting and powerful, nonetheless, now there's a role for poetry. You realize why the Greeks said that to discuss this as a legal question is not enough, to discuss this as an economic question is not enough. To discuss this in the terms of the world is not enough. This has to be brought, literally, in the case of Euripides, to the altar. This has to be lifted to another level and we have to discuss not only the written laws, but the unwritten laws. We have to ask ourselves higher questions, with higher language, and address not just where we are, but where we would like to be. We have to address questions of aspiration; we have to address questions such as, can we live up to our ancestors? They have set very high standards for us. Can we live up to our own high standards? That's where art needs to be: not just where we are now, but this place that reveals and opens the possibility of aspiration. That's why the language of pure art is powerful. Aristotle said poetry is more important than history, because history is what happened, and poetry is about what might happen.

What is stopping contemporary dramatists from moving more into this direction, do you think? There are only a handful of examples of really powerful drama now. We are not living in an age of great drama that is really dealing with what's going on in the world.

I think the prevalence of film and television have created a certain type of writing, and a certain view of a human being, what it means to be a person, and what the measure of man or woman is. Someone like Euripides or Shakespeare is using a very different yardstick. So the measure of a single human being is immense. It's, in fact, epic. We have very few writers right now that are responding at an epic level. Meanwhile, human beings' lives are epic.

Is it that reality now seems so complex, so large, so global? This whole question of the local and the global is interesting because drama has always been strong when it speaks to the local. But there's a confusion now between the local and the global because work travels, it has to appeal globally. At the same time it's also losing some sense of its locality, of its rootedness in a culture. The question is how reality or realism can come into play now, in a greater, darker dimension that goes beyond a description of reality.

What realism means is irrelevant. What it means when you're seventeen-years-old and the room you know best is an eight-by-ten cell, with nothing allowed on any walls, with no light or artificial light, and being held in total sensory deprivation—which is what we're doing right now to young people all across America and the Super Max prison boom is going full blast—is that those walls are alive. The life of the imagination is so dense and so rich. What I'm working with for those kids is the Mayan temples. The idea that of course the walls are alive. The gods are coming right through the walls; the snake is coiling around you: that's the shape of the pyramid. I've been trying to open up an image of American architecture that goes forward from Frank Gehry, which has to do with cultures where the walls are alive. Where there are beings in the Buddhist rock temples in central India, or in the Mayan temples, or in the tessellated surfaces of the Shiite mosques, where the walls are infinite. These patterns are taking you into infinite worlds within worlds within worlds. It's not a hard material surface—it's the opposite. It's that you are in all of these dimensions. And believe me, if you're being held as a fourteen-year-old in solitary confinement for weeks, you are entering such deep time-space. That's the poverty of realism, next to the deep experience of these kids who are experiencing life on all of these levels. And believe me, you start to learn about sacred space from a fifteen-year-old who's been held in Juvenile Hall in solitary confinement.

Are you working with any of these kids in trying to create works with them, or writing? This discussion of walls, rooms, prisons … they're really a metaphor for borders. The wall or border between cultures and between realities seems to be the overriding issue.

One of the first projects that I did in East Los Angeles was *The Screens* of Genet. A writer who brilliantly moves beyond realism to all these other dimensions.

By the way, I have nothing against realism.

Me neither, I'm just saying the narrowly defined realism is a profound social crisis. It's the idea that our lives are reduced to that, which they aren't. That deprives everyone of agency. That deprives everyone of that Martin Luther

King ability to do the impossible. We are called to this planet to do the impossible, every day.

As Herb Blau says, "The impossible takes a little time."

Or as Kalidasa says, "It takes an instant." In theatre, we have those two time frames. We have the time frame of generations, of centuries, of voices of ancestors, and we have the time frame of this instant. Sanskrit theatre really has a whole poetics of the instant of realization: that in your life, the most important things that have ever happened to you, whether it's falling in love, or suddenly understanding something in the world, in fact, is an instant. It's a single moment of realization. What spiritual practice is, all over the world, is how to sustain that instant. The practice of theatre is so connected to spiritual practice. It's fine to believe these things, but now how do you put that in your body?

How do you see the intersection of art and culture and spirituality in your work in different media? For example, how do these concerns transfer to video in the work with Bill Viola?

In the case of Bill Viola, the work is never an object. That's what's so interesting.

It's always an experience.

His joke is, at night, when they turn the lights off at the Rijks Museum, the Rembrandts are still there. At night, when they turn the lights off in a Bill Viola exhibit, there's nothing there! Bill's work *is* the room it's in, as much as that video. It's the atmosphere, the sound, the world, and that's why it connects to the Buddhist temples, or the Mayan temples, in that sense that it's the total environment, the spiritual space that you are occupying. The walls are speaking. Those walls are alive. The walls themselves are communicating with you. That connects to the space of the teenage gang members in solitary confinement. It's this idea of culture as the walls speaking. What is moving through the walls, what is being kept out by those walls, what is contained by those walls and, literally, what are the moral structures that shape our lives? In that sense of sacred architecture, your moral home life being shaped by what your mother put in the house you grew up in and beginning to recognize every moral structure in this society as shaping our lives. That is the spiritual architecture that we are both responding to and building and rebuilding ourselves everyday. Is that a prison culture, or is that a culture of vision? Bill is creating these visionary worlds of lives inside of lives, time inside of time, space inside of space. He can work with an actor, using his camera that takes 350 frames a minute, and take one minute of an actor's life and create an eighty-minute piece out of it. He's showing you the spaces between the emotions. The actor is giving you four different emotions in a sixty-second period.

I'm thinking of those wonderful pieces on water and fire—The Crossing.

Well, Bill has now made the next step of *The Crossing*. It will be on display in Athens for the Olympics next month. He just finished editing and shooting the piece two weeks ago. And it is overwhelming. Bill and I are working in a very interesting way. He has begun working with actors, so he's crossed into my territory.

You're going to be doing something with him for the opera in Paris, aren't you?

We have two projects on the way. One is *Tristan and Isolde*, in Los Angeles in Walt Disney Hall with the Los Angeles Philharmonic, in December. Then the following year at the Opera Bastille in Paris, and the year after that I am making a project with Amin Mahlouf and Kaya Saariaho and Bill, a kind of living altar piece for Simone Weil. Again, taking the embodiment of these spiritual convictions and testing them against the history of our times. That woman put her body on the line for her belief systems.

I'm really—stunned is too strong a word—perhaps surprised. I hadn't realized how much the whole question of morality and spirituality has been defining your projects. So much of your work is not seen in New York. In fact, you couldn't work on this level in the United States, without European support. Not many people speak about morality in theatre. Everything seems to be framed exclusively within the social or the political.

The social and political are transitory. Trying to search for something that reaches across generations and across time is what theatre does. That's moral, and that moral energy is handed on from generation to generation. It isn't just this week's headlines. It's what people keep forgetting about, because they're rushing from issue to issue, moment to moment, and they're not getting the original meaning of life work. Across our life span we have something to accomplish. It will be the work of our generation: how our generation is measured and what we have to hand on. Those are moral questions, not just social and political questions. Socially and politically there will be victories and there will be setbacks. We have to be doing something as artists that outlives all of that. As the Navajo would say, handed on to the seventh generation. I'm a very specific recipient of the seventh generation thing. For example, in the case of Mozart, who could die with his major works treated as failures, and two-hundred years later, in the eighties in America, I can take those works as a way of discussing Ronald Reagan's America. They can suddenly be the language we need to articulate a whole series of things that nobody alive at this moment can say.

What are you handing on?—is the question. Meanwhile what you can do short term is equally important in how you embody your principles. So in a very simple way, for example, in Vienna, we did the *Children of Herakles* in the Parliament. So you have this image of the Greek theatre, because the Parliament is shaped with classical columns as a Greek temple. There we are with all these classical Greek columns, this construction where you get the founding myths of your culture.

We had refugees on stage every night, those kids from the Treiskirchen Refugee Camp, who are living in conditions that are really horrifying. There they are, and they have no voice and no presence in the society where they're being held. What it means for them is to come forward and suddenly have a presence, be visible, be counted and be recognized in a place where they're being treated as non-existent. That is a very important dimension of the project. What is very interesting is that for the first rehearsals, these children are reserved, or can't even watch, sometimes collapsing in tears, sometimes severely traumatized, because since they've gotten to the West, nobody has met them at the level of their real emotional life. In fact, nothing matches what they've come from, the intensity of that, and in this theatrical experience for the first time they're being met at their own level.

The results are emotionally overwhelming. The very children who were most traumatized by the next day arrive early at the theatre because they want to be there. By the end of the week they claim their refugee status with pride, they want to take the microphone and speak to the audience, and their whole deportment and self-image is in a very different place. We collected money for those kids to have a summer camp, every night in the performance. In five performances, the audience contributed thirteen-thousand euros. Then the head of the Vienna Festival decided they would continue to collect money during all the performances in the festival. We just learned yesterday that they have collected twenty-four thousand euros for summer camps for those refugee kids. Now, that is a really simple thing that theatre can do in the here and now. Don't let me underestimate the direct social action that is possible. It's just that you can't only set your sights there.

You've sort of answered the question I was going to ask you—in a time of such malaise, what special properties can theatre manifest?

In a time of political and social paralysis it is a dynamic space where things are moving, things are happening, things are in play, human beings are meeting each other with amazing consequences. You can't act like reality is what is being painted at the moment by our political and media structure, because the minute you meet people whose lives tell you reality is something else, all of that stuff falls apart. That is what disappoints me about the Democratic party. You could bring down the Bush administration by one really simple thing—truth. Where is the truth content? That's why I'm inviting people into the theatre every night whose lives testify to the truth against the series of public lies. You can begin on that basis, with a very basic truth level. Then you invite Euripides into the room for another truth level. And those ways in which truth can be calibrated, understood, measured, acknowledged, force the political and social arguments to a whole new place.

It is a provocative format in having the discussion first, which is a commentary on the rest of the evening. A Brechtian mode, almost in reverse, because it's not happening in the play or the production, but before it, so you're carrying these thoughts and ideas with you while you are watching. And you're watching on two tracks: the contemporary and the historical.

Exactly. Again, one of the most profound things about democracy and about the Greek conception of it is theatre as a listening space. What does it mean to actually listen? The first hour of Euripides' plays is people just giving long speeches and you have to listen. That first hour of the night creates the attentiveness to argument. So you end up aware of the quality of the argument, aware of how people are expressing themselves or not, and suddenly all of those things are alive in Euripides. It's different from just an evening in the theatre. You are paying attention to how people are expressing themselves and why. What's behind the way they're speaking? That's the big question in America right now: asking people to listen with that kind of attention. The first hour sets up that quality of listening. The other thing that's going on in that first hour is that all kinds of humanity are present. You're not just dealing with people who are official spokespeople who have been selected by a mediagenic culture.

You are dealing with a whole range of people who may have difficulty speaking. Some nights, torture victims can barely say anything. That's why I use these very high quality microphones to pick up the slightest quality of people's breath, what's between the words; the difficulty of speaking about certain things, which as Beckett said, must remain unspeakable in our lifetime. That question of the unspeakable from somebody who has burn marks all up and down their back and on their private parts—that which is unspeakable also has its own type of testimony in our lifetime. One of the things I'm so moved by in the Greek theatre is virtuosic actors who were famous, celebrated for their dancing or their singing or whatever, alongside your next door neighbors, who are the chorus. You know, the Greek chorus were just normal citizens. I love that combination on stage of high art and next door neighbors.

That is, if I may say, the genius and power of early Meredith Monk and Bob Wilson. Those early Wilson pieces that matched Lucinda doing this highly articulated, hyper-developed dance next to a bunch of people standing there eating their lunch. Those beautiful notions that very high art and the most simple aspect of ordinary life need to be included in this composite picture. There's a place for the art and there's a place for the people standing there eating their lunch. Both things have their own Whitmanesque beauty, their own Gertrude Stein spiritual imminence. That's what makes Meredith's early work so powerful—the community works—that there is this combination of some people on stage pursuing a movement language and music base that is the result of a highly developed process of research and investigation. And then other people who come as themselves, come as you are, and that itself is also powerful. For me, that dynamic is also very present and very democratic, and I take that from Meredith and Bob Wilson and from the Black church and from the Greek theatre.

The way you speak is also very Steinian because not so many artists speak in such a positive way about democracy. Gertrude Stein was so American and so pluralistic, in the same sense.

Well, you know, I grew up in Pittsburgh, Pennsylvania, which is her town. I grew up knowing one of her nieces. When I first went to Paris when I was eighteen, my first week there, my mother, sister, and I stayed in Gertrude Stein's house in Garches with one of the last of her relatives. In fact, Gertrude Stein is very much a part of my direct heritage. Pittsburgh is interesting: Martha Graham, Gertrude Stein, Andy Warhol. It's a very interesting cultural scene. That is what I grew up with. The other thing that was so powerful growing up with was the Carnegie Institute there, which was this amazing building in the middle of the city that had a public library, a concert hall, an art museum, a science museum, a botanical display, and an architecture museum—all in one building. So as a child in Pittsburgh, you grew up as an interdisciplinary being, and on a Saturday, you do a nature walk and a concert and a film and a gallery tour. That is how you're wired, that is the interplay of the arts. The other thing I love about that museum is that you walk in and you see these giant murals of the steel workers at the sledge furnaces painted on every wall surface. Now you walk into most of our new museums and you see the list of corporate benefactors. That image that you're not masking the people who made this money available and whose lives make it possible so that we can have this afternoon where we can look at nice paintings because these people are at a blast furnace at this moment. That's the vestibule–I love the term vestibule: Goethe's propylaeon—the fact that it's the entrance area telling you everything, the space between the outside and the inside. In this first meeting place there are the pictures of the steel workers and your afternoon of leisure is made possible because they're working really hard right now.

I think you've encapsulated extraordinarily well a real faith in democracy, a real faith in culture at a time when our institutions seem so fragile. It is so easy to just give up and attack everything and be negative about what culture can't do. Several times you've mentioned the significance of culture in the sense of the images that it gives to people and the possibility of transforming their lives. I'm struck by the sense of retaining this positive aspect of democratic pluralism and redefining your theatre around that and really coming to what's important today—the question of ethics, morality, emotion. Frankly, I didn't come here expecting to speak about those things, but they are the most significant.

That's the starting point.

It also continues work in a theatre of extremes—I'm thinking of Susan Sontag directing Beckett in Sarajevo—a theatre of extreme conditions.

Which is what drama is based on. Which is about life *in extremis*. What destroys people, or resurrects them? That's the question.

This interview was originally published in *PAJ: A Journal of Performance and Art*, Vol. XXVII, No. 1 (PAJ 79), January 2005. A condensed version was translated into Catalan and appeared as "Representació I Ètica," in *Documents De Theatre* (*DDT* 03), Teatre Lliure, Barcelona, 2004. It was conducted in Barcelona at the Teatre Lliure in June 2004.

The Universal:
The Simplest Place Possible
A Conversation with Romeo Castellucci

Romeo Castellucci, with Claudia Castellucci and Chiara Guidi, founded Societas Raffaello Sanzio, one of Europe's most celebrated theatres, in 1981. Based in the Adriatic city of Cesena, the theatre brings together performance and visual arts in productions often featuring animals, children, and non-actors. The company has created many provocative stagings of classic and mythic texts, such as *Genesis*, *Gilgamesh*, *Oresteia*, *Hamlet*, and *Julius Caesar*, in addition to original works, directed by Castellucci. Societas Raffaello Sanzio also founded its own experimental theatre school for children and book-publishing activities. A major recent project is *Tragedia Endogonidia*, a series of independent episodes made for several European cities. The Italian critic Valentina Valentini collaborated on this dialogue which took place in Riccione, June 2002.

Much of your theatre work has been the staging of classics by Shakespeare and the Greeks. What draws you to tragedy?

A spiritual connection exists between us and the classics; through them it's possible to reconnect with the individual and with the universality of the individual. It is also possible to find the familiar as well as real solitude. A kind of reverse action shot is involved. Work with the classics demands that we confront the traditional, but that is precisely why the work can surpass the traditional, but never in a literary way. Therefore one mustn't tackle these classical texts as a superstitious person who believes the classics to be safe; quite the opposite. One must make an effort to put them to the test of fire, in order to better determine their supportive structure, which leads exactly to the revelation that they speak to everyone, to the frail and private nature of every individual. And the book, as object, is no more.

How does it relate to your work?

The new cycle of work, on the other hand, is dedicated—and it's the first time that this has happened—to a work outside the context of literature, outside the context of great books, books of the past; outside the "book," yet it's still work that is part of the discipline of tragedy. We could define the structure as classical, but the tragic form has so influenced individuals, society, and culture through the ages and has become so much a part of our psyches that it can appear in new aesthetic forms in our contemporary world. So this new cycle of work has what I'll call a universal structure, and as such it presents more basic problems. The universal is the simplest place possible to free oneself from narrative structure, from the burden of narrative, and thus also from the burden of the written word, from its visibility: the word should go back to being invisible. My tragedy project is called *Tragedia Endogonidia* or *Endogonidial Tragedy*. "Endogonidial" is a word taken from microbiology; "gonidial" refers to simple living forms that have inside them two gonads, thus both sexes, and they consequently reproduce through an endocrine system. The price they have to pay for being able to reproduce themselves is not conjunction, union, but division, a perpetual division of themselves. These living things are immortal.

The interesting thing was to contrast these two words. *Tragedia* or tragedy is something that is part of our history (or at least the history of this side of the planet); its structure has a place at the origin of our consciousness and our culture. "Endogonidia," on the other hand, is a word that falls completely outside culture, in the sense that there is no culture in this process of reproduction and survival. So while tragedy is a mechanism to expose the dead body, a mechanism whose fundamental aim is to display death, these micro-organisms are in fact immortal and reproduce themselves *ad infinitum*.

"Tragedia" or "tragedy," on the other hand, presupposes an end (of the hero). Our intention with this production is to rethink tragedy, bring it into the here-and-now. In ancient Greece, the Episodes were sections of a tragedy that presented only the facts, without commentary; commentary was left to the Chorus. In *Tragedia Endogonidia* there is no Chorus. Out of the Episodes emerge basic recurring figures and forms, themes and ideas, which make the spectators aware of their existence, their state of being.

In what way is a city involved in the spectacle?

There are various ways in which a city can be involved in the project; in some cases it can be through a specific reference to something in the city even if the city itself is never actually named. A characteristic of this project on tragedy is that it changes from city to city, therefore it is in a process of becoming, but besides being in a process of becoming it's an organism in continual flux, so the performance is never the same; but that's no reason to call it a work-in-progress. Because it really appears to be the opposite; every time it opens for an audience, it's a finished and complete production that supplies, within itself, the mechanism of endogonidial reproduction, a division of itself by itself, a sort of fall-out of spores, which provide for future and successive growth.

Furthermore, it's a system that completely eliminates the problem of repertory and therefore of reproduction, of the characteristic repetitive nature of theatre that's calendar-related, because it is a project that in some way is strongly tied to a concept of geography and of place. The cities involved are Avignon, Berlin, Brussels, Strasbourg, Bergen, London, Rome, Cesena, Paris, and Marseilles. *Tragedia Endogonidia* also includes a Film Cycle and a Travel Diary of the displacements: "Idiom, Climate Time."

In Italy, the theatre of the nineties came closer and closer to the language and forms of writing typical of film or installations. There's a big crisis in the lines of demarcation between cinema, video, film, installations, the visual arts. What has glaringly disappeared in many of our most recent experiences is the boundary between the concept of entertainment and the concept of art, and the feeling of pathos.

Yes, of course, I understand perfectly. It's a problem for me too; if there's no emotion, for me that's it, it's over, it's only a sterile idea. And that's true above all for the new generation; there's no dynamic, there's no thought. I always demand that an artist move me. I even ask that of a visual artist. For me the emotional wave is the ineffable nucleus of a work, its breath of life. But it's still difficult to be moved at exhibitions, at the biennials, where one sees dazzling and hallucinatory spectacles and stagings that remind one of amusement parks. Although even that type of irony can succeed, it's a very difficult exercise. Irony is interesting when it's fierce, when it rips your mind apart. That doesn't always happen. The artists have to be damn good.

However, one very often can have an enjoyable experience when there is an absence of irony, when there is no discussion about the world. How does European art make itself felt on the international scene?

In my opinion, in certain American artists, such as Bill Viola, for example, the relationship is obvious: his references, in his most recent works, are to the Italian Renaissance even on a formal level. The composition, I could even say the prosody, becomes a choice of colors, of placements. He's another example of work on the classical. In other situations the legacy of the European experience shines through as backlighting. Pop art itself, which is completely American, has plainly taken certain pathways left in suspension by dada and symbolism.

Matthew Barney is an artist who is completely and magisterially American. He's extraordinary because in his works he manages to trigger off a sort of language that's self-contained, cohesive, endowed with merciless logic. He presents us with this reality, this complex system of signs, but the most satisfying thing is that he does it by using the signs of our reality. He's one of the strongest artists today who is not, apparently, influenced by European art. He appears to be indifferent to the history of art, because the history of art has no bearing on his work. Brilliant.

How do you work with actors in relation to the Italian tradition?

The Italian tradition is based on characteristics of types. That is, there are character types in the Italian tradition, but meanwhile we know that Stanislavsky founded everything really on the idea of digging and interpretation, where the actor analyzes the character, the psychology of the character. In my case, neither the one nor the other exists; but these two pathways are not negated, they're simply two unacknowledged tracks, two tracks that remain suspended. My work is of a more objective nature, it relies on the body of the actor. It's a discovery, an encounter that happens with men and women willing to live this adventure. A professionalism is not necessarily required, although the actors do acquire it, in the sense that those who work with me don't work spontaneously, nor do they improvise, but they become professionals even if they weren't at the beginning. What makes an actor important in this experience is the soul, the face, and the body. The truth of the body becomes inscribed quite precisely in the fiction of the spectacle.

Two "temperatures," two expressive registers, are present: on the one hand, the logical structure of the movement principle; and on the other, the body and its truths, which is the most concise form of communication possible and also the most disconcerting, the most pointed. The body is the simplest form of communication, in the sense that even an animal understands you since it's in a position to see you, hear you, and smell you. The body is the point of departure and probably also the point of arrival, after having completed an ellipse, after having also passed through and shaken the body of spectators. So I would say that this is a fundamental idea that sustains the work of the actors; it doesn't repudiate tradition, it ignores tradition, the Italian and European tradition. And the static tradition of the East.

Can you give some examples of the difference between type and body?

In some cases the choice of an actor depends exclusively on the dramaturgy presented by a particular stage situation or by the specific text, the choice is never a personal one; the choice of a person, the shape, weight, age, walk doesn't depend on me. They're all elements that create the truth of the person's body and that spill over, willy nilly, into the dramatic fabric. So the choice depends on the dramatic characteristics of a piece of writing for the stage or even a simple text. To give an example, and to remain concrete, to the perceptive eye, the hallmark of Shakespeare's *Julius Caesar* is its loaded rhetoric.

In my production, Cicero is interpreted by a man who, I think, weighs 240 kg [528 pounds]. I didn't want to put something shocking on stage, something provocative; on the contrary, although I needed to work with a large body, in a certain way I hid it, I didn't do anything to make this already oversized choice too obvious. The body was big, in this case, because Cicero is the man who drives forward Shakespeare's text the most, who has the most weight because he inspires the conspiracy. Even if he doesn't ever take part directly in the action, he's still like a sort of weight that throws the action off balance. Thus Cicero is an enormous man who always has his back turned to the audience, because he turns his back to the action, and on his back are two treble clefs that refer to Man Ray.

Quite simply, he, in his turn, became a "rhetorical" body. In *Julius Caesar* I also worked with an actor whose larynx had been surgically removed, and it was his job to perform the voice of the character of Mark Antony. Mark Antony is the one who wins the oratorical competition, so working with someone who has no larynx meant having a new voice that came from the viscera, from deep down inside. Mark Antony's speech is completely focused on Caesar's wounds, it recalls the number of stab wounds, the blood that came out of them, the fact that the wounds are "silent mouths" which have no other voice at that moment but his, Mark Antony's. Well, this character in the shape of this actor actually talks from a wound, to make the speech truthful, outrageous, and moving. The most amazing thing of all is that this type of emotion is really stimulated by a consciously rhetorical use of the body and voice.

In what way is technology present in your productions?

Technology is present on the stage as metaphor and spirit. Technology and machines are bearers of phantoms who inhabit the set, the stage—the concept is animistic. So a machine has an entrance and an exit, it lights up, it takes up a chunk of the world; in short, it creates its own world. So it's quite clear that it's not merely a gadget, a decoration, because it is energized and it is triggered by argument with the actor, and thus it has in some way a dehumanizing function. It dehumanizes the actor, puts him in danger, places him in the paradoxical position of deuteragonist, so that finally it creates an inhuman tension.

The machine, unlike the animal, is inhuman because it's pure function without experience. The actor falls exactly between these two camps, between animal and machine, he's both things at the same time, pure function and pure exposed body, pure being. Technology becomes a central metaphor and, as such, it's often more useful to hide it in order to make it effective: it's the operation or action of the machine that's important, not the machine itself. The technology I use is very diverse and ranges from being very primitive to very sophisticated: video technology, endoscopes which reconnoiter the insides of the actor and upset the traditional relationship that the audience has with the actor, in the sense that it's possible to see the actor's interior. For example, the endoscope in *Julius Caesar* passes over and probes the vocal chords and projects a video of them upstage. The first image is the inside of an actor, not a face, not an exterior. But I only do this with very sophisticated technology, instruments that are very difficult to use, to which I devote twenty, thirty minutes of performance time without any human intervention by the actors. Pneumatic, hydraulic, oleic-dynamic or oil-pressure machines, taxidermy, automaton mechanics, microscopes, organic chemistry, chemiluminescence, techniques for breeding certain animals, acoustical physics, robotic components, but also little pieces of sacred wood that have been badly nailed together ... in short, whatever.

What is the spiritual dimension of your work? Can you describe its place in your theatre?

I can't say, I don't know anything about it, really. It's something that escapes me completely, it must be there somewhere, but I can't know it, I can't say what it is. I try to plunder the spirit of others, in order to move myself. It can happen in certain situations, in certain total creations. It can even happen in certain ancient texts that I tackle in which everything seems clear to me, even the power that they trigger. What is very difficult, however, is what happens, at least for my sensibility, with a contemporary author. It's difficult for me, if not impossible, to stage a contemporary author like Beckett. I'll never stage him, not because I'm a coward, but because we're on the same level. Beckett has, like me, like a contemporary man, the same kind of box, one might say, the same type of *aporia*. We both find ourselves in the same circumstances, and it is not possible to work with someone who is in the same circumstances as I. It's like an algebraic sum: two similar signs cannot stay together. I need a classical structure, one that's universal, pure, transparent. Being universal, it belongs to me, because it resonates in me. Beckett doesn't resonate in me, really, but I see my neighbor in him. The classical structure is pure, and being pure I can manipulate it. And once manipulated, I can purify it.

The universal allows you to dig inside yourself, to extract, to add.

Exactly, in a word ... it's possible to work, it's possible to live. In freedom. No absolute freedom exists in a contemporary author. Again, contemporary texts are all packaged, ready-made, in speech.

Do you feel that you have any "fathers" or "sons"?

I have a putative "father," a false father, and he's a shining figure, one of the ghosts of my turbulent adolescence, Carmelo Bene, whom I didn't follow in any way. For me, he's simply an icon, but the important thing is that he's an icon that is part of my adolescence; there's a personal story there. However, I reject the idea of master teachers, it has no meaning at all for me. I'm completely outside, and it would be worse still if I claimed a master teacher. Naturally there may be figures who were, and continue to be, fundamentally important to me, but they are invariably outside the orbit of theatre. That's perhaps natural and human. But following in the tracks of a method, for me that's a mistake. Following a model means taking another's path, and I want to question the very idea of a path.

In your opinion, is Pirandello relevant to present-day theatre?

I don't know. No, I'd say he isn't. Pirandello is a figure who's central to Italian literary culture, but I personally have never followed him, because he sets off a kind of self-reflection, a sort of tautology that is mirrored in the actors. It's not part of my thinking, it never has been. Pirandello's theatre is self-reflective, and a sort of new awareness happens through language. But the limits of Pirandello lie in the fact that language becomes linguistics. The energy and power are buried by the situation created, penned, by a man who knew a lot about books and short stories. "Pay attention: Pirandello is 'literature.'" That's something else. For example, when the six characters are searching for the author, that's more than a symbol, I have to say. These people are renouncing the disconcerting truth of the

stage, the rift or barrier of the stage, the alienation that is an essential characteristic of the stage experience. They are renouncing all of that, thus they are also
renouncing their stage roles. They are completely dependent on an author, on a
poet, on the script, and thus they just repeat the script. All of this was happening
at the same time that, beyond the Alps, a tortured Antonin Artaud was tearing
words from his flesh, and paying a high price for it. There's an abyss here, I would
say. These are two separate worlds that will never know each other.

In Tonight We Improvise *there's a scene where the actors send away the director, who in his turn had sent away the author, and they end up doing everything
themselves. To end that scene, Nina plays her part, she sings, etc.; and then there's
the one who doesn't die, but she does faint. This infers how dangerous it is when an
actor does without the director, without the author, because it changes from being
performance to being life.*

Yes, but it's even more ironic that it was written, fixed for all time through
artifice, through a kind of somersault. It's strange. I admit there's a great sharp-
ness of vision there, but it belongs to a piece of writing, a script that's completely dead, one that has already divulged everything. One that's descriptive,
demonstrative. *Life* on the stage.... Why are we afraid of that word on the stage?
What harm is there in it? They say it's dangerous. But I embrace the danger
that is so essential to theatre. So? I think it's really the divide, the barrier, that
causes all the furor.

Pirandello's style is to mix up the levels, but everything remains in the lin-
guistic domain. It's like the sweet yarrow, an herb with many leaves but only one
flavor. I find that—to continue the parallel which gives a sense of proportion to
the things we're talking about—Artaud is a figure who doesn't belong to the past,
he's not part of tradition. Thus Artaud represents an aspect of making theatre in
this sense; he's not simply a playwright, indeed, he really isn't one at all, and that's
a dimension I find pregnant with the future, despite the fact that academics try to
manage him, to conjugate him. Artaud won't be taken, really, he won't be held.

*The theatre of this century, of our century, does it go beyond the text and literary
language?*

No, not always. I believe that in this era theatre can really be created in all
possible ways, even by simply reading a text from beginning to end. I don't believe that there's any problem with form. I believe that in this era we can finally
say that we are released, indeed liberated, from the burden of style, from the

burden of form. You can create theatre through the written word, through a text, but theatre doesn't happen just because there's a written text, it's not automatic. What counts is the spirit, the emotion.

Does a new theatre of Europe in the twenty-first century exist?

In my opinion, it is a theatre that no longer has the problem of formal boundaries. I find that the most interesting experiences are those where certain choreographers create spectacles with very little dance, or theatrical spectacles that are really concerts. The most interesting situations, in my opinion, are those in which there's a breakdown of styles and roles, or where what happens is of a radical nature worthy of this era, and this idea can happen even when there is not much tension, when the "heat" is low. The most interesting experiences are often those that, from a formal point of view, assimilate more from the visual arts, and I believe that, all in all, the most creative energies are coming from there. There's a whole mode of theatre tied to tradition; I don't call that art, only bourgeois decoration. Essential theatre is what can be done either in the middle of a war or in a museum. I believe that, in the end, what's very important is the idea—mental giddiness, temporal suspension from this world—and presenting it for discussion, and the actual possibility of another parallel world, another language which, suddenly, as Alice knew, stops being "other."

TRANSLATED BY JANE HOUSE

This conversation with Romeo Castellucci was first published in *PAJ: A Journal of Performance and Art*, Vol. XXVI, No. 2 (PAJ 77), May 2004. It was published in Italy as "L'universale, il più semplice posto possibile. Intervista a Romeo Castellucci," in "Il Teatro Di Fine Millennio," curated by Valentina Valentini, *Biblioteca Teatrale*, Nos. 74-76, Apr.-Dec. 2005 (Centro Teatro Ateneo/University of Rome-La Sapienza), (Rome: Bulzoni Editore, 2005). It took place in Riccione, Italy in June 2002 and was conducted in Italian with Valentina Valentini, who has written and edited several books on theatre and media, including *Teatro in immagine, Dopo il teatro moderno*, and *Le Storie del video*, and a theatre series with volumes on Peter Sellars, Eimuntas Nekrosius, and others. She lives in Rome.

Art as Spiritual Practice

A Conversation with Meredith Monk, Alison Knowles, Eleanor Heartney, Linda Montano, Erik Ehn

This discussion featured the performer, composer, and filmmaker Meredith Monk; visual artist and founding Fluxus member Alison Knowles; performance artist Linda Montano; Eleanor Heartney, art critic and contributing editor of *Art in America*; Erik Ehn, playwright and director. I served as moderator for the public event, which took place at the SoHo gallery Location One on November 5, 2001. There was considerable interest in our subject—nearly three-hundred people attended the evening-long discussion—so soon after September 11, when the mood in New York City was still somber, especially downtown, and people were anxious to come together and talk. For this audience there was already an awareness of the recent controversies over religious imagery in visual arts, theatre, and film generated by the ongoing conflict between liberal values and religious conservatism in American culture.

A cursory overview of avant-garde and modernist movements, beginning in the late-nineteenth century, reveals the extent to which performing, literary, and visual arts have drawn on religious iconography, biblical themes, lives of saints, and the occult from Western, Asian, and Middle-Eastern religious traditions. In performance and visual arts there has been growing attention to the spiritual styles of artworks.

MARRANCA— The notion of the spiritual, of religion, of spiritual discipline or practice is very difficult to grapple with. One of the things we might consider is: What do we mean by the spiritual? How do we recognize it? What kinds of things do we consider to be works of spiritual grace or discipline? Often I have found in speaking to people about this theme that there is an uncomfortableness with discussions of religion and the spirit. There has come to be a taboo around them. It is so difficult to know how to speak of such ideas, images, or feelings because we have so little vocabulary today to address them. Sometimes artists think it might sound flaky to speak about them so they don't volunteer anything on the topic, but when it opens up they speak in a strong, clear way about the nature of the spiritual in their work.

A progressive discussion of the nature of spiritual feeling in contemporary artworks has not been as prominent in American culture where the subject of religion has been dominated by the religious right and more conservative forces. It can also be said that in the eighties and nineties, when so many works dealt with irony, and many took for granted the notion of unstable identities and a view of the self as socially constructed, the idea of the search for truth or transcendence was in opposition to current theory. It became suspect to speak about the authenticity of the spirit in an era dominated by political issues. Yet, the secularization of the spiritual has been a project of the entire twentieth century.

There are a number of issues we might consider in our discussion. Are certain forms more spiritual than others? What does the spiritual have to do with utopia? How is it related to politics and culture? As many of you are aware, the artworld controversies of recent years were often argued over religious iconography. In dealing with the theme of art and the spiritual dimension, we might begin by addressing the nature of spiritual practice.

KNOWLES— At the end of a book called *Ainu Dreams* my friend George Quasha, with his friend Chie Hasagawa, defined spirit. "Tamashi," the native Japanese word for spirit, is contrasted by D. T. Suzuki with the Chinese word for spirit, "Jing Shen." The Chinese words set the material against the spiritual and project a duality. By contrast, the Japanese word suggests a sense of spirit that is finally non-separable from the material. There is a certain tension between the material and the spiritual, yet never without the impossibility of an embrace between them. What is known as "spirit" is almost something you can hold in the palm of your hand. The "tama" of "tamashi" sounds the roundness of a ball, a sphere, a stone, something precious and immediate to the senses. In my view, to push the distinction between art and spirituality emphasizes a weakness in our view of both. At the root, art needs no beyond that would be exalted by a notion of the spiritual. However, art-making is a spirit practice. The homeland body, our body, we breathe into and we take a pulse for the work.

Eduardo Calderon—a *curando*, a doctor in Peru—sits in the street before his mesa of seventeen artefacts that are ringed with staffs and spears. When a patient sits down he or she listens to the story he tells and he makes a *cuenta*, an accounting of this patient's condition. He tries to locate on his mesa the object through which the spirit of the patient can speak. He tries to interrupt and disrupt the boundary between inside and outside. He looks inside to repair the balance of power. A *cuenta* puts us back in charge. It's not unlike a soup, adjusting the spices, and then knowledgeably we are in charge, before opening the cage door, releasing the bird or bowl, so to speak. We have done our best from our own seat. "We are all in the best seat." (Cage) Art simply persuades us that in fact this is the case. We are, however, not sitting together in one seat. Each has an equal opportunity to make his or her seat the best one.

I went to Pratt in the mid-fifties where I met Philip Guston, whose work I adored. He made red and orange dots circulating around an empty center in the canvas. I found that an extremely interesting comment in the midst of abstract expressionism. At the end of his career, Guston began to do socialist realist paintings such as he had done in his twenties, e.g., people sitting playing poker around a lamp. I said to a friend how disappointed I was that he let the other work go. My friend said, "No, he was making an accounting."

So, we don't know for anyone else the accounting they are making and the place they are working from. It's a great mystery. We waive judgment. We ask questions. As we make up our materials we beat the paper or prime the canvas. We are already waking up the mind spirit in beginning doing. It's the pulse we set up to do the work. A still point is reached to do from, in or out of balance with our *cuenta*. Art as spiritual practice must then include each of us and all art-making. There are many ways to engage to find the point but any route is good enough.

HEARTNEY— There's something very nebulous about the notion of spirituality. In my research, I prefer instead to think in terms of religion. I have been researching a book whose working title is "Postmodern Heretics." [The book has since been published.—BGM] It's a look at the way in which artists have been influenced by what I call the "Catholic imagination." The starting point for this was about ten years ago when the so-called "culture wars" started to kick off. I began to notice that every artist who got in trouble with the religious right came from a Catholic background. As I come from a Catholic background myself, I found that curious and began to ruminate on why it might be.

Essentially, what I have come to is the idea—and I found it well-expressed in a book by Andrew Greeley, called *The Catholic Imagination*—that there are different kinds of religious imagination. In the case of the Catholic, it is an imagination that is not simply a matter of official church doctrine—that's the least of it—but it brings together the pomp and beauty of Catholic ritual and the seductiveness of traditional Catholic art. It also touches on the eroticism of devotional literature. It is very deeply involved in what can be called the "incarnational" emphasis of Catholicism: the importance of the physical body, which runs through all of the big mysteries of Catholicism on up through the Mass, the great ritual in which Catholics actually believe that bread and wine is turned into the body and blood of Christ. There is a very strong emphasis on the body in Catholicism that becomes much more muted after the Reformation among various Protestant sects.

It seemed to me that the Catholic imagination manifested itself in the work of many artists whom we've assumed either are secular or are doing work intentionally contrary to Catholicism. For example, Andres Serrano's *Piss Christ* was read, not only by the religious right but, interestingly at the time, even by the artworld establishment, as a statement *against* religion. It was read literally as "piss on Christ." If we look at it more closely, we see it is full of reverence and has much to do with traditional Catholic notions about light and fluids. It is part of a whole series he did, using different body fluids. If we look at traditional Catholic art, we see how important is the blood of Christ, the milk of Mary, even the pus of lepers.

Similarly, probably the hardest case would be Robert Mapplethorpe who did work that was wildly pornographic. He once told an interviewer that his two greatest influences were Coney Island and the Catholic Church. You can see it in his use of light—the way he isolates images. He did a number of triptychs and images that seem to be based on traditional Catholic iconography. There is something that permeates his work in the way that he thinks about the body and sexuality that is very Catholic. In terms of performance artists, there are people like Karen Finley, a nice Irish-Catholic girl, Linda Montano, Vito Acconci, Bob Flanagan—any number of artists whose work manifests itself in a very Catholic, physical way.

One of the things that is important in thinking about such a thing as a "Catholic imagination" or a "Protestant imagination" or a "Jewish imagination" is that we are not talking about church doctrine or even about people who in their adult lives have a firm belief and devotedly practice their religion. Instead, what interests me is the way in which someone who is raised Catholic or in a very Catholic milieu gets imprinted with this view of the world, so that no matter what happens it becomes a very important part of how they think about reality.

Within my now long list of "postmodern heretics" there is an interesting range: there are some who are practicing Catholics, like Chris Ofili, who was the subject of the Brooklyn Museum controversy, or Joel-Peter Witkin, the photographer, whose work involves the very beautiful and weird use of tableaux, often made out of body parts. They are arranged in ways that make reference to religious paintings. As with Serrano, there is the assumption that he is in some way being ironic or putting down religion. But, in fact, I recently heard him speak in Arizona where there was an exhibit of his work. He is a devout Catholic and sees his work as partly in praise of religion. He talked very movingly of how when he put together these amalgams of body parts he would actually pray over the fragments, which he got from the University of Arizona Medical Department. He worked with a doctor and was very careful to be reverential. More interesting was the reaction of the audience, many of whom always assumed that this work had to be anti-religious. So, you have on the one hand, people who are actively religious. The other end of the spectrum goes all the way to someone like Mapplethorpe who, although he remained deeply influenced by a Catholic imagination throughout his life, particularly because of his status as a gay man felt very much exiled and expelled by the Church. One of the moving factors of his work is this conflict.

It is worthwhile to keep in mind that someone can manifest a religious imagination without being a practicing, card-carrying member of that religion. We need to expand our definition of what it means to be religious to encompass that wide range. One of the things that has been interesting for me in my study is that there are political implications to it. I started this research when I noticed how many of these artists were the targets of the religious right. This has to do as much with the clash of religious sensibilities: it's often framed as a clash between the atheist, secular, body-oriented, sexually-based imagination and a Protestant imagination which is quite different. It is important to start thinking about this because it helps us to redefine political conflicts right now and to realize that we shouldn't let morality and religion be the exclusive province of one group. It is also important for our understanding of art to get rid of this notion that there is an absolute, adversarial relationship between religion and art and to realize how deeply influential religion can be in the art that we see.

MONK— I come originally from a non-practicing Jewish background. For the last fifteen years I've been doing a Tibetan Buddhist practice. I started out with the secular branch of it that is called Shambala practice, but in the last few years have gone into the regular Buddhist practice. I think that why this way of thinking about things has been a very comforting force in my life and very inspiring is that as a young artist my sensibility was actually dealing with a lot of things that are talked about in the Buddhist practice. The basis of my vocal work was always silence. I was usually working from a very quiet place, no matter how much it sounded like I was screaming at the top of my lungs.

When I was teaching at Naropa Institute in the seventies and doing a performance that was quite slow in conventional terms, I noticed that the community was able to really deal with that—the idea of the body being what it was, the voice being what it was. So, in fact, what the practice has done for me has been more in terms of how I work with other people and in some ways articulating certain things I was never able to articulate. For example, one of the things that artists do is to tolerate hanging out in the unknown. That is a process most people don't want to undertake. It's trying to deal with things that are unnameable, trying to be very present.

What I try to do is start from zero in every piece, not to think about it in terms of product or what my piece should be like or doing what I've done before, but going to the edge of the cliff each time. It is really trying in some ways to follow and to delineate a mystery. That is very much talked about in terms of Buddhism—the idea that everything is ephemeral, that we have certain conceptual frameworks that keep us from experiencing what is really there. That sense of connection is something art can do. What I have tried to do in my work these last years is to offer a place where people can actually have some time to let go of the narrator or the discursive mind for a while and experience in a very direct way fundamental human energies for which we don't have words. The voice as an instrument is something I've been exploring deeply for over thirty years. The voice—the original instrument—can delineate feelings and states of being so that the music can be experienced directly by anyone. In that way, it is transcultural and it has a sense of timelessness, which I would say is a characteristic of a spiritual way of thinking about things.

Something else I think about a lot is cycles of time and human nature. Buddhism is not really a religion. It is a non-theistic study of the human mind that has been going on for twenty-five-hundred years—starting with yourself. That means no sense of judgment but just being able to observe the mind as if it were some kind of movie, really being able to accept, with a sense of compassion and gentleness, what one would call "bad" as well as the "good." That's all part of it, observing the ephemerality of thought and of life itself. These energies can be experienced very directly in art and that is the beauty of art. It doesn't matter what the form is. What we are trying to get to is that experience of "it" itself.

In a more concrete way, over the last few years I worked on two different projects that were addressing these concerns. In 1996, the Union Theological Seminary asked me if I could make a service for the Guild of American Organists, Protestant organ players from all over the United States who were coming to New York for a conference. I enjoyed working on that very much because it was also a way of thinking about what exactly is a congregation? What is an audience? I was trying to do something that was between those two ideas.

I have been thinking for many years about how to make a form that's meta-theatrical in that it is a meditative kind of piece where people can just quiet down a little bit. Even though it's in a presentational style, it is really something where the silence of the space is a way to rest the mind and rest the being and to be refreshed and look at things in a new way, to listen in a new way, to go out in the street and hear things in a new way. I had fragments of short sentences from different spiritual traditions— Rumi, an African rain song, a crazy wisdom Buddhist text, Hildegard von Bingen, Martin Buber, a Native American young woman's initiation prayer. What we did in that performance/service was to weave these texts between big choral pieces that I had written over the years. We taught one of my canons to the congregation, we did a procession which is also something that occurs in a lot of different spiritual traditions. It was going back to the fundamental qualities of what a devotional service would be and then trying to widen it out and get to its simplest elements and make it a very, very simple and direct experience that lasted about an hour and was in the middle of the day which was very nice. Your lunch hour could be this experience and then you could go back to work refreshed. That was a wonderful experience of going into the community.

Another thing I just worked on about two days ago in Ireland. I have been thinking a lot about shrines and altars. For about ten years, I've been making shrines both in a gallery situation as an installation and also as a kind of prologue to a performance piece. The first one was *Volcano Songs*. The idea of shrines and altars being something you do in a conscious way as an offering; for example, in Bali, people put a little offering outside their door everyday that is a sense of gratitude for the day. I really like that sense of articulating gratitude in objects. I was thinking a lot about what has happened after September 11 and I have been very moved by seeing that here in New York in front of firehouses people have been making shrines and altars that they add their own feelings and objects to.

Besides singing a concert in Ireland I was teaching a workshop, which I divided into groups, for people who had come from all over Europe and Ireland. They were architects, dancers, actors, a filmmaker. I finally got the courage to give the shrine as a problem in the workshop. I said to everyone that the process of making this and trying to get all of your sensibilities and visions into the shrine is what this is about. In the world that we are living in now I feel that we do have to negotiate. As human beings on the planet, it's something we need to think about. So, the first part we worked on was to make a shrine. It didn't matter what the shrine was for, it was the sense of making something that had the presence and consciousness of doing it. The second part was that each group had to make a vocal offering. The third part was to devise some kind of a ritual. What happened was that the four groups did the most moving things.

I felt that just as in the Tibetan Buddhist tradition where we have the prayer flags that are called *lungta*—windhorse—written with messages which the wind blows, the idea is that these good wishes for human beings and for the world are blown by the wind into the world. What these people came up with in the workshops was our way of actually doing something itself in reality to make the world have a sense of energy and freshness and a positive kind of action. So, the separation between making art or making an offering and living a life disappeared.

MONTANO—

Natural Voice: I must admit that I think that I have been chosen for this panel because I've performed and dressed up as a mother superior, a saint, a guru, a mystic, a priest, a martyr, a swami, and a healer for thirty years and called that play, Art. As Shakespeare, Annie Sprinkle, and others have said, "Dresseth liketh undt nuneth, duth noteth undt sainteth maketh!"

Saint Voice (as Theresa of Avila): "The first thing that we have to do, and that at once, is to rid ourselves of love for this body of ours."

Natural Voice: Art once done has a life of its own. It's our baby, a child, and as good and loyal parents we're responsible to that baby. So I'm here to be as honest as possible.

Saint Voice: "It is when I possess least that I have fewest worries and the Lord knows that I am more afflicted when there is excess of anything than when there is a lack of it."

Question: DESCRIBE YOUR EARLY SPIRITUAL LIFE (I'm using a self-imposed interview).

Natural Voice: I was enculturated early into strict Roman Catholicism in an upstate New York village right out of a storybook. Mom: Irish/Yankee/convert from Episcopalianism, was a comedienne, painter, questioner of authority in a subtle way. Dad: pious/creative/silent/focused; his parents, non-English speaking from Campobasso, both devout, silent, hard-working.

Question: WHAT WAS YOUR EARLY CHILDHOOD SPIRITUAL ENCULTURATION?

Saint Voice: "There are two kinds of love, one is purely spiritual and has nothing to do with sensuality or the tenderness of nature. The other is family love."

Question: WHAT DID YOUR ENCULTURATION LOOK LIKE LATER ON IN YOUR WORK? WE ALL IMITATE OUR CHILDHOODS AND EARLY ISSUES. THAT'S A GIVEN. DID YOUR WORK LOOK ROMAN CATHOLIC?

Natural Voice: My answer is in the form of two lists.

> LIST 1: CATHOLIC MEMORIES
> the smell of high quality incense
> the inflexibility of doctrine
> the dedication of vow-taking nuns
> the talking saint statues
> the patriarchal exclusivity
> the Tiffany stained-glass windows
> the fasting before Communion, Fridays, and Lent
> the stories of statues crying blood
> the sounds of small bells at Communion
> the sounds of the large Angelus bells
> the fear of dropping the Host
> the poetry of the Latin Mass
> the ritually-tailored vestments
> the possibility of purgatory
> the daily examine of conscience
> the mystery of Transubstantiation
> the ecstatic surrender to creed
> the nun's/priest's unavailable celibacy
> the obedience
> the stories of miracles, martyrdoms, missionaries, curings of
>   leprosy

the offering up (to God) anger, rage, traumas
the repetition of trance-inducing rosaries
the Stations of the Cross, the Stations of the Cross
the relief and humiliation of weekly confession
the prayer beads and holy cards
the May Day hymn singing and rosary at the Lourdes shrine
the belonging the belonging the belonging
the promise of heavenly reward

LIST 2: A FEW OF THOSE MEMORIES AS ART
wearing blindfolds for a week (penance)
creation of Chicken Whiteface Woman (trying to be a statue)
anorexia videos (holy anorexia)
three-hour acupuncture performances (crucifixion)
riding bikes on Brooklyn Bridge tied by a rope to Tehching
    Hsieh (miracle of walking on water)
fourteen years of living art (imitation of priest's vestments)

Saint Voice: "In every respect we must be careful and alert because the devil never slumbers."

Question: THAT IS CERTAINLY AN IDEALIZED LOOK AT RELIGION, MISS MONTANO. YOU ARE LOOKING WITHOUT THE POLITICS, WITHOUT THE PEOPLE, WITHOUT THE HYPOCRISY, WITHOUT THE COMPLEXITIES OF HUMAN FAILURE, HUMAN FOIBLES, AND FOLLIES. I WOULD CONVERT IMMEDIATELY TO CATHOLICISM READING YOUR MEMORY LIST. YOU BECAME A NUN, DIDN'T YOU?

Natural Voice: It was only logical that this intense early training eventuated in a desire for sanctity and, in 1960, I entered a missionary convent. For two years:

> I talked only one hour a day and that was "in common" (a room with all nuns present). I wore four layers of medieval, pre-Vatican II clothes called a "habit." I chanted ecstatically with over three-hundred nuns in a *Nun's Story*-type chapel and even though I was as high as a kite, I was told by a nun who was a Katherine Hepburn look-alike, "Sister Rose, go and be an actress."

I left, eighty-two pounds, anorexic and hungry for something that only art gave me. Mother art became my trauma catcher, my therapy, my confidant, my best friend, my guide, my confessor, my salvation. Art became religion. And in separating from Catholicism, I married art.

Question: WHAT KIND OF ART DID YOU PRACTICE?

Natural Voice: I sculpted/welded the Visitation (Mary embracing Elizabeth, both pregnant), made crucifixes, and eventually presented live chickens as art for the MFA in Sculpture I earned in graduate school. I later invented performance for myself. That necessity was a fascination with the energy of aliveness. When I performed I got so much attention from others, which helped me attend to myself. When I attended to me, I discovered that the three billion cells in the body, when properly treated, can produce a half-watt of electricity in all three billion cells. WOW!!! Also, I could oscillate my brain waves at a frequency that produced addictively pleasing endorphine states of consciousness. The brain waves are:

> Beta, normal, thinking, 3–35 oscillations
> Alpha, rest, 8–13
> Theta, 4–8 children, adults, dreams, strong emotions
> Delta, 0–5 sleeping newborns

By aesthetically purging subconscious material via public actions, via exposition of excesses of power, via exploration of autobiography as art ... the brain empties of obscurations, guilts, fears, shames, and goes into modes of consciousness curried by nuns, contemplatives, and all seekers of *samadhi*.

Question: I FEAR NARCISSISM AND TOO MUCH SELF. I ALSO SEE EASTERN INFLUENCES IN YOUR WORK. THIS WORK SEEMS MORE ABOUT ART THERAPY THAN FORMALIST ART MAGAZINE INVESTIGATIONS.

Natural Voice: Exactly.

Saint Voice: "We must shorten our time of prayer, however much joy it gives us, if we see our bodily strength waning or find that our head aches; discretion is most necessary in everything."

Question: WHY DIDN'T YOU REMAIN CATHOLIC?

Natural Voice: It wasn't cool to be a Catholic artist in the sixties and I regret that I followed that legend. But, I did study with my meditation teacher, Dr. R. S. Mishra, and lived in his yoga ashram and a Zen center. In the early nineties, I came crawling back on my hands and knees, broken, having taught seven years at a university, and asked for re-entry, abashed for having left my early enculturation and deeply engrained patterns. Is there a spiritual materialism at work here?

Recently, I've been able to collage together the tolerance and beauty and warmth of yoga and all of the other lineages we ALL experience and include in our art. This is currently not a detriment to my (again) strict practice of Catholicism.

Saint Voice: "His mercy is so great that He has forbidden none to strive to come and drink of this fountain of life."

Question: WHAT IS YOUR ART NOW?

Natural Voice: I'm back in life school performing and learning from my father in a performance I call Blood Family Art or Dad Art. I'm my eighty-nine-year-old dad's primary caretaker and I do this as art. It took me two years to call it art—it was very life-like. Calling it art makes it interesting and sacred. Especially, as two senior citizens, father and daughter, get to cross between the two worlds of the surreal and the real on a daily basis. He's playing with death and teaches me about that. I'm playing with aging and have not taught anyone about that yet.

Saint Voice: "Cease as I have said to have fear where there is no fear."

Question: DOES IT BOTHER YOU THAT A UCSD PROFESSOR, V. RAMACHANDRAN, POSITS THAT SPIRITUAL ECSTASY/HIGHER CONSCIOUSNESS AND THE SAMADHI YOU TALKED ABOUT IS THE RESULT OF MISFIRINGS FROM THE BRAIN'S TEMPORAL LOBE WHEN IT GOES INTO SEIZURES? IS GOD A G-SPOT IN THE BRAIN?

Natural Voice: That kind of information makes me very nervous. But it adds to my faith and doesn't shake it because even now I am practicing blind obedience. Obedience is a must. Before I was obedient only to my art muse.

Saint Voice: "The soul is like an infant still at its mother's breast."

Question: WHAT IS THE WORK LIKE NOW, GIVEN SEPTEMBER 11?

Natural Voice: The trauma of September 11 has forced the entire universe into a monastic state of THETA brain wave oscillations. Trauma elicits THETA. We are all at 4–8 oscillations, like newborns, like adults sleeping, death on our left shoulder. Artists will not be muzzled or silenced forever but we are taking our time to co-feel the ecstasy of impermanence, with everyone leveled by tragedy. As mystics of matter, we will soon know when to sing again.

Question: HOW DO WE CREATE A NEW SONG?

Saint Voice: "Remember how Saint Augustine tells us about his seeking God in many places and eventually finding Him within himself?"

[All quotations of St. Theresa of Avila taken from The Interior Castle.—BGM]

EHN— John Cage said, "What we re-quire is silence; but what silence re-quires is that I go on talking." I'm interested in the skips we make to get from the still point of certainty to the business of plot; form-in-motion. Aesthetic consistency—that's also the peril of spirituality. It can be excessively aesthetic or excessively consistent. Ideally, spirituality stays out of the way of everything. The more spirituality gets in the way of your daily life, the more it is scrupulosity—high-toned fussiness. If it gets in the way of actual meaning, then it becomes idolatry and occlusion in your soul's eye. The reason why you need leaps and why you can't argue your way from meaning to how you have to live your life is that that final thing, that ultimate thing outside of time and space, by definition, can't be described. If you described it you would give it extension in time and space. So what we are is always unknown.

Romano Guardini, a theologian, says the more purposeful we are in life, the less meaning our life has, which is good for artists to remember. Schools and the marketplace are set up to make us endlessly busy, dedicated to purpose when, more perfectly, we are meant to be purposeless. So the more purposeful you are, the more alienated you are from meaning. Here is what I've chosen to do. I create imaginary worlds. Here's the risk in that: Meaning reverberates through the world and the world knocks against me and I create an imaginary world in response. The peril here is that I become a hater of the world. I become in love with imaginary worlds. These days, weeks, months, or seasons when it is especially easy to be a world-hater, a leap of faith urges me away from that direction. So, my option has been to see that art is not an escape from the world or an alternative to the world, it's a playmate or partner of the world because the world is imaginary, too.

So I create an imaginary world out of the imaginary world. They are co-equal. The world of theatre is as phenomenal as the world itself. The world in order to continue creating, to refresh its meaning, has to constantly break. That is where Zen or spirit or God is. It's in the breaks, the fractures. Meaning—the unknowable thing—is in the moment of breaking. The way the world and art play together is that they smash into each other and the smashing itself is a higher identity than either alone can attain. Art is here to smash the world open. If you are authentic with your art, you allow your art to be smashed up by the world as well. That refreshes the meaning of the art. So art and the world take care of each other. They're siblings. I love the way they hold each other. They are both foolish and non-essential, they come *after* meaning. They are allowed to play together and break each other's hearts. That is a sentimental way of describing it, but I'm sentimental. So there's spirituality, there's imagination, and, lastly, there's religion. My religious background is Catholic, which seems to be the default religion here. I think there is a place where Catholicism, especially that of Thomas Merton and the monastic tradition, overlaps with Zen, which is what I smash my Catholicism up against. It also smashes up against Dorothy Day, which is the practice of art in the practical world, and then there is John Coltrane who smashes everything up.

In terms of form, in my art I am drawn to mystic and ecstatic states—the Spanish mystics, in general, because they are so death-obsessed and peculiar. Theresa of Avila, John of the Cross, and Lorca I'd put in the same tradition as mystics. To achieve in art ecstatic and mystical states I rely on paradox, trance, bliss, and derangement; music, rhyme, circular or open-ended narrative, and any means of abusing time and space. I like narrative that celebrates its own purposelessness. Rather than achieving any kind of closure, it trails off and collapses back on itself. Thomas Merton says that ecstasy is not union, which is a sentimental conclusion. The moment of ecstasy is defined by perfect charity. You are entirely turned out. So rather than catharsis and resolution, there is *metanoia*. You are turned forth. Zen and Catholicism have a meeting place in the idea of *kenosis*, which is an emptying-out. So rather than being filled up with the experience of a play, I would like to see work that empties us out, allows for an inflowing and weakens our structure.

In terms of content, it is less about characters and moral choices than about the shadows between self and non-self. That place where an individual ceases to become an individual: the exploded self. Economically, I like work that stands outside of the marketplace. I like art that is either free or completely unaffordable. Or art that you run across in the street. Extraordinary and disastrous—that's how I like my art. The fascination of what is difficult, in Yeats's phrase. A charitable art: That's what I am interested in.

MARRANCA— Among many things that have been spoken about is the bringing together of Buddhism and Catholicism, which is not so strange. John Cage himself took from Meister Eckhart and Buddhism as well as Hinduism and Protestantism. I'm struck by certain themes that come together here, for example, the sense of art as charity, as a gift, the sense of an offering. I would like to ask whether artists create work thinking of such concepts as grace or charity or goodness. We've also been talking about the September 11 events. I wonder if it is an issue with artists to try to capture the same kinds of intimacy and goodness or charity which ordinary people exhibited then. What kinds of artworks do we want? Are ethical issues important to artists? Meredith, what did you have in mind when you and Ann Hamilton collaborated on the new work *Mercy*?

Monk— I am always interested in human nature. The idea of doing a piece about compassion or mercy or lack of mercy was something that when Ann and I started working on the piece was pretty much there at the beginning of the process. I had not worked with someone conceptually from the beginning in a collaboration for many, many years. I usually make all the elements my-self—the music, the visual aspect, any video or film work, gesture and move-ment. In her work Ann is in charge of all the perceptions. Both of us are very interested in how perceptions are woven together, perception actually being the door to another way of looking at the world, which can be called "spiritual." In a sense, this ethical thing that you are talking about had to do with letting our two sensibilities have total integrity and at the same time renunciate certain aspects of the work each of us would usually do.

When we talked about the idea of mercy, Ann was very interested in the mouth and the hand. We went right to the body. Help and harm. When I was in Columbus working with her, I happened to see on television the event in Israel in which a man and his son caught in a crossfire were pleading for their lives. They were shot anyway. The idea that they couldn't stop the battle for five minutes and let these people go home was something I started ponder-ing—mercy and lack of mercy. What would that state of mind actually be?

Working in a non-verbal, more poetic way, both of us then did a lot of read-ing. There was a central part of the piece that was almost like three haikus, based on actual people who had a sense of personal courage. One was a doctor in England who in the fifties and sixties had come from an Oxford education and gave it all up to live in a working-class mining town. He became the person in the town who listened: healing as listening. Another was a woman in World War II who along with her husband—they were Protestants in the south of France—saved about six-thousand Jewish children. The whole village of Le Chambon hid them in their homes. The third is someone alive now, the Java-nese writer Pramoedya Ananta Toer, imprisoned by the Dutch government, then by the Sukarno government. All his writings were confiscated. In prison, not being allowed pencil and paper, he memorized the novel he wanted to write and would tell each chapter every day to the other prisoners to keep up their courage, then after twelve years he wrote the book from those memories.

What we realized very early on in this non-verbal form—not being politi-cal critics but trying to work with a meditative form—was that we couldn't do a piece "about" mercy. We did it in July but have performed it since the Sep-tember 11 events. I was worried about it because it is an extremely somber piece. What we found is that it has really had a sense of power for audiences. In a way, it allows for these feelings, makes a kind of environment for feelings that have come up in the world that we're living in and shows in a very strong way the hunger and longing that we have all been feeling for a long time. Live performance—the figure-eight of energy between performer and spectator or participant—cannot be replaced by the computer or ninety-nine percent of movies and television, and is an experience of community that we are in danger of losing. This is a time of great power for art in the world that we live in.

KNOWLES— I was just thinking of Shakespeare, "the quality of mercy is not strained/but falleth as the gentle rain from heaven upon the earth beneath." Mercy is a quality; there's no strain. It just grows from these elements. It isn't forced in there.

EHN— That's striking to me, too. If there is a project we have of reclaiming religious language from the right, the task is not to replace one definition with a new one, but to restore language to the environment. To allow a word like "mercy" all its complexity and perversity and savageness and strength and strangeness, rather than replace an intolerable orthodoxy with our own intolerable orthodoxy.

MARRANCA— Why don't we open up our discussion to questions from the audience. Would anybody care to make any comments?

FIRST QUESTION— My name is Anda Rothenberg. I come from Warsaw where I was the director of the National Gallery of Contemporary Art for several years. I lost the position after having shown the Maurizio Cattelan work *The Ninth Hour*. I was told I did it purposely to harm the religious feelings of the Catholic majority in Poland. I would like to hear your comments about that.

HEARTNEY— Perhaps you should explain the piece.

ROTHENBERG— It is a hyper-realistic figure of the Pope lying on the floor, hit by a meteorite. It was shown in a huge room, on a red carpet, totally alone; it looked terrifying. I thought the public didn't know how to cope with it because the piece is very strong. Some people came and prayed. Others felt strongly but couldn't interpret their own feelings. They thought it was probably something against the Pope.

HEARTNEY— I've seen the piece. It has been quite controversial. There is the distinction I have been trying to make between religious feeling and the orthodoxy of religion. I read the piece as attacking the orthodoxy of religion.

There is the suggestion that the Pope is not speaking for the true Catholic faith. Then it gets into the realm of politics. I can imagine, especially in Poland, that this is extremely inflammatory. Andres Serrano did some early work which were assemblages of dead animals, a chicken Christ, and a dead cow which appears to be sacrificed, even before he did *Piss Christ*. He did some very pointed critiques of the Catholic Church ...

ROTHENBERG— It was censored in Poland and couldn't be shown.

HEARTNEY— ... and how it had lost its way from its original mission. An artist can have a very strong spiritual and religious sensibility and still be very critical of orthodox religion. The problem is that there is often this tendency to identify the one with the other and then to see this as a condemnation of all religion rather than to see it as a critique, coming from a place where the person is heartfelt in feeling that the Church has fallen so far from its original goals.

SECOND QUESTION— What are your feelings about the interplay between a personal spirituality and a collective spirituality, respecting what the effect of our work on other people's spiritual unfolding is going to have?

HEARTNEY— In the case of *Piss Christ* that was really used by the religious right and most people who initially raised all the furor about it never saw it. I have a lecture that I give in which I open with *Piss Christ* and when I show the image to people who have never seen it, they are amazed at how incredibly beautiful and reverential a work it is.

KNOWLES— Once you have an interior accounting as an artist, that is about all you can do. You put the work there and people may or may not be offended. You've done your best. Whether or not you are on the side of Satan or the divine healer, that is the balance of your accounting.

EHN— I think there is something moribund in a lot of contemporary religious thinking. We're speaking about Catholicism. There has traditionally been lots of room for deep problems. We seem to be afraid of problems now, in a very idiotic way. For example, in the fourteenth century Meister Eckhart says that to be with God first we need to get rid of God. He was very iconoclastic in his insistence that orthodoxy and image-making not be such a fixed thing. I am reminded of Ikkyu, the fifteenth-century Zen poet, who said, even if I saw Buddha he still wouldn't mean shit to me. And he was no less Zen or Buddhist for saying it. Serrano stands in the tradition of iconoclasm that is important to the interiority of the Church.

Third Question— [*For Monk*] What distinction do you make between soul and spirit? You mentioned a word like "thought" and, to me, that comes from the realm of what emanates from the soul. Spiritual is more like "goodness" or "truth," something that is out there, and will always be beyond ourselves.

Monk— So you are talking about spirit as being the environment and the soul responding to that. I don't make those distinctions for myself, particularly. When I was talking about mind it was really about the impermanence of thought: that thoughts are only one aspect and it's much more about getting to energies that are beneath those thoughts. I think of it that way rather than as soul and spirit.

Fourth Question— I want to try and play devil's advocate about this. For many years artists have considered themselves shamans and have implicitly taken on the role in the culture of priests and priestesses. Part of that is the deprivation and denial that many artists live with and even glorify, in fact, in a very Catholic way. I wonder if any of you can answer this. To me, that is an implicit part of our lives as artists. Will it change things if it becomes explicit? Will it change our self-image in how the culture relates to us if we explicitly see ourselves in a spiritual practice, without the denials cultures enforce? Is it possible to escape self-righteousness on either side?

Montano— I can only talk about right now. As a people we're stripped of cynicism, we're stripped of irony, we're stripped of bitterness. For a while, or maybe forever. It is a very incredible time. The monastic gathering of fragility and vulnerability is absolutely essential, even if we have to go to church and still call ourselves artists. We are in a very "I-don't-know" place.

Marranca— What actual spiritual practices might one do in preparation for creating? Are there specific practices to put one in a state to write or perform or think about work?

Monk— I think the daily work itself is the practice. As a performer I sometimes feel that it has this simultaneous pinpoint focus and at the same time complete openness to whatever comes in the moment. From the point of view of meditation practice, it is very much that combination of things. As a performer going on stage, my preparation is very physical—warming up my voice, warming up my body—even if I am just singing a concert. It is getting back to the very essential thing of the beginning and end of life, which is the breath. That is how I prepare myself to perform. As far as the daily work it's in some ways, as hard as it is, accepting what comes up—that letting go of intention.

Just accepting what comes up as being part of whatever this process is going to be. It is like a journey without a goal.

Going back to the question of shamanism, the process of making work is actually that idea of letting go of intention so much that whatever work is going to be made literally comes through you. It has to do with not knowing what the result is going to be. In the incredible time we are living in now, it has to do with affirming that process and not giving in to the consumerism and the product-oriented culture that we have been living with for a long time and going more and more in the direction of business and commodification of everything. This is a chance that we have now to actually go back to some of the values of process and inquiry, curiosity and discovery, which is, I think, what it's about.

This conversation was part of a series of five public panel discussions on the contemporary arts, entitled "Performance Ideas," that I co-curated with Meredith Monk in 2001-2002. The year-long series, held at Location One in SoHo and White Box in Chelsea, New York, included several artists working in performance, media, and visual arts. "Art as Spiritual Practice" was held at Location One on November 5, 2001. It was edited for publication in *PAJ: A Journal of Performance and Art*, Vol. XXIV, No. 3 (PAJ 72), September 2002.

.

Art and the Imagery of Extinction
A Conversation with Robert Jay Lifton

R obert Jay Lifton had written numerous books, among them *The Broken Connection*, *Death in Life*, and *Home from the War*, by the time this discussion took place in March 1982. Nuclear warheads were aimed at Europe and the threat of annihilation seemed very possible. Lifton was heavily involved in the anti-nuclear movement and active in Physicians for Social Responsibility and International Physicians for the Prevention of Nuclear War. The distinguished author and psychiatrist would later publish influential studies such as *The Protean Self* and *The Nazi Doctors*, remaining to this day one of the country's widely admired public intellectuals.

Can you outline a particular kind of character, in film or theatre, who offers a psychological profile of a person living under the threat of nuclear war and possible extinction?

I don't think the theatre can be expected to have caught up with a "character of extinction," if there is such a character. The terrible problem for art is that an artist is asked to create a narrative or a set of symbols around our own collective and total demise. We resist the narrative, understandably, and it's a tough one to enter artistically.

In my work I take three dimensions that you can roughly connect with postmodernism, or with our contemporary situation. The first is the breakdown of traditional symbols and of modern parallels or developments of those symbols; the second is the mass-media revolution; and the third is imagery of extinction or threat of extinction. This last is the most difficult for art to confront, and I don't know if it's really been represented yet. But maybe the way art has begun to confront it in the theatre and elsewhere has been through increasingly radical discontinuity.

Do you mean in terms of narrative?

Yes, in narrative that hardly exists or is circular or recurrent rather than continuous or linear; in terms of characters who feel cut off from a past or future.

If you're cut off from a future, your past is threatened also.

I don't know if I could suggest the particular kind of character because it's always difficult to figure which came first and what, in effect, people are reacting to. But I think there are some manifestations of new feelings and responses in the theatre. For example, take a piece like Satyagraha, *the opera that Philip Glass and Connie De Jong created, also the ACT company from Buffalo under Joseph Dunn, and some of Meredith Monk's work. I think these are examples of a new expressionism or a holistic approach to theatre. Some of the expressive work we're seeing now could be a different kind of spirituality.*

Well, I wrote a piece a few years ago called "Survivor as Creator" in which I took up three writers: Camus, Vonnegut, and Grass. Each saw himself as a survivor, and creatively, a survivor has to imagine that death encounter in order to create past it, to stay in it and use it, yet move beyond it. There the artist and the writer parallel and anticipate some of the thinking and politics necessary to stem the nuclear threat. You must imagine what the end of the world is, as Jonathan Schell tries to do in his book *The Fate of the Earth*, in order to prevent it.

For me, then, the problem is to get a handle on this, and the psychological handle is death and the continuity of life and the larger symbolization of human connectedness, or the "symbolization of immortality." So the theatre has the task of expressing, symbolizing, and representing how, in the face of or threat of extinction, one imagines human continuity. Perhaps that spiritual theatre or expressive theatre you mention is one way of imagining it.

Or turning away from it—

Something in terms of feeling is happening that's important—after the decades of numbing that followed World War II—the numbing is beginning to break down. That's got to affect the theatre, too. It's a breakdown of the kind of collective arrangement, collusion, and "not-feeling"—especially not feeling what happens at the other end of the weapon, and especially what might happen to us. People are afraid. When I talk to audiences now, kids at colleges are frightened, sometimes at secondary schools, and ordinary audiences. The polls show that most Americans fear and even expect a nuclear war in the not-too-distant future. That's new. There's a movement now towards awareness or a shift in consciousness that's quite hopeful.

One of the things you mention in The Life of the Self *is a human hunger for an evolutionary leap, that it will produce a new kind of art. Do you see a manifestation of this new art?*

Not really; now I question what I wrote. Yes, there's an appropriate moment where an evolutionary leap would be parallel to the technological leap, and perhaps that evolutionary leap would be parallel also to this incredible demand on artists and on all of us that we imagine the end of the world. People have been thinking of the end of the world for a long time. Every kind of millennial imagery and major religion represents the end of the world in some way, but there's a distinction between that millennnarial imagery where it fits into a system of belief and structure, and millenarial imagery which has to do with the nuclear holocaust. In Christian religion, God will punish all sinners and there'll be a judgment day after which everything will begin again. Not so now, when it's a matter of doing ourselves in with our own tools in an absolutely meaningless way.

For an artist, that kind of end-of the-world is a very demanding artistic requirement, so we can't expect artists to suddenly move into an evolutionary leap any more than anyone else can. Incidentally, Alvarez in his book on suicide claims that the recent increased incidence of suicide among artists—and he means writers and painters and artists broadly defined—has to do with reaching a point where it's impossible to find meaning or words that express life's continuity in the face of extinction. He draws upon my Hiroshima work to make this argument. Therefore, artists shout more loudly or more desperately but can't get through with the words or the images they need, and that's why they become desperate.

But isn't there another side of the issue—more and more people wanting to be artists? I don't mean necessarily that the average person wants to drop his or her career to become a painter or a writer. But you do find people—and I find them often outside of the city—taking up painting or creative writing, and it's become a major involvement. It's a much more philosophical impulse than, say, a leisure-time activity.

If meaning is harder and harder to come by, and the ordinary symbolic structures are crumbling, they're burdensome rather than liberating. One can feel the increasing appeal of art because art is constantly trying to resymbolize, express symbols; and probably art does thrive, or at least increase its energy, where there is a threat to the existing structure. For instance, there was the extraordinary resurgence of German literature, film, and theatre after World War II.

The problem is what artists do when becoming artists, and maybe it's only a certain extremely brave and talented vanguard that really moved towards this kind of abyss, or challenged it, and then faced the kinds of issues that Alvarez writes about, or that I write about, too. Or there's a sense in which there's absolutely nothing you or I or any artist encounters in everyday life or art that's totally caused by nuclear weapons or the threat of extinction, because we still have our work and our struggles with our love lives, our children and our parents and our marriages and friends. On the other hand, there is nothing in our lives that is not affected by the threat of extinction. I guess it's that double life we all live in in which the artist has to create. And I think that's quite possible.

In the seventies there were a lot of plays around the subjects of cancer and death, plays such as The Shadow Box, Whose Life Is It Anyway? *and* Wings. *Simultaneously, we've also seen disaster films and an exceptional amount of violence. Would you say that while these things are not about the nuclear power issue, they are manifestations of paranoia about destruction and death?*

Absolutely. As soon as you have the threat of imagery of extinction, death and life are out of kilter, and that's why I called my most recent book *The Broken Connection*: the connection between the two is radically threatened. That feeds back into what Vonnegut calls "plain old death." We're creatures of our own history and so we're influenced in what we think and study about. This is true in all of the arts, with a great focus on death in the sixties and seventies, and the nuclear threat creates or contributes to that preoccupation with death.

America has been notable in repressing death and maybe reaching the most radical form of denial of death that any culture has ever "achieved." So there's a kind of rebound reaction here along with the nuclear threat and some other influences, with a great sense in America that it's now discovered death. Twenty years ago nobody in America ever talked about death because as a young culture we're not supposed to die. It's Europeans and Asians who die. All of a sudden Americans are talking about nothing but death, it's the way Americans embrace things. But with that—again that's the seeming trivialization of the mass media—something happens, some kind of struggle with death and with pain that has been taking place in America is expressed. The plays you mentioned reflected that. They can go just so far, though, can't they?

Because they drift into sentimentality. And they create a vogue for certain kinds of death plays or cancer plays and young playwrights follow the lead—and then there are a rash of plays on these topics. I'm more interested in the shape of "character" and how that can change. For example, at the turn of the century, and in the twenties and thirties, there was a certain type of character, the hysterical woman. You see this in Artaud, in Witkiewicz, Strindberg, Musil, to name a few. Now that kind of Freudian character doesn't exist. Except for some remnants, say, in Tennessee Williams and others. I want to pin you down and see if you can create a model of the contemporary character.

The hysterical character you're talking about began to disappear twenty or thirty years ago. To have an hysterical character you need a whole life pattern, a full individual. Even if that woman or man has gone a little berserk, it's still a life that's relatively intact and has a beginning and a middle and an end, or a sequence. We don't have that now. Freud believed in reason and in cause and effect, and in a linear sequence to lives, and of course we still live around those principles. But here I think art does move ahead of everyday life, and has, in contemporary theatre and films.

There's a kind of transition between Freud and proteanism, shape-shifting, multiple selves without a linear process, that's more characteristic of a contemporary character. And in between somewhere as a transitional or connecting figure is the character of identity struggle. You find them in Miller and Williams, for example, some of the American playwrights who are transitional, Freudian in their influence, but they're also a little post-Freudian in no longer portraying straight neurosis. Strindberg is straight neurosis with hysteria or whatever, but with Williams and Miller it's a lot about identity and confusion and who one is. That isn't the question Freud asked. That's the question Erik Erikson asked. Freud asked, "What does one do with one's instinctual drives, and how does one tame them and become human or live a human life?" Erikson asks, "How does one maintain a sense of sameness over incredibly shifting environments and themes and influences?" That's the question Williams and Miller and a lot of other playwrights are asking. The protean or postmodern question is, perhaps, "How does one maintain a sense of life—continuity in the face of the threat of extinction, and in the face of the breakdown of all the symbols by which our lives are organized?"

Didn't absurdism dramatize those feelings in the post-war period, with playwrights like Beckett, Adamov, and Ionesco?

Beckett is very much asking the question of identity, but he does it beyond identity; he's very much in the realm of extinction. Beckett has his characters so constricted to accentuate by contrast the richness of life. I take from Beckett not a positive message, that would be putting it too strongly, but a great imaginative vision that is very much touched by extinction, but is a little bit beyond it. Beckett is the best example still of a theatre that does something with extinction. He's the only one I can think of who can really talk about having a profound sense of the imagery of extinction or death-in-life, yet preserving that notion of continuity. You mentioned Ionesco. He certainly explores and plays with some of these issues, he's a little more concrete. He talks and writes in his journals about the threat to life continuity, but he doesn't transmute them as powerfully as Beckett, and his plays are more limited or cerebral. Maybe that's why when we read and see Beckett, he does something for us that nobody else does, because he has really immersed himself in this ultimate image of extinction and come up from it.

In an interview PAJ published with Susan Sontag in 1977, she mentioned something Joe Chaikin had said about Beckett, which is that the problem for Beckett is what to do the next minute. It's a profound, concise statement. That's not the problem in Ibsen, if you know what I mean.

Ibsen assumed that a life would be led and that it would reach its conclusion, that there would be old age unless there was some kind of tragedy.

But we begin to see Beckett's vision in Chekhov, whose sentimental side is, unfortunately, what is stressed in most productions, and yet he dramatizes broken conversation, society falling apart, inertia.

With Chekhov, yes, society is falling apart and his relationship to time takes a new direction. Chekhov is not worried about what happens the next moment. He's worried about what you do now in your life when all the fundamental structures no longer pertain. Part of the power of Chekhov is that along with the symbols and values breaking down there's an odd timelessness created because there are no meaningful actions to interrupt the flow of time. Chekhov's characters try desperately to carry out meaningful actions, but they never quite succeed. I don't know of another playwright who gives us that odd suspension of time, or timelessness, because something that is supposed to happen never does and never can happen because people are not hooked into time in a meaningful way.

The question of time is interesting. During the sixties, a lot of the experimentation in theatre had to do with space. I felt it coming that at some point in the last five years or so there would be a switch to time and to narration. In fact, with the rise of autobiography and more interest in writing as a craft, the theatre is moving again towards narration and use of writers, back toward dealing with time. I think we've gone through our experimental theatre period when there was an attempt to control the environment or space.

If there is a return in the theatre to the writer and the experience of time, it might partly parallel the return in painting to the figure, but if it's to be at all powerful it's got to do that along with retaining considerable doubt and absurdity or, worse, some of the influence of extinction. One thing that is crucial to this, both pre-dating but reinforced by the threat of extinction, is the use of absurdity, and then more intense developments of absurdity in the form of extreme mockery.

As opposed to satire, or do you mean the grotesque?

The grotesque has always been with us, and that has to do with the threat of death and the threat of unacceptable death. Maybe the grotesque is especially a modern genre, but it's still not new. Irony requires a strong sense of self because it must reflect on itself in order to be ironic. Absurdity slips off that a little bit, and a lot of theatre and modern art, particularly contemporary art, has to do with a kind of absurdity which I think has to do with death. Mockery is absurdity with a lot of doubt about the self. When you mock something, you take a look at someone else's self or claim to a self and do something with it. You're not clear about your own self, you're not self-observing in the way that genuine irony is. If there's to be a return to more formal elements of the theatre, it has to have some of that edge of mockery, absurdity, doubt about the flow of time, along with a reinstatement of it.

There's been a resurgence in comedy, not only in the theatre world, but also in the artworld. There have been a lot of stand-up comedy performers, a renewed interest in the clown, and the New Museum recently had a show on humor in art. It's often more like television comedy, only a bit more arch. Nevertheless, it's comedy, and comedy is classically considered a form about self-survival or about limited achievement, as opposed to tragedy, which is about unlimited goals. When you think about popular, contemporary playwrights you think of someone like Christopher Durang who's mocking Catholicism and bourgeois family life. Or, in film, you think about someone like Woody Allen, whose work exemplifies the humor of disjointed, contemporary characters on the edge. Would you agree?

Yes. Woody Allen is a good example. He is constantly self-absorbed, he's worried about his body and what it does or doesn't look like and what it will or won't do, and his precious little sense of self in this world in which the self takes such a beating. But underneath that, what gives Allen power is the more primal fear of coming apart, disintegrating. And the way of evoking humor, quite wonderfully at times, humor and connection, because he does, I think, rather touchingly, portray love. *Annie Hall* is a good example in which the contemporary sense in all of us of falling apart is embodied by Allen, and he moves into and through it, and beyond into a self-mocking rendition of it. The self-mockery is central—obviously, it's Jewishness universalized—and then beyond into something like love. *Annie Hall* does say something about love; if not permanently or enduringly or perfectly, love is still possible in the face of this threat of disintegration.

Do you watch much television?

My television is limited to special programs, sports and news and occasional pornography. From what I've seen I guess there's a lot more death and extremity in comedy-situational dramas and soap operas. Soap operas are a lot more serious and have a lot of death, mourning, fear, neurosis, and trouble in them. They're struggling with a mass cultural rendition of what we've been talking about, and that's difficult.

In discussions about violence on television, I find myself a little reserved. Most television violence is very exploitative, horrible, and harmful psychologically. The trouble is that people need some kind of rendition of violence in order to register and reflect the threats as well as the inner violence they're feeling, in order to avoid recourse to actual violence.

In The Broken Connection *you quote Franz Fanon who talked about the "shared violence" that a culture goes through providing "therapeutic knowledge." What you're saying is that an audience, or American audiences who watch television, need to go through this violence to express what they cannot do in reality. Do you mean psychologically or physically?*

Well, psychologically, and creatively, perhaps, touching on the actuality of violence. It's a problem of art, though, because nobody would want to prohibit any rendition of violence in any art form. The problem is it's really bad art, so the violence becomes exploitative and I think violence is the issue around which good art and bad art make such a profound difference.

Did you see Route 1 & 9? *It's a brilliant piece, and the only one in years that really divided an audience. It's about nihilism and images of death and life, and social violence.... You've written on the Living Theatre—do you think their work is useful violence?*

I think it has been. I guess something like the Living Theatre finds a metier, works in it, then loses it. In those years it had something to say about violence—the late sixties—and it did connect violence in our lives with some kind of transmuting process of the theatre. The moralistic approach to the question of violence flattens it, and reduces it to a simple cultural good and evil, and misses the whole point.

A good example of the border of this in film is the *Dr. Strangelove* theme. It's very literal, it's about nuclear weapons, but consider the end of that film where the captain goes roaring down with the bomb, straddling it like a horse and yodeling in a great expression of triumph. It's a brilliant mockery of the whole nuclear madness; on the other hand, there is more than a suggestion of a kind of ultimate nuclear high—going down with the bomb. And that's attractive to some people.

Isn't this what you refer to as "nuclearism"?

Yes, and in the new book that Richard Falk and I are just finishing, *Indefensible Weapons*, I have a whole section on what I call "nuclear fundamentalism." I take this up again as an ultimate nuclear high, but nuclearism is the ultimate fundamentalism in regard to the weapon. There are a lot of people seeking high states through fundamentalist religious or political movements, and I think they have a fairly direct relationship to nuclear threat.

In Stanley Diamond's book, In Search of the Primitive, *he talks about the problem of violence in contemporary culture, that unlike in tribal times we don't have rituals to exorcise this lingering need for violence.*

Violence in my kind of theory—I develop this in *The Broken Connection*—all violence probably, and this is the irony of violence, is in the service of more life. "More life" is a phrase used by Ernest Becker. There's a search for vitality around the expression of violence. For instance, in the initiation rites, which can be quite violent, with scarification or other expressions of violence to the body, violence is in the service of a death and rebirth ritual, initiation. That channels tremendous energy around anger, rage, fear, and their transmutation into some sort of adult constructive work or pastime, like hunting, or whatever adults do in a particular society, and adult rules and rituals around which the society is built. The theatre doesn't have sufficient power in our culture to be an initiation rite, but I think people can experience through powerful theatre something parallel to that.

In the last fifteen years or so there's been a strong movement towards what Richard Schechner and Victor Turner, among others, refer to as "interculturalism"—it brings social anthropology into theatre, creating a kind of global theatre field in which all communication is seen as one kind of social drama or another. There's been a lot of talk in all this about shamanism, ritual, healing, and other rites. I think there's a significant need among many theatre people in the world to turn away from theatre in the conventional sense, while at the same time viewing all human activity as a theatrical paradigm.

That has parallels with what I would call an experiential mode. When it is strong it looks for pre-modern truths and pre-modern sources of psychological power. Also, this gets complicated because, take the figure of the shaman, and shamanism, it's a key figure both for pre-modern human power and power over death, which is what a shaman had as a precursor of the physician and as a kind of priest. The shaman is a figure of life power, power over death. He or she is a kind of ideal figure to go back to because shamans touch upon magic and that life/death axis. I find myself now confronting the negative side of shamanism—my work with Nazi doctors and the shamanistic legacy is what the Nazis called upon in a murderous way to enlist doctors in the killing process—and probably some of the interest of the theatre in anthropology and shamanistic ritual has to include its murderous capacity or the murderous or more negative use of magic, though the pre-modern shaman could never begin to approach the modern physician enlisted by Hitler.

I think that when the future is threatened one reaches backwards, and rightly so. I speak of the mode of restoration that can be a form of reaction or a reactionary mode. Reactionary—if you try to restore a past of perfect harmony that never was, something like the Moral Majority. On the other hand, you do need elements of restoration. You've got to look back and see what the shaman really was like, and then combine this with very contemporary motifs where you feel some fundamental threat to human continuity, so it makes sense.

Often what they're doing really goes way beyond art; it's more a way of life, really, and it seems almost religious. What Grotowski is doing is also beyond any expression of art. The reports of his rituals in the woods or his theatre of sources sound a lot like what I remember in the sixties—"T" groups and retreats and group encounters. What is problematic about some of these manifestations is the authoritarian male figure involved in all of this—the guru aspect.

That reminds me, there are certain elements of the late-sixties and early-seventies which had a tyrannical authoritarian component and expressed that totalistic component in the name of liberation. It usually had to do with a demand to liberate the body, and there would be certain rituals and arrangements of the group which were immediately and totally legislated by the leader. I have an aversion to that—how can I describe it?—an allergy to any kind of totalism. What we're also talking about is a severing of the experiments of the self from what we consider theatre, from the discipline of creative performance, from the discipline of creating an experience that can be shared by an audience and that has some relationship to a tradition.

Since you mention it, there is a trend to do performances without spectators. Allan Kaprow has done this kind of work in California, and this is what Grotowski is doing now, and sometimes Barba. It's an attractive idea to a lot of people. This boundary between the spectator and the performer is largely breaking down, and who knows where it's going to go. My feeling is that those people interested in linking cultural anthropology to theatre, while often meaning well, assume too many universalities for the audience and the artist. I question the feelings and the assumptions they have about the theatrical experience. There is something too ordered in the anthropological view of the community, and contemporary society is not like that.

One can have a kind of retrospective wisdom. It's hard to make a judgment of how much that tradition is being struggled against and how much it's been abandoned, and it is a kind of critic's own personal judgment about it. I would sense that the anthropological theatre has lots of possibilities, but it just depends on what one is doing and it has a kind of responsibility to the tradition of the theatre even, and especially, as it breaks off from it. You can make your most extraordinary innovation by being grounded to some degree in your tradition.

Can you apply the notion of being "grounded in tradition" to the ability of today's artists to successfully use the imagery of death that's all around us, to turn it into life-generating imagery?

Yes. I think that people need discipline—you can't impose classical authority on them anymore because even mentorship and discipleship, or learning and teaching, have different dimensions now. But one needs rigorous teaching and learning, still. You can't be grounded in the theatre or in any other art form without a period of real study. It requires a disciplined exposure towards what is known and what has been learned over decades and centuries in the theatre. Then, when you have that—as a sensitive writer, director, or performer in the theatre—you can connect that grounding and relate it to life/death issues that are imposed upon us. Grounding can give one the strength and courage and innovative potential to immerse oneself in a terrifying imagery of extinction and death-haunted issues that we have to face.

What kind of theatre then do you envision that faces these issues?

A theatre with elements of a struggle back toward and forward from ritual. A theatre that struggles with nothingness and beyond and that has to be post-Beckett. It's hard to be influenced by Beckett without being drowned by him. A theatre that is concerned with death but not narrowly and not necessarily concretely, but with what death symbolizes, and with different forms and dimensions of death and its grotesquerie but that transcends it. A theatre that can imagine the end of the world and create beyond that.

A theatre then that can imagine the end of the world but that also believes in tomorrow.

Exactly. Therefore it's a theatre of faith. It can be a religious faith or a kind of secular faith—it has to be for many of us—but you require faith, and faith is something that always goes beyond evidence but not totally without evidence in the idea of a human future. But in order for the faith to be powerful, it has to really immerse itself into precisely what threatens the human future. It's got to do that in its own way and that way is hard to come by.

Do you think that because theatre is built on the notion of representation it has a special power to help an audience go through a catharsis—to go through that way in the experience of the performers?

For instance, Joanne Akalaitis's *Dead End Kids* is a relatively more concrete work about the nuclear and radiation issue. It's the most successful play on that issue because it uses a lot of contemporary imagination, very protean in spirit, it's death-haunted but mocking while joyous and humorous, with a lot of gallows humor, which to me is a great plus. Humor is liberating, deepening, pedagogic in the best sense—a theatre without humor at all is worthless. The more threatening and serious things get the more humor that's needed. There are different kinds of humor, and of course it's the quality of the humor that's important. If you only stay in the death immersion without the humor you're in some degree perhaps getting pornographic.

Joe Chaikin always seems able to combine death and humor in his work. But he is out of fashion now with audiences who are more used to highly imagistic or technological work. The thing he provides that no one else involved in group work does is the evocation of real emotion, and he's always been able to do that. That's the problem some people have with Chaikin. They're not used to seeing genuine sentiment anymore.

Yes, he seemed to be in his earlier work, and probably is now, too, on the edge. The issue of emotion becomes very important. Another way of putting it is, emotion is a form and you need formed feeling in the theatre. Experiments in the late-sixties, seventies, and some today, too, have difficulty giving form to feeling and therefore giving it depth, and feeling becomes all too forgettable, or transient. Perhaps a man like Beckett is committed because his way as an artist one can take as a commitment to the world. That means stepping over a line in which one relates one's life to dealing with the world in some important way, as opposed to simply stepping back from it. And that may be an issue for the theatre from now into the future, I don't know.

I think it's a kind of Sartre-like drama, a special kind of theatre of commitment, of ethics.

But now the Sartre-like question has to be altered. Yes, it's a similar question but it's already a different time, because it's infused with extinction which gives it a kind of mixture of terror and amorphousness, and a greater imaginative requirement. It gives it a more wild and extreme dimension. The theatre can't shy away from that, either, but it's that grounding that may give it the freedom to be wild or extreme.

But, dealing specifically with death imagery; it's beyond humor, it's beyond the comic wildness, say, of an Innaurato or a Durang, but actually dealing with death and felt emotions, getting back really to a classical drama.

It may be possible that one can embody the nature of nuclear threat in other metaphors. The limitless symbolizing capacities of the human mind are the same source of either dooming us or saving us. It's that same gray matter that constantly recreates and symbolizes, and it's very hard to imagine how to subsume human extinction to some kind of artistic or theatrical metaphor. The art generally suffers, and the theatre suffers in the effort, as you know. It needn't literally be a death-haunted play about nuclear weapons or about actual death and destructiveness.

There has been a school of theatre, an extreme kind of realism primarily by French and German writers, the "theatre of everyday life." Perhaps even in some cases with those kinds of plays the attention to detail is more of an involvement in the life process.

Yes, it could be, and it's the power of realism of a certain kind. And any worthwhile so-called realism or focus on everyday life has to be touched by madness and the imagery of our time.

It will be interesting to see if we go back into a period more like absurdism or like the period between the wars when there was the greatest experimentation, and perhaps some of the strongest questioning of representation in the theatre. But the most recent movements have been realism, back to naturalism—a kind of flat, stylized naturalism without the heavy psychology. Kroetz, Botho Strauss, David Storey, some of the early Edward Bond is like this. It hasn't been a movement that's influential here because Americans are more into the psychological factor of character, and less formalistic and artificial dramatic techniques of stylization. Part of that has to do with the lack of class consciousness, I think.

If the realism is too bound to a kind of old-fashioned version of realism then the theatre is holding on tightly against the threatening images. But art can't follow rules, it has to be anti-historical, and in my terms some of this realism would be moving back into a restorationist mode almost with a vengeance, almost with a caricature, and it may have to abandon that. Something will be learned in the process.

188 □ PERFORMANCE HISTORIES

At a time, now, when people are moving more and more towards art because that kind of experience fills some kind of void in their lives, I think the culture is moving towards seeing itself as spectacle, in terms of seeing its citizens as performers. The media has caused this to a certain extent, but I think it's also a human development. Maybe now we can begin to discover again what it means to go into the theatre and go through certain experiences as a culture, which is what live actors should do to live audiences.

I think so, too. An awful lot of people are now "imagining the real," in Buber's phrase. The "real" is the threat of nuclear holocaust in the most extreme way. It's a terribly demanding and difficult thing to imagine. But with more and more people forced into making that imaginative effort and never fully organized in an orderly way, that means more and more people are open to art in the best sense, art that has the courage to do something like that.

The fact that this numbing could break down is what I take to be a significant beginning shift in consciousness. It's what I call a movement from a fragmentary awareness to a struggle for formed awareness. The struggle has two sides: one, cognizance of actual danger, being wary, and the other, awareness in the way that theatre and artists and visionaries have always understood it, the sense of special insight or vision. There's a struggle for awareness on both of these levels that's more widespread in the culture now, and that I think enhances the possibility of a theatre that can say something. Because the theatre becomes part of this awareness, this dreadful but possible moment in our culture, it can also have an audience to join in that process.

The conversation with Robert Jay Lifton was first published in *Performing Arts Journal*, Vol. VI, No. 3 (PAJ 18, 1982), accompanying my essay, "Nuclear Theatre," in the same issue. It was taped at the author's home in New York City in March 1982. Lifton also included it in his collection of essays entitled *The Future of Immortality and Other Essays for a Nuclear Age* (New York: Basic Books, 1987). It was later published in *Conversations on Art and Performance*, Bonnie Marranca and Gautam Dasgupta, eds. (Baltimore: Johns Hopkins University Press, 1999).

Mediaturgy
A Conversation with Marianne Weems

M arianne Weems is artistic director of The Builders Association, a cross-media performance company, which she founded in 1994. She has directed all of their productions, including *Faust, Jet Lag* (with the architects Diller and Scofidio), *Extravaganza, Alladeen* (with the British company **moti**roti), and *Super Vision* (with dbox). In addition to her work with the company, which tours worldwide, Weems also collaborated recently on a new theatre/music event with David Byrne and Fatboy Slim, and completed a multimedia performance workshop with Disney Imagineering. She was a dramaturg of The Wooster Group during the years 1988-94 and worked as a dramaturg with Susan Sontag. Weems is the co-author of *Art Matters: How The Culture Wars Changed America*. This conversation took place in December 2006.

It has been twelve years since you founded The Builders Association. In the early productions, like Master Builder *and* Faust *and* Jet Lag, *more of the architectural elements were apparent. In recent years, you moved on to work that has to do with digital performance and global perspectives.* Alladeen *focuses on call centers in Bangalore, India, and* Super Vision *takes on dataveillance and data bodies. But it also includes a family in domestic space, where a father is stealing the identity of his son. In using the tools of media, does your work embody more of a critical attitude toward them than may be apparent to audiences?*

It is both a celebration and a critique of our culture's use of technology. We can't avoid using the tools of technology to create this stage picture, but we're using technology to talk about its impact on the world. The critique is in the content—our stories often have a certain implicit melancholy or, some would say, pessimistic view of where our connections to this network are leading us. I don't think that I'm in a position to answer that, but we are in a position to hold up a mirror and reflect where we are right now.

So, for instance, *Alladeen* addresses how the technology of fiber-optic phone lines gives the illusion of bringing people closer together when, in the case of corporate outsourcing, it's driving them further apart. We staged this piece about the call centers of Bangalore before they really became public knowledge. We went to India to observe the training process of how the Indian operators learn essentially to "pass" as Americans, and to watch the operators in action, and to shoot video of phone calls from American customers being handled in the call centers by Indian operators often deploying their American personas.

This confusion of identities, distance, and proximity is teased out in the production through the phone conversations staged between the Indian operators and the American customers. Also, in the interview excerpts, you hear Indian operators talk about their "cultural schizophrenia" that's brought on by working in call centers. One sees the alienation produced on both ends of the phone line, and the audience is left to draw their own multiple conclusions. To me, the critique is difficult to miss, but the productions are both an entertainment and an interrogation. Because if they're purely critical, they are not going to play in theatres.

It's interesting how your politics is elaborated elsewhere, for example, in your piece Avanti, *which centered on displaced car industry workers when the Studebaker plant closed in Indiana. Perhaps you could speak about the* Invisible Cities *project. Clearly, you have a view of the world, of globalization, of economics, and maybe we can explore that. Themes of social consciousness run through the work, and they become more or less difficult or easy to decipher depending on the tools. Also, perhaps audiences don't have as much sophistication in the critique of imagery as in listening to stories and texts. What I'd like to address is the sense of the social that runs through your work, and how that's manifested in* Invisible Cities, *beyond what you've referred to in terms of globalization and corporate culture in* Alladeen.

Invisible Cities is a small arts and education project we just finished developing with "at-risk" high-school kids in Brooklyn, mostly coming from the surrounding housing projects. This project was motivated by looking at the digital divide and attempting to put some of the tools that we use in the hands of kids who don't necessarily have access to those tools. We were meeting with them in a computer lab at Brooklyn College where they had access to computers, and where many of them were already busy building video games. This project focused on the psychosocial space of the city, and the idea that parts of the city are visible to some of its inhabitants, but not visible to other people who are just passing through, and vice versa. For instance, what does New York mean to a first-world traveler staying in a luxury hotel as opposed to a kid moving daily through the city on the subway?

Our next project, *Continuous City*, begins with this on a much more global scale. We're looking at megacities and megaslums, urban networks, and social networking in general. It's a modest undertaking.

Are there other scientists or engineers involved in it?

We're working with the National Center for Supercomputing Applications through the Krannert Center in Urbana, Illinois.

A few years ago you were working with Columbia University's computer music division. It seems that each Builders Association production requires a whole new set of relationships and partnerships. That in itself must be exciting. Do you have a vision you're moving toward, or is it a question of whoever can fulfill such a project with their tools is where you go? How does an artist work like this? In a way you're work is so much about place, and yet you don't have a place. You deal with sites, but you don't have a site. Do you know what I'm saying?

I do! I think that's key, Bonnie. What you just said is an enormous part of why we make the kind of work we make, and why I have the kinds of ideas I have, and also where we are in this generation of artists. We have never had a theatre in New York. That has been a blessing, because we've been able to be light on our feet and be on the road a lot. But also I think it is ultimately detrimental in terms of having any kind of stability or keeping the company stable. A sense of location provides all of that, so operating outside of that is often daunting.

Speaking metaphorically, I think this has to do with the dramaturgy behind the projects. The issues of place and placelessness, the collapsing of geography, and confusions of location and identity are all woven into the work, and have all been observed in our touring lives on the road. The way the pieces come together is I come up with a central idea, often drawn from a contemporary issue or topic, and I bring it to my core collaborators to kick around. Then additional new collaborators are found depending on what the idea requires. So, for instance, right now I'm interested in this idea of global networking, so I'm looking around for ways to forge a connection with the engineers and technicians who are working on this topic.

When we started *Alladeen* we had just done a kind of "studio visit" to an engineer at IBM. He had created a software called Dynovision that they were developing for security purposes (using motion-sensitivity to spot intruders, or any unusual movements). But he understood right away when we asked to fool around with it in the show. The way we worked with it is, the actors would move their faces very subtly, looking into a camera, and other images would ghost in and out, appearing almost subliminally over their features. So, for instance, we used the images from the television show *Friends*, which is one of the shows that the Indian operators study, to play over the faces of our performers. The software became a tool for expressing the idea of cultural masking.

Is there any possibility of working in the future with IBM—any funding there? By the way, in his piece Come home Charley Patton *Ralph Lemon worked with a special IBM program, Face-to-Face, that could draw a person's face during the performance—it was James Baldwin's.*

It's somewhat idealistic to imagine that corporations are really interested in experimental theatre. Even though we have toured a lot and we have sold-out houses all over the world, to them, it is a tiny percentage of the audience numbers they're looking for, through television, for instance. Also there's the nagging issue of the actual critique which exists in this work. We were very close to receiving some corporate support for *Alladeen*, but they wanted us to eliminate one section of our Website which was titled "Corporate Colonialism"—it addressed outsourcing in the developing world. So that conversation quickly came to a close.

If we consider the development of the performer and the technological tools that call into question the notion of "presence" in theatre, is there a new concept of character, of dramaturgy, in such work? Have you thought about what kinds of people might populate the plays, what kind of characters you want to create? If you're dealing with storytelling you are dealing with character. Domestic spaces, airport spaces—these are conventional sites—the family, the home, the public world. Social interaction as a theme remains. What is the new dramaturgy for this theatre? How do you look at objects in your work? What about light? How do people move in these worlds? I wonder if you have had to rethink a lot of these things, or simply rely on the performers.

Good questions. The work is developed very, very minutely in the rehearsal process—in fact, there are so many layers that they are almost undetectable to the human eye because every moment in the performance is tightly designed and scored. For instance, in rehearsal the performers have to spend a lot of time standing in one place on stage so that we can get the light and the video in exactly the right balance with them, physically. They know that every single second of the show is built around where they are on the stage, and they work very closely with the technical artists to align with video projected behind or in front of them, or with a camera picking up their image. Their sense of extending into the network that then extends out to the audience is very visceral, and very closely created in alignment, in every moment of the show. They know they need to work in concert with the media—it's there to extend their reach but it's a force to be grappled with. The performer Dominique Dibbell, who was in *Jet Lag*, once said, "Technology is the diva in this show."

For instance, with the Traveler, in *Super Vision*, our idea was that in each one of the scenes a different field from his body of information (his "data body") is revealed. First he's questioned about his national identity and information comes up on the screens all around him that reflects his dual national identity, Indian and Ugandan. The second time you see him it's about his financial identity, so all of the images show his credit lines, bank accounts and transactions, etc. The audience is allowed to compare information about him on the screens with things he is actually saying, and it creates a much more complex and full picture of who the Traveler is. The point was that we have many different data bodies that float around us and that the more electronic information is available, the less you need to be there physically. Through the course of the show the Traveler becomes physically redundant. And, in the end, he disappears. There's a complicated moment where the light on him fades very slowly as the video becomes more and more dense around him. So—as much as one can accomplish in live theatre—he is meant to disappear into the data. There are several levels of story construction and character construction that are told through the line of video as well as what the actor is doing on stage.

Even though one is used to all these tools around us and we're told we live in a visual culture, still, people are very literary when they go to the theatre. Most audiences are interested in the plot of a play, basically. So it does require a different kind of spectator to be able to understand and analyze imagery. That's why one needs certain new critical tools as a spectator and as a critic.

Yes, but at the same time, everyone can relate to this frictive relationship to technology—we struggle with it and depend on it daily. We definitely are refocusing the stage picture by bringing the media into the foreground. But don't you find that that's an old problem? When people write about Richard

Foreman's work, and try to describe the storyline, it's absolutely beside the point. The point is that you have the pleasure of visiting Richard's mind for an hour-and-a-half. His stories often have the same elements more or less, but it's the idiom in which he tells it, and the kind of mind-bath that you get from being in this completely multivalent experience that is the pleasure of entering into his work. I sort of feel the same way—though I'm not comparing our work to Richard's—in that there is a complete world created that you're entering into. All of it is carefully choreographed to convey to the viewer the visceral, palpable, sometimes overwhelming sense of being enmeshed in, surrounded by, almost functioning through technology.

Audiences today are not exposed as much as they were in recent decades to works of the imagination, like Foreman's, which create a total world. While people may be very sophisticated in terms of computers and iPods and all of that, their viewing habits are still conditioned by psychological realism. People get hung up on stories and make everything complicated by trying to get the exact plot line. And of course nobody can ever tell the story of a play. I see this also with students. They're using all these technological things, they're on MySpace, they're using iPods, and yet, they're very plot-oriented. I find this dichotomy extremely interesting. People are still conditioned by linear narrative—we're in the twenty-first century and theatre audiences are operating as if it's the nineteenth.

I completely agree. It's exhausting. It's beside the point. While we tell stories that have to do with these struggles—*Jet Lag*, for instance, was about a woman who flew back and forth across the Atlantic 167 times consecutively until she died of jet lag—I hope the *telling* of the story gives the audience the visceral experience of jet lag. There's a mesmerizing soundtrack, an endless panorama of video showing the antiseptic space of the airport, and the impossibility of actually living there. The "story" is take-off and landing, take-off and landing, until she is worn away. So there's a kind of ambient story—the skeleton is there—but it's the experience created by the performers and the media that has impact, and that is recognizably contemporary.

I'm glad you mentioned MySpace because to me that's a great example of how this generation could look at a theatrical experience like this. Social networking embodies the myth and desire of being constantly connected, and it is complicating the ideas of exterior and interior, public and private, in the virtual and the physical worlds. A student at California College of the Arts printed out the MySpace pages of everyone at the school and hung them in the lobby for all to see. There was an enormous and immediate reaction; people were so upset. The printed page in a public space carried an enormous distinction from its direct equivalent in the electronic world.

That's really fascinating!

Yes. And to me that's what the Builders' shows are more and more about. How do we experience this gray area between "real" reality and mediated reality? Can we really hold onto these distinctions? Theatre is actually a great place to experiment with that—we have the live bodies, and we can create the mediatized world around them—how do they bleed into each other?

I want to go back to an issue that I've hounded you with for a year or two. Something I remember you saying in an interview—from Glasgow, I think—that referred to another artist who creates more personal video performances. You said that you didn't like the work very much because you were tired of artists' ideas about things. I've always been intrigued by that, and wonder what you mean. Are you saying that works of the imagination are less interesting than work as documentation? That you are more interested in real-time than an artist's representation of an event?

I'm not so sure it's that. However, given the cultural moment that we're in, I appreciate work that has a social consciousness, and a critique that has some kind of social engagement or relevance. I'm not saying that it needs to be a concrete political message. But there needs to be some kind of information in it that has to do with what the rest of the world is dealing with. The fantasy of artists who are completely removed from everyday concerns, and who just want to make things up, is not really relevant. I'm not that interested. Are you?

I would have to say that it depends on the artist. It depends on the quality of mind. I am interested in some artists' private worlds. I wish we had more works of the imagination and less of replicating social crises in simplistic works. By the same token I don't always believe that the personal is political. I think there are different realms—the aesthetic realm, civic realm, political realm. Sometimes they spill over. I don't think we can assume that everything an artist does is political, or need be. Probably I'm defining things in more of a Hannah Arendt distinction. Maybe that's my classicism. I think it's too easy to say that the personal is political.

I do, too. I cut my teeth on literary criticism and late-feminist critique. I went to the Whitney Independent Study program and I studied with Mary

Kelley, Martha Rosler, Yvonne Rainer, and many others who birthed a generation of conceptual artists creating stridently critical work. Yet I don't think that one approach inherently validates the other. There still needs to be some artistry involved.

It's funny you mention the term "conceptual art." I was speaking with someone the other day who teaches at UC-Irvine, where, incidentally, Yvonne Rainer recently has accepted a professorship. She was talking about the difficulty students have with conceptual art. One of the things that is problematic for younger generations is the question of accessibility. Art that's difficult immediately is put in the category of "inaccessible," or it is accused of being uninterested in communicating to an audience. Sometimes works are beautiful and mysterious and are inaccessible to us from the start. Sometimes they become more accessible as we know them or know the artist more. Some works gain meaningfulness after years or decades. What do we do with the "difficult" or the "inaccessible" now? We don't have that many artworks created any longer that are really so challenging and exceptional, and that require so much work to understand. I'd be afraid to lose that kind of work in the world. It really comes down to the issue, how do works speak to us?

There are many forces brought to bear on this—the stranglehold of consumer culture, lack of time, lack of art history, lack of any history besides autobiography, lack of continuity, etc. The problem is also what remains in the "experimental theatre" world. The work of younger U.S. experimental theatre artists seems to be, for the most part, very self-referential and self-indulgent. I think this is partly because there is a sense that nobody's watching, nobody cares, and there's no support anyway. There's no critical writing, or rigorous discourse around the work. So they're rehearsing the experiments of the previous generation in a kind of vacuum. But I think Romeo Castellucci is somebody who manages to do what you're talking about. He has a private world that is displayed very elegantly but also has deep political currents that run through his pieces.

That's also because Italian artists have a rich philosophic, poetic tradition. For example, the recent London section of his eleven-part Tragedia Endogonidia *project, which many of us saw last year in the Montclair State University performance series, included the writings of St. Paul. I've seen his* Julio Cesare, *which is quite extraordinary in terms of its vision of a post-apocalyptic world, and its ideas about rhetoric and Roman culture. Castellucci's theatre brings a whole world of civilization to a work, a philosophical worldview. What I'm afraid is happening here is that so much new work seems like television or mass entertainment. Audiences don't want difficult works. Of course, the artworld is very different from the theatre world.*

There's an ongoing critical discourse in the visual arts world, which is now informing performance again. The artworld's economic standing gives their focus on performance it's own credence. They're not dependent on Broadway or mass media to validate their practice.

How would you define that? There seems also to be a return to performance in the visual arts world and a move away from video, to some extent.

As we've discussed, in the artworld, there's more of an acceptance of conceptual work, there's even cachet in it. In the artworld, there is validity in work that is more academic or intellectual, which in theatre is unacceptable. Don't you think that's part of it?

I think the art audience is certainly more sophisticated. There's ongoing regeneration through exhibitions, through catalogues, through the development of art history as a field, but mostly through criticism and critique, which is really missing in theatre. Though nowadays one of the big topics in the artworld is the irrelevance of the art critic in the current art market.

To state the obvious, the artworld is driven by the economy. It's not even late capitalism now, it's "killer capitalism." And this makes the artworld relevant to the rest of the world. There's only going to be wide interest if there's money to be made. In theatre—where's the money? Unless you're working commercially, which seems to be a completely different field.

But you have been able to do large, complicated works with overseas partnerships and, on the technical side, with scientists and engineers. Everybody is working together with cutting-edge concepts and ideas. The organizing principle is the collaboration.

Very true, and despite everything I've just said, I'm not complaining. Because our productions are often generated around an idea with real relevance, they do reach out to a large audience and an unexpected set of participants. There's a kind of dramaturgy about technology that takes place.

I think of it as mediaturgy. One analogy I can make is a reference to Cocteau who talked about poetry of the theatre and poetry in the theatre. So there's media of the performance vs. media in the performance.

That's great! To me it is relevant in both ways—we start with a contemporary trope or dilemma and then we tease it out with the contemporary tools. Practically speaking, the technology and the technicians are present in the rehearsal space from the very first day of our rehearsals, as well as the performers, and I firmly believe this is how the pieces end up the way they do. It's not as if the technology is brought in during "tech week." It's not even simply a design idea. It's an integral part of the storytelling.

The dramaturgy aspect is what I'm interested in. What you describe is a concept of dramaturgy that moves beyond the play into an entire construct of research, collaboration, technicians and actors. We could say now it's really moving toward a new conception of collaboration that was begun in the sixties in such events as 9 Evenings: Theatre and Engineering and EAT, which John Cage, Robert Rauschenberg, Yvonne Rainer, Deborah Hay, and James Tenney, among others, helped to create with scientists. But the technology wasn't available to do the experiments easily. These are very seminal, historical moments when artists and technicians tried to work together. But everything didn't always work out and there's a lot of controversy about whether they were successes or failures. It seems to me that you want to be in the theatre, that you came out of the theatre and you're staying, so far, in theatre. In your explorations of new forms of dramaturgy—or what I am calling mediaturgy—the technicians are not just technicians, they are artistic personnel.

Interesting. I used to worship Cage's writing. And because my background is in music and composition, I've always been interested in how lines of information are woven together. I played viola, and always found string quartets the most satisfying—there's no conductor and the ensemble depends on each other to draw the music out of its center. In these shows, the spectacle is dependent on this ensemble acting in concert, there's no stage manager telling the tech guys what button to push and when. The music comes out of the center.

If we try to think of a new conception of dramaturgy, one of the first things to consider is writing. You never talk about text, you talk about stories, which is even more "old fashioned" to talk about.

I'm just an old-fashioned girl at heart.

You're just an old-fashioned girl at heart, right! I'm interested in the vocabulary you use. You talk about storytelling. So we're not just talking about text as material. How do you reconcile the most advanced kind of technologies that people are using in theatre with more traditional forms, for example, in the concept of character and story?

It's extremely complicated to work with writers, there's an enormous discrepancy in expectations of what their role will be, and in particular, what playwrights have been trained to expect. That's why my most successful experiences have been with non-theatre writers, like Martha Baer who worked on *Alladeen* or Jessica Chalmers who worked on *Jet Lag*. Once you have our tools on the stage, there are other things you don't need—there's an old film saying—"Show it, don't say it." I think playwrights feel the burden of conveying everything, whereas sometimes it's much more concisely told in a video image or a sound cue. There's a lot of scaling roles and evaluating expectations whenever we start working with a writer.

What do you consider are the demands of storytelling in your work? How much of it do you want? What if I said I think there's too much in Super Vision of the Traveler who keeps coming and going in airports, as more and more data about his life is revealed in his speech and in projections? Sometimes I thought there was too much narrative, more than we needed to get the story.

The story is like a container or skeleton that the ideas are hung on. For me it's a way of providing a road map for the audience to move through a set of constructions. It's a complicated stage picture, and there are many different levels to what's going on, so the story is often pretty broad. For instance, in the case of the Traveler in *Super Vision*, each picture becomes increasingly dense as his data cloud increases, sometimes with contradictory or elusive information, and the audience has to work to catch it all. I think of structuring storylines like a network, which connects many "nodes" or layers in the piece. Calvino refers to this kind of structure as "accumulative, modular, and combinatory."

It's not surprising that storytelling would gravitate toward fictional strategies. But with regard to imagery, one of the most interesting aspects of the story was the Father, who was live and visible on stage and a real person, accompanied at times by a huge projected image of a part of his face. I consider that perhaps a technique that media could use in terms of offering a different sense of portraiture in the theatre. Do you see yourself wanting to do something different with the actors? Does what I said about having the digital image do that have any meaning for you in terms of portraiture or fragmentation or dramatic character?

Do you mean because the camera was primarily focused on his eyes?

Yes—while you saw his actual whole body on stage.

It amplifies a certain kind of performance. David Pence (the performer play-ing the Father) was able to do very subtle things and communicate a heightened amount of anxiety or tension or paranoia because he is delivering a very cin-ematic performance with the assistance of the video. At the same time, on stage, he's certainly using a more theatrical kind of acting. And his acting partner Kyle DeCamp wasn't on video at all, so there's a subtle spectrum of acting styles flowing between the two of them. Also, quite honestly, the reason we ended up focusing on his eyes was because the sound was out of sync with his mouth.

Great!! That always interests me—the exigencies of theatre. A few weeks ago at Meredith Monk's opening at BAM of Impermanence *I saw Ann Hamilton, who had collaborated with her on* Mercy. *I couldn't remember exactly how the video monitor worked when the image of Meredith's throat was projected in real-time in the opening section. I asked Hamilton about it and she said her uncle was a dentist and he created a special palate in which the video camera was embedded in Mere-dith's mouth. I thought it was a marvelous story. Yours is the same kind of thing.*

Exactly!

I think most people don't realize how so much artistic process is involved with technical problem-solving.

I'd say it's at least half of what we do.

It's more and more intriguing to me how little is known about how things work. Sometimes elaborate concepts are created, or schematic and theoretical issues are overlaid on productions, where it's typically just technical problem-solving.

Very true. It's related to an ongoing issue with *Super Vision*. People think it's very slick—that's the response we get a lot—almost a kind of suspicion from the audiences in non-profit theatre spaces, especially in the U.S. One question I get is, "How much did this cost?" And the other one is an overall, "How did you do that?" They don't see the trial and error, the sweat of my heroic collaborators, and absolute jerry-rigging and duct tape that goes into making the production look as good as it looks. Also, usually, "slickness" delivers a commercial spectacle without any challenging content. I think it's doubly disorienting when there's a critical commentary embedded in this very high-end delivery.

What were the technical issues in that piece, or some of the other things that you find yourself solving from production to production? Maybe you could talk about the work with dbox in creating it.

The members of dbox are intelligent, big thinkers, and their trade is fabricating photorealistic images, mostly for architecture. So it was a great match for *Super Vision*. We were both interested in making the invisible visible, and envisioning an "electronic *doppelgänger*" or data body that could shadow the performers. One of the things that was revolutionary about being able to work with dbox at the scale of *Super Vision* was that although they had created some of the backgrounds for *Jet Lag* and *Alladeen*, to bring them in as primary collaborators meant that there was going to be an enormous resource of designers and of computer processing power that we hadn't had access to before, to create the sophisticated 3-D images that we used. But they had never worked in the kind of improvisatory way that we work with technology. Our first *Super Vision* workshop at the Wexner Center in Columbus included dbox, me, our other designers, some actors, a pile of material, a couple of cameras, and a couple of screens. I had compiled a lot of material about dataveillance, identity theft, and the idea of a data body. We had two weeks to improvise with the material, to create some sketches of the data body, and figure out how to stage that.

As always, it was rough, very rough. It looked terrible. You have to imagine that ultimately it's going to look like something. You have to have faith, based on our track record, that it's going to shape up. For dbox though, it was absolute torture. In fact, James Gibbs from dbox had an absolutely classic rehearsal dream of being hanged by the neck repeatedly but not being able to die. Because the idea of looking at something unfinished, or just sketching something and then throwing it away, which is ninety percent of the process, is absolutely antithetical to the way they work, which is extremely painstaking, time-consuming, and visually meticulous. So they learned a lot through that initial trial by fire, and almost a year later we ended up with an opportunity that I think very few theatre people have had.

After a series of design workshops we had our final six-week rehearsal at St. Ann's Warehouse in Brooklyn. James Gibbs was there every day with what amounted to a sweatshop of programmers from dbox who were working around the clock to create these enormous images. They would put something up on the stage, we would talk about adjustments, and then James would send it back upstairs and they'd spend another twenty-four hours modifying it. It was truly like making a high-tech animated film and a theatre piece at the same time. It was the closest they've gotten to improvising. And it was the closest any non-profit theatre company has gotten to working with that scale of visuals. We created a unique system that allowed us to generate animations on the spot, more or less, to work in concert with the performers. It was a great, very interesting, and radical way of working for both of us.

They probably can't afford to spend a year or two on a project.

No. But they are going to continue to participate in the next project.

How long does the process take from start to finish? How does something like that start?

It really takes two years from the first drunken concept meeting to the actual premiere. Granted, a lot of that is fundraising. But within that there is a series of ever-growing concept meetings, workshops, design sessions, and then a final big rehearsal period. Back to back, it's probably five or six months of straight work.

So was dbox in for the whole time?

Yes, they were in for two years. When we showed the piece in San Francisco, the editor of *Wired* magazine said that that was the most labor-intensive thing she'd ever seen. And it's true—it is an enormous amount of material.

The performance styles seemed to work in contradistinction to each other. For example, the virtual world of the domestic scenes differed from the reality of the Granddaughter in New York involved in a narrative that unfolds in real-time video conferencing with the Grandmother in Sri Lanka. The Traveler is another one. They seem to be in different performance modes. I felt that the domestic scenes were cinematic in the manner of a strange realism that's come into film now, like in Far From Heaven. *That kind of flatness. The tone of voice is extremely interesting. Whereas the Granddaughter and the Traveler seem to be doing more conventional acting. In thinking about the performance, was there a style that actors in one environment perform that is different from those in another? Did different kinds of language create multiple performance styles? Is that something that concerns you?*

I love that analogy to *Far From Heaven* and I'm a big Douglas Sirk fan. There are things about surface that can be very deep. Anyway, each story calls for its own performance style. The Traveler and his Border Agent are a kind of comedic drone, two people trapped in an endless repetition, while the Grandmother and her Granddaughter are reaching out to each other through technology to chat naturalistically about everyday things—recipes, boyfriends, old photos.

A certain quietness and lack of inflection in the domestic scenes made them more dramatic than the real actors in so-called more "emotional" or repetitive story narratives. They seemed to have much more feeling.

Why do you think that is?

Well, it's the way in Far From Heaven *that Julianne Moore became much more tragic through the slow, flat stylized speech. It's also the stark and heightened realism. There is a certain kind of mechanical quality that produces a really different dramatic world.*

I think that's beautiful. "Starkness" is right. Certainly this isn't a new idea, but it remains true that if a performer strips back, can calm down and withhold, and let the audience come to them instead of indicating and telegraphing what they're supposed to be feeling, there's a lot more space in the audience for emotion and experience.

The other two stories in *Super Vision* hark back to the structure of *Jet Lag*. There's no teleology, it's like a pendulum. The Grandmother flies back and forth, back and forth. I really enjoyed making that without it having an ending. But in these endings, the Traveler disappears into his own data field, and the Sri Lankan Grandmother slips away from communicating with her distant Granddaughter.

The minute those extraordinary visuals come in for the airport environment that was created by Diller and Scofidio, the actors become less interesting to me. I can't help it. How compelling are live actors when there is a huge flat screen or grid? Or the live performer and virtual actor or animation? It's really a question of the appeal of different kinds of performance styles. I don't think theatre has produced enough radically new modes of performance to work with media, especially regarding the issue of live presence/mediated presence.

We're all learning to become "smart viewers." In real life we can seamlessly link several modes of information at one time and the audience can bring this skill into the theatre. Balancing the screen and the stage has to do with the *mise-en-scène*, and it's the responsibility of the director. It's been a long lesson for me—balancing live performers against the media, or letting one overwhelm the other at certain times. This is something I started to observe in a basic way in my years at The Wooster Group, now some time ago. I think you could roughly trace this trajectory as something like this: The Performance Group and The Living Theatre were frequently ideologically opposed to media and based their work on physical ritual and the sanctity or at least the undeniable presence of the performer.

Then there was a transitional period in which forms of media encroached on stage, but the live performers are still privileged as the unquestioned source of the performance. The Wooster Group and Mabou Mines fall into this camp, for instance. Now there is a branch of contemporary theatre that is fully "mediatized." We are working in the gray area between live performance and "live" media, and the world that we create is dependent on the presence of both. In these performances, sometimes the media becomes the protagonist, and the stage becomes a laboratory for the interactions between human presence and electronic presence. That all sounds pretty dry, but it's a spectrum of experience that we're moving along, and of course it depends on the stories you tell—Indian operators studying *Buffy The Vampire Slayer* for hints about American culture is a lively part of that spectrum.

I see it as a kind of exploratory time in which we're evolving new performance styles in the same way that one is evolving new ways of using words in theatre or using media. It's just that we're moving toward different languages. Still, a lot of theatre has conditioned people to accept an idea of theatre that has become like a TV show. What are the audiences like for your work?

We've been very fortunate. As I said, our productions tell stories about global issues, and usually there's some recognition of that. Also, the way the company has managed to survive is that we receive co-production support from European and U.S. theatres. Less so from Europe in the last three or four years.

Because they can't afford it?

Yes. And because presenters in Europe are experiencing the kind of chilling effect that we had here in the early nineties. They are receiving pressure from their own governments and constituencies to produce nationally and not internationally. Certainly not to support American companies.

Is that a reaction to the U.S. government or U.S. foreign policy?

Yes, it's simply another response to the drastic isolationism of our current Administration.

For at least the last four decades most of our avant-garde, whether in dance or in theatre, could not have survived without European commissions and festivals.

Well, I think it's changed. In my lifetime, I've seen it go from being a given that you will receive half of your co-production support from Europe to having it be very minimal.

Is that because Europeans are tired of the same artists and there aren't enough new ones to support, or is it anti-Americanism? Or is it just that governments have changed in their social welfare policies and they're moving toward a more commercial sense of culture or cultural nationalism?

I think it's all of the above. Granted that there are some younger American artists who are getting support because Europeans are always looking for the "new." But I know that they're not being supported at the level that we were, and we've never been supported at the level that The Wooster Group and their generation was. It has definitely diminished.

What are the options then? Do you think that your theatre might survive in universities through workshops or a touring network? In other words, if the European situation dries up and there's not that much here, how will the work be funded? Do corporations and scientists have much interest in thinking about art and science projects?

There is university support, and it is absolutely critical. There are also a handful of courageous and essential U.S. presenters—at the Walker, the Wexner, the Krannert Center, On the Boards, The Museum of Contemporary Art in Chicago, REDCAT—and those producers continue to be valiant pioneers. But their funds are limited.

I know you are working with The Presence Project in a transcontinental partnership between Stanford University and the University of Exeter which is set up to explore issues surrounding telepresence and telematic installations. Where does your work fit in with the current thinking about interactive environments? The evolution in a media-driven theatre like yours, from set to installation, seems to me a significant move. But, I am not looking forward to the prospect of theatre resembling games, with audience-driven narratives, if that should come to pass. I would prefer to see theatre as the philosophical critique of the proliferation of performance modes online. Then again I am an unreconstructed Pirandellian.

I have never been a fan of old-fashioned audience participation, and I have not seen many successful theatre projects that incorporate interactivity. In many ways the myth of interactivity runs counter to the spectacle of theatre—once the audience becomes an active controller, the gaming aspect overwhelms the more subtle dimensions of staging and storytelling. And too many times it becomes only about the technology, e.g., "Everybody get out your cell phones ... " then you're looking at your phone and not at the interactions on stage.

The Presence Project is tracking several artists to see how we articulate levels of presence in our work—in the Builders' case, the spectrum of play between live performers and live technology—meaning technology that is played live, and that has an intense and in some ways "live" presence on the stage. But these levels of presence are still carefully choreographed by us, the artists, as opposed to, for instance, Second Life, where many players are experimenting with being present in the virtual world.

Finally, I'm glad you mentioned the critique of online performance modes. Our next project, *Continuous City*, looks at social networking—a huge event in the minds of the middle-class, white participants who want to be constantly telepresent to the networked world. What will happen when surprising incursions are made in that network, and when people who are not yet networked gain a presence in that space? That moment is just a few mouse clicks away.

This conversation was taped in New York City in December 2006 and is published here for the first time.

Present Tense

Berlin 2000

In 1998-99, I had the occasion of a nine-month stay in Berlin as a Fulbright scholar teaching at the Free University. This extended trip provided the opportunity to meet with many journalists, artists, academics, diplomats, historians, corporate and cultural representatives, as well as to experience day-to-day life in a city whose theatre culture I had always admired. Berlin was a city I had been familiar with over many years, as a theatregoer and publisher of German plays.

In this particular period and immediately afterwards, there had been several events of historic significance: Earlier in the summer President Clinton came to Berlin to celebrate the fifty-year anniversary of the Berlin Airlift; November 1998 marked the commemoration of sixty years after Kristallnacht, eerily coincident with the date, November 9, the Berlin Wall fell, in 1989. In the spring of 1999 the Reichstag reopened, with Sir Norman Foster's newly-built dome. Some months later, Germany would count fifty years of its post-war constitution.

Germany has been the focus of considerable press attention ever since the fall of the Berlin Wall and subsequent reunification, and with the recent move of the government to Berlin from Bonn the two Berlins have been joined in a massive rebuilding effort. Reconstruction is occurring on every level: political, social, cultural, economic, spiritual. No one knows yet what the new Berlin will become, though there are plenty of skeptics and naysayers, whether on political or aesthetic grounds. Berliners are highly articulate about their politics and social realities, and over a long period of time one can't help but be drawn into the discourse of a society in which the subject of cultural life is so central.

But trying to unravel the complexities of Berlin and the role of the new Germany is no simple matter, for the perspectives change according to generations and social and economic classes, and whether one is from the former East Germany, or from Berlin, or another part of Germany, where it matters less. There are those in the former DDR who feel themselves "occupied," their culture totally obliterated by the juggernaut of the West German economic miracle. As for questions that had preoccupied me during my stay—What is socialist culture? Where is it?—I cannot say that I found many answers, other than a few social generalities which even former East Germans now question as they begrudgingly acknowledge the good things that have happened in their transformed lives. What I did learn is how little Eastern Germans and Western Germans know of each other and their different ways of life, and how unbridgeable the gaps are even now. About forty percent of West Germans have never even traveled to the eastern part of the country, though people in the communist countries know far more about the West.

Today everyone speaks of the invisible wall inside the heads of Berliners, and some hold the view that the former two Germanies comprise entirely separate peoples and cultures who should not have been reunited, though for students and younger generations these issues matter little. Many others are still frozen in variations of Cold War rhetoric or sixties leftism or Marxist theory, each purveying some political distortion or another. Mostly, everyone agrees that it will take a generation to ease the transformation. By that measure, Germany is already halfway there.

Still, the insistent questions: How much of Germany's past to remember, how much to forget? After half-a-century there is no agreement on an appropriate response. In many ways, it is hard to be in Germany; Berlin itself has a tough, masculine feel, corroborated by the groups of young men one sees in the streets and train stations and who can turn ugly when threatened by the presence of people of color. One is never fully a tourist here but a student of history. It is unusual to have a conversation in Berlin without attention turning, sooner or later, to the subject of Germany, or more than likely to the new Berlin. How can this be otherwise in a city and a country in search of a new identity? At times the dialogue can be oppressive, for who can bring clarity to unresolved phantoms? History and memory are the gravitational poles of thought around which circulate the great political and cultural themes of the twentieth century, which we are still not done with. All of them have passed through the Brandenburg Gate. The fixation is even more intense in the debates on memorial sites and commemorations that have preoccupied Berlin for years. Martin Walser's controversial speech upon receiving the Büchner Prize a year-and-a-half ago, in which he stated that the Holocaust should not be used as a moral tool of intimidation or exploitation of German guilt, was one of the most talked-about events of my stay. It is time to move on, many, especially the young, agree. How dare he propose that Germany can ever be normal? others argue.

In Germany, one never escapes the feeling of history, especially in Berlin, where it is all around you: in the architectural hodge-podge of a city rebuilt from the ruins of war and division, in the war memorials and monuments, in the ghosts of Jews, in the corporate sell of the new Potsdamer Platz offering the amnesia of consumerism, in the repeating war documentaries on TV, in the curatorial sweep of museum shows, in the sorrows of public spaces. But, it is also in the faces and hearts of many Germans who cannot rid themselves of a terrible shame. An aspect of the post-war condition Americans do not often realize is the continuing impact of World War II on the psyche of Europeans, not only Germans, but anyone with a sense of the continent's history. If in time Berlin becomes the cultural center of Europe, the idea of Germany as a "great power," which the new Schroeder government has no difficulty in asserting, makes many Europeans fearful.

For anyone who has never seen the Berlin Wall it would challenge credibility to describe the psychology of fear that pervaded the streets of the old East Berlin, with its surveillance huts planted on city corners and machine-gun toting soldiers lurking near official buildings, ready to jump out at you at the flash of a camera. When I first went through Checkpoint Charlie as an exchange student at the University of Copenhagen, in 1969, there were posters of Walter Ulbricht fixed to lampposts lining the gray and empty silent streets. Some of the war's ruins were still uncleared from them. Later, when I would return in the seventies, it was a real feeling of accomplishment just to get past the border police at the Friedrichstrasse station and a few blocks down the road to the Berliner Ensemble, and then to hop a tram to venture a few stops into the foreboding city, which was irresistible. Shortly after the fall of the Berlin Wall, as I lingered before Bertolt Brecht's desecrated grave in the cemetery next to his home and not far from the theatre, a middle-aged German remarked, "The new old Germany."

Now, these same streets in the former Soviet sector of the city mark the center of the new Berlin—the Mitte—where clubs, cafes and restaurants, bookstores, opera and theatres, museums and galleries, and newly renovated hofs and residential blocks attract lively crowds. Farther north, in Prenzlauer Berg, even in DDR times the center of a counterculture, is a growing alternative arts and youth scene. Music clubs seem to be the most exciting arena of Berlin nightlife. There has never been any strong contemporary experimental theatre tradition in Berlin, the most important work occurring in the very bourgeois *stadttheaters* which absorbed all the best young artists. What was surprising after almost a year of theatregoing (including a brief trip for a few months in the summer of 1998, before returning again in the fall for the long stay) was the apparent inability of the theatre in Berlin to address the most serious contemporary issues and the diminished role of the theatre as a significant institution of public dialogue. As for the visual arts, the art market is not yet developed enough in Berlin to give it any sense of variety or fashion comparable, say, to London or New York, which the tepid response to the first Berlin Biennale that year confirmed.

Traces of the Wall are all but invisible. Building by building and street by street the old East Berlin is being overwhelmed by "development"—shopping, fashion, restaurants, and entertainment—just like any other Western city. It is practically impossible to find a café or store that doesn't look like it was newly designed, and the wood-paneled bars and restaurants of the DDR, with their framed photographs of the old Berlin and rippled yellow glass, are fast disappearing, with pasta now frequently overtaking wurst as the food of choice.

Driving the sixty or so miles to the Polish border from Berlin one can see the old villages and towns of the former DDR in their gradual change from dilapidation to modernization, with the addition of bus, tram and train lines, as well as gas stations, banks, movie theatres, shops, car dealerships, street lights, expanded roads—all of which have been built in the last decade. For all the difficulties reunification has brought about, and their have been many in the massive unemployment and disenfranchisement of the former communist state, there has not been enough acknowledgment of the remarkable visible changes in infrastructure and business services and the transformations in public space.

There are enormous expanses of forests and lakes for those whom nature served in the absence of free and various social activity. Besides, the outskirts of Berlin, unlike urban centers everywhere else in the world, did not become ringed by suburbs in the decades after the war. It is abnormally underpopulated since no one wanted to move to a Berlin surrounded by the DDR. In the Berlin of today, about a quarter of which is wooded—and with the environmental degradation of the East abated—one can walk for miles and miles through the city along paths in the Grunewald, Tiergarten, or any *Volkspark*, and along the embankments of the Spree River and the city's canals, or even bike along the same routes. But the experience is different from, say, walking in the parks and boulevards of Paris, for example, which are made for looking and being looked at. The German way of walking, preferably briskly, is to be alone or with a single companion on private pathways, away from onlookers; it has more of the Romantic feeling. Not surprisingly, when Walter Benjamin wrote about the *flaneur* he had Paris in mind, not Berlin.

My stay in Berlin revealed what travels in Europe elsewhere last year—to Warsaw, Dresden, Copenhagen, Milan, Prague, Madrid—confirmed: societies exhibiting simultaneously a cosmopolitanism and a cultural nationalism, global interest and pan-Europeanism. There is a general rise in the standard of living everywhere but also high unemployment, struggles between the new free market philosophies infiltrating the continent and a commitment to the older social welfare systems, the custom of independent shopkeepers and a gradual awareness of more service economies, fear of foreigners conflicting with their necessity in countries defined by drastically falling birthrates, and the rise of conservatism, especially with the young. For many in the Eastern countries, freedom has come to be less important than job security.

While the increasing influence of American culture and ideas and the attraction of young people to it is evident, there is also a backlash against America. Just as it seemed the anti-Americanism was beginning to wane in the decades after the Vietnam war, especially with European youth who are traveling steadily to the U.S. and are less influenced by the leftism of the continent's intellectuals, it has started up again with fears of being swallowed up in American-led globalism and military adventures. There are numerous variations on the American imperialism theme: cultural, economic, military. Yet, many older Europeans speak with gratitude of the American soldiers who fought on the continent in World War II. Berliners have a special feeling for Americans who airlifted food and supplies during the Soviet blockade of 1948.

For the first time I heard Germans, including the new Minister of Culture, Michael Naumann, speak critically of their university system, which is desperately in need of reform. In fact, all over Europe bulging universities are homes for unemployed youth and hangers-on. Students who have been to America are now openly envious of its university facilities, flexible programs, and library collections. The social welfare system, one of post-war Europe's most prized creations, is under scrutiny everywhere. It is not so much that Europeans want to change to an American-style system—they are more pro-government and not apologetic for it—as much as they wonder if their countries can maintain the social security they have been used to, and have often seen abused, for so many decades.

Everywhere people feel insecure, even in Austria, one of the most secure societies on the face of the Earth, where the entry of the right-wing Freedom Party of Jorge Haider into the government has brought about a crisis of the European Community. But it seems that Europeans, even with the proliferating freedoms of choice, money, and independence, like Americans, are unsettled by incomprehensible global economies, proliferating technologies, the loss of traditions, and cultural transformation. In fact, Germany, whose wealth out-strips its technological capabilities, is at least a decade behind America in being wired, even forced recently to import computer experts to fill jobs available since its own population is not well-enough trained for the positions. No one knows for sure if Berlin will attract enough business to make it a prosperous city, or enough people to fill its vast, anxious spaces. Whatever kind of city Berlin becomes in the future, it will have provided for itself the extraordinary opportunity—or is it the illusion?—of starting over, almost.

Now it is May, the most beautiful month in Berlin, a season when it comes to life and abandons itself to northern light after the unbearably long, gray, chilly days. Throughout the sprawling city huge chestnut trees spread their limbs over the streets and squares, their shadows hovering over the gaiety of outdoor gardens and restaurants. Sometimes, on a warm night, it is so fragrant that one forgets the dark secrets of the rebuilt neighborhoods, blurring the history and memory and poetry they house. From my vantage point on the Wannsee there was something of everything, the modest lake site that marks Kleist's suicide and the imposing villa where Nazis convened to plot the Final Solution, and a little farther on the Glienicke Brücke, which eased the exchange of prisoners and spies between East and West; nearby, Cecilienhof, host to the Potsdam conference that was both an ending and a beginning. Tourist boats on the Havel and Wannsee can now take one all through this part of Berlin, past palaces and parks and little islands and villages and through many canals into once forbidden waters, gliding for miles and miles along Heiner Müller's despoiled shores.

This essay served as the introduction to a special issue entitled "Berlin 2000," in *PAJ: A Journal of Performance and Art*, Vol. XXII, No. 2 (PAJ 65), May 2000.

Barcelona Contemporary

Barcelona holds a special charm in my dreamlife of cities. It was the starting point for a first grand tour on the European continent, in 1969, when I had arrived there after a semester at the University of Copenhagen. I went to Barcelona alone that June, by ship from Majorca, having left behind there a college friend who was supposed to travel with me for the summer. Even though the island was filled with Scandinavians practicing what was then fancifully called "free love," she had fallen for an Algerian guy and went off with him to North Africa. Those were the days.

Indeed, the world was such a different place when I began my travels abroad. Another country I went to that year, Greece, was under a military dictatorship. Ironically, during this era the Middle East and Asia were popular student destinations, and I recall many advertisements then for overland bus trips across Europe to Afghanistan. By the following decade, after I had made it all the way to Kathmandu, now the scene of a Maoist insurgency, there were so many Europeans and Americans there, dropped out, drugged out—and it wasn't on yak butter—that one of the roads in the center of the city was called "Freak Street."

The Barcelona I first encountered was existing as less than itself, rhetorically impoverished under Franco, its inhabitants forbidden to use Catalan in schools, publishing, or any official capacity. Even the Catalan national dance, the Sardana, was banned, though now in the square facing the Cathedral older inhabitants of the city form several large circles to perform it on weekends to the delight of onlookers who often join in. Today one of the most cosmopolitan of European cities, its visitors can enjoy an all-night life in the shadows of free verse architecture along its splendid boulevards, or dine by the sea on the new cuisine its chefs are inventing.

Like many people who have suffered under repressive governments, the Spanish are fiercely demonstrative of their new standing in the world, coming from near Third World conditions three decades ago to the economic and cultural miracle that is contemporary Spain. They have been among the most vociferous citizens in the world exercising their democratic rights, in previous years demonstrating in public squares against the Basque killings, and, more recently, the country's involvement in the Iraq war which, urged on by the March bombings at Atocha station in Madrid, brought down the conservative government of Aznar. The Catalans, especially, take pride in their modernity. More than once, I heard it said—by a Catalan—that Barcelona is really "Europe," and the rest of the country is, well, Spain.

The age- and Fascist-blackened buildings of the Barcelona I remember from decades ago have by now given way to a well-tended city that has grown enormously in size and reputation since the Olympics were held there, in 1992. This summer it was host to the Universal Forum of Cultures Barcelona 2004, a four-month program of performances, public dialogues, congresses, and exhibitions, organized by the Barcelona City Council, the Catalan autonomous government and the Spanish government, and with the support of UNESCO, reaffirming the city's pride and its urban renewal plans jumpstarted by the Olympics. Like Paris, which has turned dilapidated and often outlying parts of the city into parks and cultural centers, Barcelona's local government has also taken the opportunity to transform the run-down facilities of an industrial zone on the Mediterranean, a few miles from Port Olimpic, into state-of-the-art water treatment and incinerator plants, including a solar panel that brings power to the Forum. Exhibition grounds and parks, hotels, a convention center, a congress hall, and apartment buildings have paved the way for the economic and ecological revival of this peripheral area of the city.

While a diverse assortment of exhibits, spectacles, and public dialogues took place on the Forum site, cultural institutions throughout the city sponsored hundreds of theatre, dance, music, and art events, with guests from several continents, including The Wooster Group, Peter Sellars, Mikhail Baryshnikov, Peter Brook, Pina Bausch, Sting, Norah Jones, Gilberto Gil, Cesaria Evora, Bob Dylan, Tibetan monks, Khaled, various European symphonies, and artists from all over Spain. However, during my stay in the city over a period of weeks, and well past Forum Barcelona's opening, none of the people I spoke to had visited the Forum site itself. There had been a considerable amount of controversy surrounding the cultural event, focusing on the inevitable real estate boom in the area that would displace people and businesses, the high ticket prices for a daily pass (about twenty-one euros for adults, thirteen euros for children), lack of interest in the on-site spectacles offered, criticism of the mayor's grand vision, and the tremendous expenditures by the city. Local politics are always difficult for the outsider to sift through, and given the nature of the autonomous status of Catalonia, even more so in Barcelona.

For my part, having spent a considerable amount of time at the site itself, I was generally impressed by the ambitious cultural and social reach of its organizers, who developed three themes around which the entire program for the Forum events was conceived: cultural diversity; sustainable development; conditions for peace. The public dialogues/seminars/international meetings that took place, led by writers, politicians, scientists, and social activists, addressed such topics as "The Role of Europe in the World," "Linguistic Diversity," "International Justice." I saw two of the big expositions at the entrance to the Forum that further emphasized the broad goals of cultural awareness and urbanity. *Cities, Corners* focused on the kinds of buildings made for corner sites—how they create meeting places, intersections of simultaneous random events, points of conflict and exchange—in various cities around the world, such as New York, Vienna, Bombay, Milan, Moscow, and Barcelona. Maps, models, and maquettes were combined to reflect the exhibit's themes, along with a film which collaged scenes from international cinema that took place—where else?—at corners. *Voices* carried along the diversity theme, with an especially apt seriousness in the bi-lingual city, focusing on the languages people speak around the world. This show, using high-tech displays of images and text, went beyond merely enumerating linguistic difference to make a point of demonstrating that the distribution of media in the world is related to the disappearance of languages unrepresented in global communications.

Forum events presented at the exposition grounds were very family-friendly and youth-oriented. There were spectacles all over the site day and night, featuring international performers, such as the Kavkasik Circus from Azerbaijan and Thanglong Water Puppet Theatre from Vietnam, as well as local artists and those from around Spain who work with highly theatrical effects, like Escarlata Circus and La Machine's Giant of the 7 Seas, the Comediants's *Memory Tree* constructed out of objects and fabric, or the large puppets—*Fantòtems*—that floated in small boats and barges on the waterfront at night, created by puppeteer Joan Baixas. Admittedly, performances were of the street-theatre and popular-festival variety, and such exhibits do not challenge the serious museumgoer, nor are they meant to. But make no mistake about it, the Forum is not a theme park, nor is it a world's fair. It is its own new form, combining cultural events, EU ideals, urban planning, tourism, and global awareness in a demonstrated commitment to progressive political and social issues. Joan Clos, the mayor of Barcelona, described the impressive undertaking in these terms: "A new kind of international event that brings together people rather than states.

Its central aim is to provide a platform for global civil society to make itself heard and a framework for reflection, dialogue, experience, festivity, and celebration of all the arts."

The clearest expression of this philosophical view was the construction of the Haima, a huge tent area coursing the main thoroughfare of the Forum, housing fifteen exhibitions on such themes as Practopia; Water Talks; Biodiversity; You Consume, You Decide; Ethical Banking; Women and War; Refugees and Displaced Persons. These exhibits were intended to educate the public in ethical, economic, and cultural perspectives surrounding the significant issues of our time: consumerism, immigration, war, and natural resources. That they were produced in conjunction with United Nations agencies, NGOs, and other humanitarian organizations gave them something of the self-satisfaction of a foundation's annual report, but the focus on global issues reinforced the stated core goals of the Forum. This is really a new concept in exhibitions for the general public. The fact that the term "practopia" defined one of the exhibits demonstrates a commitment to finding new solutions to the world's problems, not simply viewing change as utopian and, therefore, unattainable. More importantly, the ethos of Forum Barcelona was built around the assumption that visitors to the site are citizens, not customers.

In its comprehensive approach, the organization of the Forum reflected the European way of working toward interconnected networks, regional cooperation, and social consciousness on a global scale, an integrated approach that Jeremy Rifkin, in his new book *The European Dream*, regards as characteristic of contemporary thinking in Europe. Likewise, at the heart of the Forum's *Statement of Principles and Values* is the Universal Declaration of Human Rights and the founding themes of the UN. For Spain, isolated so long under fascism while the rest of the continent was developing sophisticated social and economic policies in the post-war period, being part of Europe is a highly-valued status. From a Catalan viewpoint, an event like this establishes Barcelona as a cultural leader in southern Europe, since ancient times a passageway in the Mediterranean between Africa and Europe.

Spain just elected a socialist Prime Minister, José Luis Rodríguez Zapatero, who immediately appointed women to hold half the positions in his cabinet. Furthermore, the first bill he presented to Parliament proposed wide-ranging new legislation to combat what he calls "criminal *machismo*" against Spanish women, confirmed by the recent newspaper coverage of several murders of women or attacks on them by husbands or lovers. It is worth noting that Zapatero is the first premier since pre-Spanish Civil War days to visit the annual Madrid Book Fair (the sixty-third) in Retiro Park, accompanied by the Culture Minister and head of the National Library, both women. At the Europe Pavilion, *El Pais* reported, many authors from Europe's new member states met with Spanish intellectuals and the public to discuss the cultural and political future of Europe. The King and Queen, whose son and heir to the throne was married on a rainy day in May in a city still nervous about the recent terrorist bombings near that very park, also attended the fair. During my stay the EU Parliament elections took place as well, with Spain voting on fifty-four of the 732 seats available to the twenty-five countries.

Another historic event was the sixtieth anniversary of D-Day, June 6, which included a visit to Normandy by Gerhard Schroeder, the first by a German chancellor, underscoring the new spirit in Europe as it moves further and further away from the divisions of the Second World War. I could not help but wonder what the Spaniards were thinking that day this year, having been abandoned by Europe and America in their efforts to create a Republic, and watching bitterly as Europe was liberated, then rebuilt after the war, while they had four decades of fascism. The Spanish Civil War remains an open wound for the country. Lately, a significant number of memoirs and personal narratives has been published, chronicling the life and death of many people who had previously chosen anonymity, or who could not face until now the conflict that divided so many families.

With peace as one of the three major themes of the Forum, throughout the city major exhibits were organized around the subject and, by extension, its opposite, war. *Picasso, War and Peace* was at the museum devoted to the artist. The Center of Contemporary Culture of Barcelona (CCCB) mounted *At War*, an overview of global conflict. Cultural diversity shaped the focus of several museum shows, one on Confucius and others dealing with Mediterranean, Mid-East, and Oceanic cultures; the Forum site offered the highly popular Warriors of Xi'chan. Besides bringing to town his Indonesian folk piece, *I La Galigo*, Robert Wilson was given the opportunity by the Barbier-Muller Museum to create new installations for the pre-Columbian art in its collection, which he did by situating it comfortably in newer settings of popular imagery, abstraction, and minimalism.

At the Fundació Antoni Tàpies, *Tour-Isms: The Defeat of Dissent* showed several artists working in video, film, photography, and installations that addressed tourism, the dissemination of cultural imagery and myth, and the new life of cities. In *T.P. Interrupted Trip* Pedro Coelho designed a wall of postcards chronicling the difficulty of conveying the uniquely personal experience of travel. Lisl Ponger's film *Passagen* reconstructed the mentality of immigration and travel, with a moving narrative and "found" film material. In one of the more compelling installations, Rogelio López Cuenca showed several examples of the same photographic image of a town on the Costa del Sol, in *Nerja, once*, with accompanying texts that placed it in a historical and political continuum, e.g., the Spanish Civil War, as a site of drug trafficking, a home to immigrants, and, finally, as a unique Mediterranean coastal ecosystem at odds with its mayor's vision of developing tourism. Videos of the region and inhabitants expanded his theme. Having just passed through the southern coast of Spain and seen firsthand the spoliation of the landscape by hideous overbuilding, this particular work stood out among several others in the urgency of its linkage of landscape and history.

As I left this gallery, I picked up a brochure published by the public space interventionist group Tourism Tactic entitled, "La ruta de l'anarquisme," which featured a map of sites marking Republican scenes of conflict during the civil war, so many of them in what is now the heart of the tourist district, in and around La Rambla. One of the Forum theatre events I saw was a British-Catalan adaptation by the West Yorkshire Playhouse of George Orwell's great memoir of his months as a volunteer in the Spanish Civil War, *Homenatge a Catalunya* (Homage to Catalonia), directed by Josep Galindo at the historic Teatre Romea, which had been a stronghold of resistance when Orwell was hiding out nearby. I found the production full of bombast, in comparison to the understatement and refusal of military glamour that Orwell himself exhibited. Here was a man who described three days and nights at a watch post on the roofs of buildings in Plaça de Catalunya with a modesty that surpasses calm: "Sometimes I was merely bored with the whole affair, paid no attention to the hellish noise, and spent hours reading a succession of Penguin Library books which, luckily, I had bought a few days earlier; sometimes I was very conscious of the armed men watching me fifty yards away."

Another performance I attended, which also reflected the all-out efforts of cultural events to reflect the Forum's social and political themes, was a performance of Mikis Theodorakis's thirty-year-old oratorio *Canto general*, based on the poetry of Pablo Neruda. Theodorakis, who had left Greece under the dictators when he wrote it, referred to his work as a "a gospel for our time." It was sung by the widely-admired Greek singers, Maria Farantouri and Petros Pandis, in the Palau de la Música Catalana, one of Barcelona's glorious *modernista* buildings, designed by Lluís Domènech i Montaner. The Ensemble Barcelona Ad Libitum, conducted by Josep Vila i Casanas, gave the rousing piece its passionate due as a testament to life and freedom. For sheer delight, and focused more on culture than on politics, at the relatively new Catalan culture palace, Teatre Nacional, Philippe Decouflé showed off his accomplished international company in *Iris*, a cross-media work which brought together pantomime, dance, music, and video. Though it had the feel of a government-sponsored festival piece—specifically Franco-Japanese—that characterizes many productions on the circuit these days, *Iris* managed to combine a charming insouciance and philosophic integrity in a series of vignettes that explored the human condition, body, and image.

One of the most compelling official events of the Forum was installed in the large complex of the CCCB, the exhibit *At War*, which was spread over two floors and organized around several themes related to the twentieth-century experience of war all over the world: the socialization of violence; the construction of the enemy; hostilities; victory and defeat; memory. Bringing together painting, photography, sculpture, installations, objects, film, and documents, *At War* amassed a remarkable amount of material. Among the objects were European children's war toys and games; a Catholic priest's traveling box with instruments for saying Mass; the medical case of Magda Goebbels holding poison; cutlery for disabled French World War I veterans; pieces of weapons made into furniture in Mozambique. If a number of the paintings or drawings—by Severini, Grosz, Dix, Malevich, Golub—are well-known, there were plenty that are not, such as the drawings by British surgeon Henry Tonks who studied facial wounds of disfigured soldiers from the Great War; World War II art by Dame Laura Knight and Henry Moore, and the American Tom Lea. There were also drawings and photographs done by the Vietnamese, culled from the British Museum and Imperial War Museum, and others from the National Museum of the U.S. Army in Washington; children's drawings from Sarajevo and Rwanda.

I found the photographs to be the most powerful documents—the image of a row of prosthetics in sneakers attached to children who lost limbs on landmines (Gervasio Sánchez); Robert Capa's original notebook for the Spanish Civil War; Dresden after the Allied raids; James Nachtwey's "Passion of Islam" series; José María Rosa and María Bleda's contemporary views of landscapes that are part of the history of war; Gusi i Las's front pages of a newspaper burnt directly onto photographic paper, protesting the mediatization of the war in Kosovo. Among the installations in the show, two were particularly moving, from the last section of "Memory." Francesc Torres who with Antonio Monegal was a curator of the exhibit (José Maria Ridao was the third), and wrote the introduction to its very fine catalogue (featuring essays by Michael Walser, Jeremy Black, Chris Gray, and Andreas Huyssen), was represented by *Memorial*, his installation made on the first anniversary of the Gulf War, consisting of a military cemetery marked by hats placed on the end of rifle butts that invade an entire living room. Bringing together strategies of minimalism, conceptual art, and photography, Alfredo Jaar created a heartbreaking archive of photographic boxes, *Real Pictures*, with texts from the thousands of photos he took in Rwanda after the massacres, each one offering a description of the photograph but not the actual image. Instead, the boxes stood upright or were laid out in grids on the floor like the stone slabs of cemetery plots.

At War is a superb curating accomplishment, reflecting a profound understanding of war and warfare—its preparation, duration, and aftermath—as a state of being: how it is socialized, how it is fought, how it is represented in art, and eventually memorialized. Like the exceptional exhibitions I have seen in Europe over the decades, particularly in Germany, the subject of history is intertwined with the subject of art.

Another large-scale exhibit, *Art and Utopia: Action Restricted*, was installed around the corner from the CCCB, at the Museum of Contemporary Art (MACBA). Taking as its inspiration Mallarmé's view of poetic action as a limited but powerful gesture for reflecting human experience and social consciousness, it encompassed the period of the late-nineteenth century through the seventies, the intention being to examine the exchange between art and poetry. Mallarmé's project of the book as a "spiritual instrument" pointed the way to the visual anthropology of symbol and image, text and word, the sacred and the ordinary. Artaud, Duchamp, and Cage were positioned as central historical figures, and of contemporary artists, Marcel Broodthaers, Dieter Roth, and Öyvind Fahlström assumed prominence. Essentially, every influential modernist and avant-garde movement or style was represented here, with countless works of European and American artists in painting, drawing, sculpture, books, photography, film, and video, extending from symbolism to post-conceptual art, and passing through futurism, constructivism, expressionism, dada, surrealism, pop and abstract art, and performance.

Another way to consider the exhibit, curated by Jean-François Chevrier, is that in terms of the poetry of the performing body, it ranged from Loie Fuller (the spiritual) to Judson dance (the ordinary); in terms of the literary, from symbolism to conceptual art and concrete poetry. In general, European curators are much more likely than their American counterparts to consider theatre and body art in the history of modernism and the avant-garde, as this one does in bringing together the likes of Wagner, Craig, Appia, Meyerhold, Bauhaus performance, Carolee Schneemann, Trisha Brown, Simone Forti. Indeed, Mallarmé's insistence on the mystery of the quotidian, his assertion of the poetic gesture in art, is credited here with the opening up of modern space, both visual and performance varieties.

In my view, the death of John Cage, who technologized the sacred in the sound of everyday things, and made notation and the essay forms of visual poetry, signaled the end of a long line of avant-garde utopianists who believed that a revolution in art would lead to social revolution. The exhibit challenged that notion in pursuing the idea of utopia as the very language of art and of modernity. Despite the overwhelming inclusion of so many artists from so many countries, movements, and generations, which invites serious questions about the relevance of some work to the theme, *Art and Utopia* insists that the project is ongoing. Perhaps in Europe it is still possible to pursue that ideal.

If *Art and Utopia* proposed a seemingly French-influenced view of modernity organized around language (the aesthetic), Swiss curator Harald Szeemann offered a Germanic view centered on the politics of community (the social), in his controversial show *The Beauty of Failure/The Failure of Beauty* at Fundació Miró. For him, the history of art is replaced by the history of failure: of revolutionary politics, of the total work of art, of architecture, of globalization, of religion, of communication, of peace. Beauty and failure are interchangeable in modern consciousness. The dream began for Szeemann in Romantic political and artistic movements, culminating in the utopia of Monte Verità, at Ascona, and in subsequent modern art experiments, and ended in the horrors of the twentieth century continuing into the twenty-first.

This high concept, eccentric exhibit was installed in a series of twelve rooms, organized around such subjects as: revolution in art (Artaud, Duchamp, Kandinsky, Malevich, Mondrian); Wagner and the total work of art; visionary architecture of Albert Trachsel and Bruno Taut; Viennese Actionism of Otto Mühl; an installation on media and war by Thomas Hirschhorn; Thomas

Virnich's collapsed St. Peter's Basilica; September 11 and after; Chen Zhen's negotiating table. One of the most disturbing pieces was Zhou Kiaohu's film, *Beautiful Cloud*, featuring an audience of cloned children watching films about the twentieth century, the cloud being an "image" of the atomic bomb. Shocking in its prophetic nature was a 1973 postcard by Joseph Beuys, the revered European utopian, of the World Trade Towers on which he had written the words "Cosmos" and "Damian." In contrast to the more formal and affirming stance of *Art and Utopia*, *The Beauty of Failure/The Failure of Beauty*, while sharing a number of the same artists, focused on the failure of utopia as a political and social force in our time. Taken together, the two exhibits offered a serious opportunity for debate of this perennial issue at the very heart of the idea of Europe. They have led me to believe that the current interest in the theme of utopia, besides acknowledging the absence of radical politics today, is an attempt to reinsert in contemporary thinking the question of the spiritual in art.

Everywhere I turned there was one more exhibit to see. The CaixaForum, a large exhibition building under the auspices of one of the major financial institutions in the city, situated in the Parc de Monjuïc, presented a large show on Confucius at the same time the smaller *Documentary Fictions* was taking place, which I chose to attend the day before I left the city. This was an international group show of video, Internet art, and installations that put into contention both the documentary work's status as a truthful representation of reality and the process of documentation itself. A research project for the Internet unraveled the notebooks and films used by Walid Raad and the Atlas Group to construct the history of Lebanon, with "The Fadl Fakhouri File" documenting car bombings there. In *Videos des villes*, Santiago Reyes created a series of one minute-and-a half videos featuring a man and a woman having a conversation in non-descript parts of several European and British cities, using the found speech of everyday desires. "I feel happy today." "Life is good." The multiplication of the couples and the simultaneous diminishing of their vocabularies gave the work its poignancy.

One of the most intelligent videos I have seen of late is Zineb Sedira's *Mother Tongue*. The artist installed three monitors of five-minute segments each: the artist speaks French and her mother Arabic (they understand each other); the artist speaks French and her daughter British-accented English (they understand each other); the daughter speaks English and the grandmother Arabic (they don't understand each other). The conversations are about ordinary things, like friends, school, etc., but the drama resides in the awkward pauses, the framing of the women on each monitor exposing their levels of communi-cation, tension, or relaxation, and the distance that is emotional, cultural, lin-guistic, and physical. Video was used as an intimate medium to create three separate portraits whose exchanges address the issues of immigration, language and gesture, intergenerational communication, and speech and emotion. In its relation to the theme of the show, *Mother Tongue* presented an actual docu-ment that explored the fiction-like narrative of the women's lives.

I had arrived in Barcelona too late to see the CaixaForum's big Dalí exhibit, which traced his work and influence in mass culture, but since this was the artist's centenary year plenty of other shows in the city featured hundreds of his paintings and drawings, many on religious or literary themes, which I had not seen before. Dalíesque motifs in black, white, and pink served as settings for the mannikins in the large windows of Loewe's, the deluxe leather-goods shop on Passeig de Gràcia whose violation of Domènech's splendid Casa Lleó Morera frontage made Robert Hughes, in his fascinating book on Barcelona, call for its boycott. Down the block, the harlequinade façade of Gaudí's Casa Battló, one of the dandiest examples of performance architecture ever imagined, was still dazzling passersby. (Truly, can anyone just pass by?) North of this undulating wonder stands his Sagrada Família, surely the oldest work-in-progress in the Western world, having begun in 1882, the year after Picasso was born, and sev-en years before the Eiffel Tower was built. Through the miracle of technology a Barcelona advertising executive, working with numerous technical experts, has had a vision of the church in its final form—virtually speaking—which is now available on a CD-Rom for those who can't wait any longer for its completion, probably several decades away. The Sagrada Família may simply always exist as an icon of the Barcelona imaginary.

All the same, for the summer of 2004, Forum Barcelona had presented its more secular version of a holy family to reign over the city, though with no less sacred a purpose: cultural diversity; sustainable development; conditions for peace.

This essay provided the introduction to a special section on Barcelona in *PAJ: A Journal of Performance and Art*, Vol. XXVII, No. 1 (PAJ 79), January 2005.

The Crossways of Istanbul

This year marked the fifteenth International Istanbul Theatre Festival and the fourth International Theatre Olympics, brought together under the theme "beyond the borders." The Olympics were initiated in Athens in 1994 by a number of world theatre figures, including Theodoros Terzopoulos, Tadashi Suzuki, Robert Wilson, Heiner Müller, Nuria Espert, and Wole Soyinka. So the current border-crossing reference—coupled with this year's theatrical representation from Europe, Russia, Japan, and the U.S.—amply serves to reinforce the organizational aim of recognizing the diversity and achievement of many cultures.

Though I had come to Istanbul for the arts events, it was an inescapable fact that besides aesthetic borders at this historic moment I would be confronted by more volatile cultural struggles across social, political, and religious lines. Certainly among the most explosive of current issues is the woman's headscarf, which is outlawed in government offices, Parliament, and universities. This highly sensitive subject moved to the forefront early on in my stay because of daily news reports concerning the recent assassination at the Council of State in Ankara of a Turkish judge who had refused to relax the rules on the wearing of headscarves. No sooner had I settled in the city in the latter part of May than I witnessed a demonstration by Turkish lawyers on İstiklal Caddesi, in the Beyoğlu district near my hotel. A statement was read by the head of the Istanbul Bar who said, "I call on all people and institutions that are partly responsible for the attack to respect all the institutions of the republic and obey the judicial rulings." Based on my observation, it was also true that the vast majority of women walking day or night around lively Beyoğlu, home to numerous restaurants, shops, galleries, theatres, foreign embassies, and cultural centers, was not wearing headscarves.

Not long after this disturbance, it was reported in the June 1, 2006, edition of *The New Anatolian* that the Turkish president, Ahmet Necdet Sezer, and his wife refused to attend a recent dinner for the King and Queen of Sweden due to "their reluctance to sit at the same table as the 'headscarved wives' of politicians." The prime minister of Turkey, Recep Tayyip Erdoğan, whose AKP (Justice and Development Party) regularly undermines its own pledge to uphold the secular principles of the country and create a bridge between Turkey's more religious citizens and those identified as secularists, recently had created an incident in Berlin, publicly embarrassing the Turkish Ambassador over the complaints of Turkish women living in Germany concerning the inability to have their passport photos taken while wearing a headscarf. Pondering the complex emotions this issue elicits, which is difficult in so short a stay for an outsider to understand beyond its simple outlines, I was reminded that in the great drive toward secularization after the First World War Atatürk had outlawed the male custom of wearing the fez because of its reference to the old Ottoman Empire.

Far more worrisome than the headscarf issue for those secularists who want to see Turkey fully embraced by the European Union is the ongoing censorship and trials of Turkish writers, journalists, publishers, and scholars who have referred to the post-World War I Armenian "genocide," whose million-and-a-half deaths Turkey officially defines as the result of a "war" that followed the breakup of the Ottoman Empire. Furthermore, those who satirize politicians, disparage the military, and insult Atatürk's memory can also be prosecuted under Article 301 of the new penal code. Last winter Orhan Pamuk, Turkey's most well-known writer, was charged with "insulting Turkishness" for mentioning the Armenian massacre in an interview with a Swiss journalist. The charges were later dropped for the author who gave the Arthur Miller Freedom to Write Lecture sponsored by PEN and Cooper Union in New York last April. [He received the Nobel Prize for Literature before the end of 2006.—BGM] Pamuk's translator, Maureen Freely, in the *New York Times Book Review* of August 13, 2006, reminded readers that Nâzim Hikmet, Turkey's great modern poet, died in exile, having spent much of his life in prison, and that "during the seventies, eighties and nineties, so many writers, journalists and scholars were imprisoned for their views that prosecution became a badge of honor." PEN reports that more than sixty cases have been brought against writers and artists, though no one has been imprisoned. On September 21, in the latest case to be brought to trial, and watched closely by the EU and international organizations, the Turkish court dropped charges which had been brought against the novelist Elif Shafak because one of the characters in her new novel, *The Bastard of Istanbul*, refers to the Armenian "genocide" as a part of family history.

The issues circulating around free speech and a free press are especially important at a time when Turkey has just conducted its first round of negotiations in June toward attaining membership in the European Union, with almost three dozen in all to complete in a continuing process expected to take a decade. EU members have warned Turkey that continued prosecution of writers threatens its membership in the organization. The move toward integration pushes beyond the phraseology of the "new Europe" and "old Europe" to considerations of the "other Europe." Indeed, many Europeans have expressed concern about the acceptance of Turkey because it would be the first essentially Muslim, albeit secular and democratic, country to join the EU. The secular establishment in several realms of Turkish society has accused the government of resisting the EU process to appease conservative Islamist forces, while Europeans have been rethinking the number of members—now twenty-five, soon to be twenty-seven—in the EU in the years ahead. Unfortunately, the prosecution of writers and publishers helps those inside and outside the EU who want to undermine Turkey's eligibility. Only last year Austria had inserted into Turkey's application to the EU the phrase "absorption capacity," which has become a euphemism for those members questioning how far the EU can expand. In the September 8 edition of the *Financial Times*, it was reported that Turkey's chief negotiator in Brussels called any breakdown of the process bringing Turkey into the EU "devastating ... for the future of the world" because it is important to show that the "values and ideals" of the EU could be congruent with those of a Muslim country.

Since European voters in France and Holland refused to accept the proposed EU constitution, the sense of what the European Union means to European citizens, where Europe begins and ends, and what defines European values, remains in flux. The question of "borders" within and beyond Europe is constantly shifting and brought under interrogation—geographically, spiritually, historically, economically, and culturally. This year's "beyond the borders" Istanbul Festival theme offered many perspectives from within the art forms presented and, more aggressively, beyond the borders of art into Turkish society itself.

Coming to this part of the world for the first time, I was captivated by the idea that I could go to the Istanbul Modern in the morning and in the afternoon hop a Bosphorus ferry to Asia Minor, having a look at painting and video, and then a walk in the ancient land of Chalcedonians, a place which I had recalled from reading Edgar Allan Poe. The trip to Istanbul brought to mind references from school days that I had not thought of for many years. Did I ever really know where the Thracians or the Phrygians came from? Well, here I was in their former home. Chalcedon, so mysteriously described in Poe's "Silence," and drawn into the poetic imagination of Nerval and Gautier and Flaubert, who wrote famous accounts of their travels to Istanbul, was now a luxury shopping area of Kadiköy whose main boulevard looks like any thoroughfare of European capitals farther west of it.

I tried repeatedly to get to Troy, 220 miles and a five-hour bus ride from Istanbul, but the logistics of tours and festival scheduling prevented that. Besides, all the *Istanbullus* I spoke to disparaged a trip—there was nothing there, they said. (Oh, the jaded luxury of coming from a ten-thousand-year-old culture!) I had wanted to see the sky over Troy, the first city mentioned in Greek literature, or breathe the air in that part of the world. Alas! *The Iliad's* "broad streets of Troy" were buried deep in layer upon layer of destruction, natural and man-made. Now I could only console myself with a visit to the Archaeological Museum where all the artifacts of Troy are displayed in glass cases, anyway.

Troy hadn't really been on my mind for quite some time, except for the fact that around the time of my trip to Istanbul I had been preparing a new seminar on the rewritings of Greek classics, featuring many plays dealing with the Trojan War and its aftermath. Now Troy was very much in my imagination, Homer's heroic epic of death, destruction, and enslavement coursing through the other side of history in Charles L. Mee's contemporary vision interfacing Euripides, Hiroshima, the Holocaust, Yugoslavia, Hannah Arendt, and a television talk show.

None of the festival offerings dealt with any of the plays that were related to the Trojan War, but continuing the contemporary interest in classics Theodoros Terzopoulos staged for the first time in Turkey Aeschylus' anti-war play *The Persians*, in a Turkish-Greek production, before I arrived at the festival. Yuri Lyubimov brought his Taganka Theatre from Moscow in *Medea*. A "barbarian," Medea (played in an operatic Russian manner by Liubov Selyutina) had originally come from this part of the world. In Lyubimov's staging Jason and the other men in the play were dressed in military camouflage—even the King, visibly an old man—as if this were a time of perpetual war. The stage was bordered with sandbags. Unfortunately, the director's conception of Greek tragic form seemed terribly out-of-date, with its prominently featured chorus of robed women wailing in a style long gone in contemporary theatre (the choral texts had been written by Joseph Brodsky). Coincidentally, the handling of the chorus was the chief problem in the recent British production of *Hecuba*, which featured Vanessa Redgrave. After new visions of Greek tragedy by the likes of Andrei Serban,

Robert Wilson/Heiner Müller, Ariane Mnouchkine, Peter Sellars, Peter Stein, Romeo Castellucci, Deborah Warner, and Tadashi Suzuki, it is difficult to accept this heavy-handed staging which, surprisingly, premiered in 2005.

At the opposite pole from the wooden Russian production was Peter Brook's direction of *The Grand Inquisitor*, which British actor Bruce Myers performed as a monologue, in an adaptation by Marie-Hélène Estienne. It was set in a spare room with Myers standing and directly addressing the audience in his long black robe, a picture of deadly formality and fierce eloquence dissecting the use and abuse of human freedom. The other voices in Dostoevsky's text were eliminated, highlighting the painstaking clarity of purpose in the delivery now by one sustained voice and mood while the figure of Christ sits, silently, across the room. Listening to the complex inner dialogue of the work provoked the same response I had had recently while attending the London production of Schiller's *Don Carlos*, featuring Derek Jacobi and the superb cast around him. The dimension of such theatrical experiences and the demands of concentration they make of an audience in their long reflective passages on power, religion, and human will are almost without exception absent from the short sentences, and even more limited philosophical dimension, of contemporary drama now seen on Western stages.

Brook, who was given a special Honorary Award at the festival, also brought to Istanbul the Théâtre des Bouffes du Nord production of the Fugard/Kani/Ntshona international success from 1972, *Sizwe Banzi is Dead*, continuing his interest in African themes, as the recent *Tierno Bokar* demonstrated. Here again the staging was a *tour de force* for the actors, Habib Dembélé and Pitcho Womba Konga, who, in a simple setting of cardboard props, propelled their robust comedic spirit into this story of mistaken identity, restricted borders, and everyday struggle under the apartheid system.

Coming as well from France was an excellent production of Beckett's *Endgame*, directed by Pierre Chabert who had worked for many years with Beckett in Paris, and featuring two well-known Turkish actors, Genco Erkal (Hamm) and Bülent Emin Yarar (Clov). A number of Beckett plays were done at the festival in memory of the one-hundredth anniversary of the author's birth. (There was also a celebration of Lorca for this seventy-fifth anniversary year of his death.) Here Hamm is an elderly dandy with velvet robe, silk foulard, and two-tone shoes. Clov made a marvelous tramp, his body angled slightly by lifting his left shoulder and lowering his right side. His movements were mime-like, his face pasty. Suspenders were attached to his cuffs. What made this staging so rich is that each actor exhibited a varied set of gestures to create a lively repertoire of facial expressions and individual peculiarities. The tone was affectionate rather than masochistic, and very funny. Nell and Nagg (Meral Çetinkaya and Erdem Akakçe) were also full of feeling in this highly-charged humanistic view of the play, which is also part of the International Paris-Beckett Festival 2006.

If the productions from these and other so-called "master" directors whose work (only some of which coincided with my visit) was shown in Istanbul— namely, Brook (*The Grand Inquisitor*), Suzuki (*Ivanov*), Strehler (*Arlecchino*), Nekrosius (*Othello*), Terzopoulos (*The Persians*)—focused on classics, it was evident from the offerings of many of the younger Turkish artists that the drama was not central to their thinking about performance. It was markedly true of *A Play for Two*, conceived, designed, and directed by the well-known graphic designer Bülent Erkmen for a male and female performer (Yelda Reynaud, Altay Özbek), dressed in white, who climbed in and through a labyrinth of black steel poles, at times moving in perpendicular relation to the wall or ceiling. This obviously digitally mapped grid, like a minimalist sculpture, encircled the audience of less than thirty who were perched on small swivel seats, turning this way and that to watch the performance. The performers spoke in Turkish as a woman who acted as translator of the text by Yekta Kopan walked in the space, offering their fragmented and largely failed attempts to communicate in single words or small phrases, such as "Crazy," "Passionate," "Enthusiastic," "Tempted."

Even though the performers didn't have the skill to sustain text and movement, and their lack of variation lessened the effect over its approximately fifty-minute performance, *A Play for Two* signaled the explorations in contemporary work that are bringing dance, theatre, and the installation closer together, the implications of which have yet to be fully realized in any center of performance, here or abroad. The recently formed Dot Theatre, which has produced such writers as Churchill, Harrower, and McDonagh, hosted the event. An example of the same tendency toward movement was demonstrated by *Misfit*, directed by Emre Koyuncuoğlu for more than a dozen actors and non-actors in another new Istanbul performance space, The Garage. Here again the performers, an unconventional-looking cast, were called upon to execute exaggerated configurations of body work, all of the action taking place on and around a bed. Solos, groups, pairs—various combinations of seemingly nutty but ordinary people meet in this dreamy/nightmarish/passionate/funny space where the language (a group creation) seemed to arise spontaneously. There was an aspect of this production that elicited the outrageous effect of throwaway, "found" speech, even though exceedingly relevant to our time, similar to the wildly satiric language of Germany's Rene Pollesch—part television, part sociology.

The festival performances demonstrated that even when the more conventional theatre work was of a generally good quality there remained a sense of tiredness with the old forms, even though those theatres aspiring toward more cutting-edge work did not always have the technical proficiency to accomplish their goal of moving theatre toward dance or visual arts. I have had the same feeling about theatre in other countries as well, where dance seems so much more appealing to younger artists and audiences. With few exceptions, drama on its own—in the form of a complete piece of writing—seems to be losing ground as a vital expression of contemporary energies, and much of it is not so different anymore from television, independent cinema, or mass culture. It may take some time before theatre forges a new identity and generates new languages for itself, in the process of absorbing the influences of video, installations, live art, dance, and world music. New performance thinking seems to prefer image to drama and the body rather than dramatic language, which is not to say that artists are not interested in "text" or "texture." That use of writing is different from "dramatic literature," which is steadily falling away from theatre, here and in Europe, accelerating the decline of its cultural significance.

Certainly the biggest artistic explosion abroad, and some of the most passionate performance experiences in the past two decades, have come from the world of dance. Anne Teresa de Keersmaeker, one of the international favorites, brought her Rosas Dance Ensemble from Belgium in an elegant two-part work, *Raga for the Rainy Season/A Love Supreme*, created with Salva Sanchis. In the first piece, the Indian "Mian Malhar" raga (featuring a singer and musicians on tape) accompanied the eight women and a single male dancer in a joyful picture of a community expressing a range of human feeling as they wait for rain, the women clad in billowy white dresses to underscore the swirling emotions and extended sense of time flowing through the space. An entirely different and more formal world opened up for John Coltrane's classic "A Love Supreme," which featured two couples in a more improvisational, spatially contained exploration of the divine. Though they looked so visually different, and the choreographic structures were autonomous, Rosas demonstrated with a magisterial beauty that they were simply two different paths to the ecstasy embedded in spiritual bliss, and that there exists multiple varieties of religious experience, which is sensual feeling, too.

Another marvelous evening of dance also presented at the Atatürk Cultural Center was offered by the Turkish choreographer Zeynep Tanbay, who showed the work of her young company Dance Project in a blast of energy called *Four Legs*. The conceit of the piece is that all of the many vignettes given as solo, duet, trio, and group events are set in, on, and around chairs, tables, beds, benches. Tanbay brought together the intelligence of the body and international experience from both New York and the European continent to create a post-Judson/post-Bausch work for ten dancers (and at times herself) alternating pure dance, social commentary, and everyday-life occurrence for each "scene," regardless of how long it took to play out. Not all of them were performed at the same technical level and at times young dancers struggled with a chair in the Robert Wilson-like "knee plays" that punctuated each longer dance, but it was always worth watching the vocabulary of human gesture the company put forth. Tanbay's approach was humanistic, often evincing a touch of light humor. At times the confrontation of two men or a couple marked a simple moment of stress or an expression of love; a meeting between a man and a woman might provoke an elemental struggle, powerful in the swiftness of its movement into disturbing psychological terrain. On the opening night performance I attended, the company was clearly an audience favorite. For sure, it was difficult not to feel the kinetic power coursing through the theatre in the music of the many musicians—Veloso, Glass, Pergolesi, Tiersen, even Marlene Dietrich—who accompanied the spirited dancing.

The mood changed drastically in other dance performances I saw, demonstrating the range of work in dance in Istanbul these days. *Phronemophobia/F* (The Fear of Thinking), with concept and choreography by Tuğçe Ulugün Tuna, was a somber dance piece in two parts: The first, a strongly emotive, even disturbing solo by the choreographer rubbing her feet on the ground over and over, and the second part featuring five dancers who formed what appeared to be a post-apocalyptic community. Their misshapen bodies, with odd head turns and leg twists suggesting Butoh influence, struggled to move on and across a grid-like floor often highlighted in white blocks of light. The section ended with a series of tableaux as the dancers crawled toward the audience. This was an ambitious evening of dance by young performers, which also included black-and-white video segments (by Vahit Tuna) featuring close-ups of a man's face making slight movements, shown both above the space and on floor monitors, accompanied by an electronic score. The overall feeling of *F* was a sustained sense of doom whose effect would have benefited from being shortened and more focused for greater clarity in the relation between its parts. The title of the work and the strong element of resistance in both solo and group movements suggest that the piece had moved beyond formal elements to an underlying social commentary.

Sometime during the festival I started seeing posters for upcoming dance concerts by the Galata Mevlevi Music and Semâ Ensemble. The Mevlevi are the whirling dervishes, a branch of the most famous Sufi sect that had been banned by Atatürk in the process of creating modern Turkey. The original dervishes were followers of the great Sufi master, Rumi, who died in the thirteenth century. Having seen this sacred dancing twice before in New York City, I was overjoyed to find that I might be able to attend a performance in Istanbul itself. The dervishes were performing a *semâ* (ritual dance) at the Mevlevi Monastery in an eighteenth-century lodge next to an old cemetery. Three dancers and a holy man who read prayers, all in robes and tall hats, performed the ritual in an octagonal room with a wooden floor, around which sat the spectators.

Musicians played in the balcony above us. From the start it was distracting to concentrate on the spirit of the ritual, with its highly codified system of gestures and movements, because of all the tourists; eventually I was forced to give up any thought of a focused, much less spiritual, experience because my neighbor was incessantly taking pictures. And as if to mock the ecstatic moments in dance that I was anticipating, I saw the short and stocky dervish whom I had deemed the most otherworldly, only moments ago twirling round and round with his head tilted over his right shoulder and eyes closed in an image of utter entrancement, leave the monastery after the performance in jeans and polo shirt, the hairy chest of a mortal poking through at his neck. He held a nylon sack likely shielding the holy robes, as if he were a dancer in Chelsea. The actual ritual enveloped me much less than the performance I had witnessed in New York several years ago at Town Hall. Oh, the perils of cultural tourism.

What would a trip to Istanbul be without going to the grand bazaar to witness the great theatre of shopping and to Cağaloğlu Baths for the luxurious theatre of hygiene, and to its mosques for the theatre of prayer that begins with beseeching voices calling forth believers throughout the city. Standing in Sultanahmet Square, to my left was Hagia Sophia, the architectural wonder of Byzantine religious life for nine-hundred years until the 1453 fall/conquest (depending on your vantage point) of Constantinople, towering just beyond the Topkapi Palace, and to my right the great Blue Mosque, while behind me marked the site of the old Roman Hippodrome. There is something strange about this view: the obelisk in the square was stolen from Luxor by the Romans for Constantine; the four bronze horses that once stood here were carried off to St. Mark's in Venice during the Fourth Crusade; four minarets surround Hagia Sophia. In every direction I saw another perspective of Istanbul. Here I was in the former Eastern Roman Empire, the former Byzantine Empire, and the former Ottoman Empire. A walk across any one of the main streets brought me quickly to museums that held treasures from great civilizations existing before the invention of writing, and when writing developed it was from this part of the world's Hittite culture, in one of whose languages the first story, *Gilgamesh*, was written in stone.

The mix of ancient empires representing so many cultural, political, social, and religious systems that flowed into the wrenching modernization of Turkey in the twentieth century, makes the present-day culture abundant in artistic traditions and forms. The music especially, with its great earth-dwelling sounds combining East and West—sax and *saz*—seems to float in the air block by block through the city. I cannot recall ever being in a city where so much music sounded through the streets. Turkish music combines old folk instruments and electronic sounds, and rock and jazz, in high voltage sensual rhythms whose extraordinary instrumentation and vocal techniques draw on Balkan, Eastern European, Byzantine, classical Persian, southern Mediterranean, and Central Asian traditions. It is apparent that a significant part of the crossover spiritual and New Age music—what is now identified as world music—emanates from this ethnic mix.

The distinctive music of Turkey is the subject of a new film entitled *Crossing the Bridge: The Sound of Istanbul*, directed by Fatih Akin, who also made the recent Turkish-German *Head On*. That film's explosive soundtrack by Alexander Hacke initially drew my attention to contemporary Turkish music. The new documentary opens with the band Orient Expressions and scenes from the Istanbul club Babylon where I had seen them perform in front of a high-energy crowd only some weeks earlier during my stay in the city. The charismatic Sabahat Akkiraz sang with the band, her throaty laments in rippling scales, her outstretched hands and beatific smile generating an emotional response from an audience obviously familiar with the singer. On this night new technologies mixed with ancient string and reed instruments and songs from Anatolia.

Another meeting ground of international culture is, of course, the art scene. The Istanbul Modern was just opened in 2004. The day I visited it offered the opportunity to see among a great deal of work that, admittedly, is more concerned with identity issues than art-historical ones, a special exhibit of the extraordinary output of Turkish painters Fahrelnissa Zeid (1901–91) and her son Nejad Devrim (1923–95), who worked and traveled in several cities East and West. Zeid's modernism—passing through the great styles of constructivism, cubism, and abstract expressionism—brought to her work the feeling of calligraphy and ceramic tile, and Eastern colors and iconography. Both artists spent their lives in many centers of art away from home. Her son commented on an influential 1980 trip to America, "I did large paintings there and started using rhythm and violence in my work. There is a pointless struggle in America ... they mix up art and fantasy and American politics." At the risk of stating the obvious, both painters, particularly Zeid (her life extending from the Ottoman Empire to the fall of Yugoslavia), have not been as much a part of modernist narratives as they might have been due to the exclusivities of twentieth-century cultural politics.

The museum also featured an exhibit of new video works called *Painting as a Way of Living*. The most powerful of these was Lida Abdul's *White House*, a silent black and white video projected on the museum wall which shows her in black robes painting with thick white paint two bombed-out houses in the countryside of her native Afghanistan. When a man, also dressed in black, appears from the rubble she paints his clothes. Mountain goats meander among the ruins. Abdul, who now lives in the U.S., demonstrates a remarkable resiliency and life spirit in reclaiming devastated spaces with her art. Equally culturally specific, in this case for its Eastern-European irony, was Albanian artist Adrian Paci's *Pictori/Painter*, a single-channel video shown on a plasma screen, in which the camera slowly moves through the painter's studio cluttered with paintings, advertisements, signs, paintbrushes, and books. The artist (on camera) bemoans—with a text in English running at the bottom of the video—the uselessness of his traditional education, now that anything can be considered art. Having already created a sign for a mosque (with good wishes for Ramadan), and another one for a church at Easter, he is now working on a death certificate. Taken together, these two video performances demonstrate widely diverging paths in video performances of artists; one, social documentary; another, Duchampian.

The independent gallery known as Platform Garanti Contemporary Art Center was showing an exceptionally intelligent and well-conceived installation by the xurban_collective (Hakan Topal, Güven Incirlioğlu), entitled *Void: A View from Akropolis*. At the entrance to the gallery a large mound of dirt, rock, and grass was wedged into a corner. Large scale C-prints of native plants, a grid of time-lapse shots of ruins and landscape, and a four-channel video were installed in the gallery rooms. The ruins documented in the work are Anatolia's Bergama Akropolis from the second century BC whose most famous section, The Pergamon Altar, was excavated in the 1880s by German archaeologists, and carried off to Berlin where it has resided for decades in its own museum. As if the sacred area had not been violated enough, a gold mine near the village of Saganci, where the artists worked, continues to deface the land through the use of large earth-moving trucks.

The artists have videotaped and photographed the site and also performed "actions" (shown on video) of taking rocks out of the ground and filling the spaces with objects, in some places even stuffing crevices with other plants, re-generating and recuperating the "void" with new life and the human hand. In one of the videos a text is shown moving across the countryside, as if to re-mind viewers that human history is written in the landscape and that natural history is part of the history of the world. Seeing this work, carefully created over a substantial period of time and elaborated in different media, natural and artificial, I was reminded of Robert Smithson's ecology of devastated spaces, though less history-weighted ruins than the ones in this pre-historic terrain of Turkey. He pointed to the understanding that sedimentation is a way of exposing unwritten histories. Now the xurban_collective is writing new texts in the landscape that will someday also disappear into the earth, reversing the process of archaeology. In their definition, site is not the surface containing the monument/ruin but the "non-monument"—in other words, what they view as a Beuysian "social sculpture" constructed by the collective through millennia.

For Orhan Pamuk, the idea of ruins is closer to our own time, though he too reads the history of Istanbul in the sadness of its architecture. His method of telling time unfolds through the photographs documenting the city that are distributed plentifully throughout his recent memoir, *Istanbul*. Pamuk devotes a special chapter of his story to the concept of "*hüzün*," the profound melan-choly that he inscribes in the soul of his city and in the people who live there. His grief is a world away from the nationalistic, nostalgic, anti-modern Islamist politics. Pamuk's perspective is cultural, aesthetic, cerebral, sensual—an intellectual's history of his world, a form of sensibility. It resides in windows and doorways and crooked streets and burning yalis, it breathes in certain nouns and Sufi poetry, it describes the color of light at certain times of day, and the way men stand on street corners. For him the greatest loss was the effacing of Ottoman culture in the process of modernization that has characterized the twentieth century of his beloved city. It is a yearning for cosmopolitanism that comes after the confidence of modernity.

I returned from Istanbul not having experienced the profound *hüzün* that casts its shadow on the pages of Pamuk's memoir. Where was it? Had I not understood it? How could I discover this sentiment in so short a visit? And yet, I think I know what he is writing about. I could hear it in the city, though I could not see it. This spiritual feeling resides in the music that has a deep attachment to place, even as it has produced the universal sound of "world" music.

Though I found works to admire, I did not find a flavor of Istanbul in the performances created here. They could have been done by American or European artists. The nature of any contemporary festival is that it draws work from abroad to educate its local audiences as well as providing an opportunity for its own cultural achievements to be seen. It has long been the case that so much art now making the rounds of biennials looks the same, but art is a different matter because of its status as a commodity. Theatre is not like that. The vast majority of work does not have an international life. Dialogue with its own society is the foremost priority. In the Turkish performances that I saw, international performance vocabularies have largely overshadowed the particularity of individual cultural (I do not mean "ethnic") expression. I would like to have seen performances that could not have come from somewhere else. The continental drift is more pronounced in a country that is both Europe and Asia, modern and traditional, and now swept up in the EU drama. At this transformative moment, perhaps what I witnessed is a kind of theatrical manifestation of *hüzün*.

From Istanbul I brought back an 1838 W. H. Bartlett print of the Galata Fountain that I had passed by so many times. In this engraving the artist recast Islamic architecture in the vocabulary of European painting. Once back at home I put it in the same room with other Bartlett prints of the Hudson Valley, whose scenes of the Catskill Mountains are inflected by the British landscape tradition. Together, they are a reminder that to construct a narrative of another culture than one's own always involves an overlay, a rubbing of surfaces against each other—the doublevision that asks: How do I see? What do I see?

This essay was originally published as "Afternoons in Asia Minor, Beyoğlu at Night" in *PAJ: A Journal of Performance and Art*, Vol. XXIX, No. 1 (PAJ 85), January 2007.

In Memory of
Her Feelings

◘

Art and Consciousness
A Conversation with Susan Sontag

I remember very well the day we taped this conversation with Susan Sontag. Fledgling editors of *PAJ*, Gautam Dasgupta and I were already waiting in her apartment at 106th Street when she arrived and, smiling, said "I'm all yours," before settling down with us. She had just returned from a chemotherapy treatment. She was wearing brown slacks and a brown sweater, with a gold silk Indian scarf folded at her neck. It was February 1977. Susan Sontag was forty-four years old.

It was perfectly natural to include her in an issue whose other pages featured a special section on experimental theatre, with contributions by Sam Shepard, Megan Terry, Carolee Schneemann, Stanley Kauffmann; articles on contemporary dance, text-sound art, Fassbinder, and European festivals; a new Edward Bond play. Unusual for American intellectuals who have largely ignored the non-literary arts, Sontag had a far-ranging knowledge of world theatre, opera, and dance, in addition to film and painting. She was a passionate theatregoer, sometime playwright and director, who could be seen frequently at BAM or Lincoln Center or in downtown spaces. While her literary work is widely known and celebrated, it is perhaps less evident how much she cared for and wrote about and supported the world of performance over four decades.

I am grateful for the encouragement she gave to *PAJ*. Like any young person in the downtown scene at the time, I wanted Sontag to acknowledge our publication. She always understood the new, the avant-garde. She appreciated work outside the mainstream. She valued independent small presses. Mainly, she cared about what you were doing if she respected your endeavors. She had critical perceptions that went in complicated directions and yet made fine historical distinctions. In this interview she demonstrates her knowledge of the then-new theatre of artists such as Robert Wilson and Richard Foreman, linking many of the concerns of the seventies, such as perception, consciousness, and imagery, to the modernist legacy. (I was already preoccupied with these issues in *The Theatre of Images*, which was published a few months after our discussion.) No matter what the era, Sontag was always our contemporary.

It was the rare writer, performer, filmmaker, or artist who didn't want to be noticed by her luxurious mind and discerning eye. The intellectual landscape of New York is forever changed at her death. Who remains to distinguish the ecology of images?

Sontag was always supportive of our publishing activities, not only the journal from its early stages, but in the next decade when we started to publish fiction and other non-theatre titles. I can recall a long afternoon at her place, by now she had moved downtown, during which she pulled out from her bookshelves several foreign-language editions, suggesting possible projects for us to consider. One of them that comes to mind is the untranslated autobiographical writings of Robert Musil. We sent her every journal we ever published and most of the books. (*Could they be hardback copies?—OK, sure.*) It gives me great pleasure to know that so many PAJ publications are in her beloved book collection.

In the last conversation we had just over a year ago, by telephone, I made some remarks congratulating her on *Regarding the Pain of Others*, then launched into a discussion of several older artists I knew who were doing such good work. But when I lamented that it was a struggle for them in this culture, how hard it was to keep going, Sontag wasn't interested in such complaints. Did I think Goya didn't struggle? (*You're right. You're right.*) I could find no defense against her steadfast belief in the exemplary. She respected struggle.

I had seen examples of that up close. One summer evening, in 1999, Sontag was the guest of honor for dinner at the home of her dear friends, Bob and Peg Boyers, editors of *Salmagundi* who run The Summer Writers Institute at Skidmore College, in Saratoga Springs. Sontag had come there for a reading though she was again facing a severe health crisis. Her current treatments created neurological damage that affected her walking and she was unsteady on her feet. (*How are you? We don't want to lose you. I hope to have you around for many more years.—I'm planning to be.*) But she was as interested as ever when, newly arrived home from several months in Europe, I told her of the brilliant theatre work of the Italian director Romeo Castellucci. A short while later, she walked onto the stage at the college and gave a reading from her then novel-in-progress, *In America*, whose central character is the Polish actress Helena Modjeska. She was living in the moment, in her writing, in her thought. She was showing that life is worth fighting for, you do your work, you go on.

What performances in the past few years have you felt were worthwhile experiences?

Lucian Pintilie's *Turandot*. Robert Anton's puppet theatre. Merce Cunningham. Peter Brook's *The Ik*. Beckett's Berlin staging of *Waiting for Godot*. Plisetskaya doing Ravel's *Bolero*. Watergate. Franz Salieri's *La Grand Eugene* (the original Paris production, not the one that went on tour). Strehler's production of *The Cherry Orchard*. The invented Act Three of the Met's recent production of *Lulu*. Maria Irene Fornes's staging of her play, *Fefu and Her Friends* ... Shall I go on?

Why haven't you written about these events?

I'm writing other things. Mostly fiction.

Don't you want to go on writing criticism?

I don't consider that I ever was a critic. I had ideas, and I attached them to works of art that I admired. Now I attach them to other things.

How do you view the current critical scene?

You mean monitoring productions and giving out grades—the kind of consumer reporting that decides whether something is good or not good, well performed or not well-performed?

If that is what people are satisfied with, isn't it due to the lack of a new critical vocabulary with which to treat the new theatre?

I don't expect ideas from critics. They come from poets and painters and novelists and even playwrights—doing a stint of writing about the theatre. And from directors who found their own theatres.

But the current experimental theatre is such a radical break from our theatrical past, not part of a developing American tradition. No one seems to know quite how to deal with it.

I think the problem is that the more than sixty-year-old international tradition of modernism has bequeathed us a surfeit of critical perspectives—constructivism, futurism, Brecht, Artaud, Grotowski, et al. And that we give an open-ended but increasingly limited credence to them all. It's not lack of familiarity with experimental theatre that explains the critical vacuum. It's the mounting disenchantment—partly justified, partly shallow and philistine—with modernism. And a widespread boredom with high culture itself.

You mentioned Artaud and Grotowski. Their theories—which go back to the origins of theatre in ritual and ceremony—seem to be a negation of everything that's transpired in Western culture. Isn't that a regression? And doesn't their kind of theatre remove one from the immediacy of the moment?

There's no opposition between the archaic and the immediate.

I see such theatre as a form of hermeticism, a withdrawal into a world that we have no contact with whatsoever.

Well, I've no objection to art that is hermetic. (Some art *should* be hermetic, I think.) But, far from being hermetic, the theatre influenced by Artaud and by Grotowski is very much about immediate, present experience. The difference is that both Artaud and Grotowski believe in the reality of evil—the reality treated superficially, or denied by so-called realistic theatre.

Why do you emphasize evil?

First of all, because it exists. And because an awareness of the reality of evil is the best defense against artistic trivialization and vulgarity.

The modern attack on "dialogue" or realistic theatre seems to have taken two directions. One, represented by Artaud and Grotowski, explores feelings. The other, represented by Foreman, is more interested in exploring the thinking process and modes of perception.

Perception in and for itself?

Yes. In order to perceive better.

Perceive *what* better? Doesn't the material offered for perception have to be trivial, precisely so that the audience can't be distracted by it and can concentrate on the process of perceiving? If you are invited to consider the relationship between a chair and a grapefruit—that is, what's on the stage is a chair and a grapefruit and a string connecting them—then you will indeed perceive something about how they are alike and how they differ. But it's no more than an interesting perceptual problem (and that largely because it's a problem one does not ordinarily consider).

You don't think being interesting is enough?

I used to think so. But I don't anymore. You know, that notion has a his-tory—a rather brief one. To apply the word "interesting" to a work of art was an invention of the Romantic writers of the late-eighteenth and early-nineteenth centuries, and one that seemed very peculiar at first. (Hegel, for example, thought it was not a compliment to say that something was "interesting.") The notion of "the interesting" is approximately as old as the notion of "the boring." Indeed, it seems to me that "the interesting" presupposes "the boring," and vice versa. One of the proudest claims of the modernist theatre is that it is anti-psy-chological. But "the interesting" and "the boring" are psychological categories, nothing more. They are feelings, assumed to be of limited duration, and to be capable of mutating into each other—categories of the solipsistic, narcissistic worldview. (They replace "the beautiful" and "the ugly," which are attributes—hypostasized, quasi-objective, assumed to be permanent.) An "interesting" ob-ject has an arresting quality: It seizes our attention, we take cognizance of it, and then let it go. An "interesting" experience is one that has no lasting effect. The notion of "the interesting" arises when art is no longer conceived of as con-nected with truth. (When truth comes to be reserved for science, for so-called rational inquiry.) In continuing to consider something to be valuable—valu-able enough—because it is interesting, we perpetuate a Romantic attitude that needs reexamining.

Foreman's theatre is about thinking, about the-being-consciously-aware at the theatre event of the working of the mind in the theatre. I can't think of another kind of theatre where one feels so consciously in the present. It's Foreman's attempt to actively engage the audience that is important.

I don't agree that consciousness-as-such is Foreman's subject. Or, if it could be—and I don't think consciousness-as-such is really a subject at all—that it could be very engaging.

What about Beckett?

Beckett is dealing with emotions, however abstractly, and there is a progress from one emotion to the next that feels inevitable. Not only are his plays nar-rative but, as Joe Chaikin once observed, Beckett has actually discovered a new dramatic subject. Normally people on the stage reflect on the macrostructure of action. What am I going to do this year? Tomorrow? Tonight? They ask: Am I going mad? Will I ever get to Moscow? Should I leave my husband? Do I have to murder my uncle? My mother? These are the sorts of large projects that have traditionally concerned a play's leading characters. Beckett is the first writer to dramatize the microstructure of action. What am I going to do one minute from now? In the next second? Weep? Take out my comb? Stand up? Sigh? Sit? Be silent? Tell a joke? Understand something? His plays are built on reflections leading to decisions, which impart to his dramas a real narrative push. Lessing was right about the irreducible difference between spatial and temporal arts. A play—or a novel, or a film—can be non-narrative in the sense that it need not tell a story. But it has to be linear or sequential, I think. A succession of images, or of aphorisms, is not enough to give a play the linear cohesiveness proper to the temporal arts.

Do you feel the same way about Peter Handke's works—his Sprechstücke, *particularly—which resemble Foreman's plays in the lack of dialogue, in the attempt at consciousness-raising, in the dialectical relationship of the stage and the audience?*

No, because Handke's plays are about specific ideas or problems (not about consciousness or perception as such), dramatized in a sequential form. The ideas matter dramatically.

In Foreman's recent Rhoda in Potatoland, *there are many quotations—from Breton's* Nadja, *from Wittgenstein, et cetera—allusions to paintings, and so forth. How can the contemporary artist cope with the radical strides made in art in this century without alluding to them in his work?*

Modernist self-consciousness can take many forms. Painters like to quote other painters. But one can't imagine Beckett quoting anybody or making allusions to predecessors and models—as Wittgenstein didn't. The demands of purity and the demands of piety may be, ultimately, incompatible.

Consciousness is the principal subject of modern art. Is that in some way a dangerous tradition?

It seems to me that its biggest limitation is the value placed on consciousness conceived of as a wholly *private* activity. Modernist art has given the central place to asocial, private fantasy and, in effect, denied the notion that some intentions are more valid than others ... It's hardly surprising that so many modernist artists have been fascinated by the diseases of consciousness—that an art committed to solipsism would recapitulate the gestures of the *pathology* of solipsism. If you start from an asocial notion of perception or consciousness, you must inevitably end up with the poetry of mental illness and mental deficiency. With autistic silence. With the autistic's use of language: compulsive repetition and variation. With an obsession with circles. With an abstract or distended notion of time.

Are you thinking of the work of Robert Wilson?

Of Wilson, for one. More generally, of the long faux-naïf tradition in modernist art, one of whose great figures is Gertrude Stein. (What *Four Saints in Three Acts* started, *Letter to Queen Victoria* and *Einstein on the Beach* continue ...). But the symptomology of mental deficiency recurs in most of the really seductive productions I've seen recently: Pintilie's *Turandot*, *The Ik*, Carmelo Bene's *Faust* fantasy, Patrice Chereau's production of Marivaux's *La Dispute* ...

Twelve years ago, in "One Culture and the New Sensibility," you advanced the argument that the function of art is to extend and educate consciousness. You seem now to have moved away from the ideas expressed in that essay.

I don't disagree with what I wrote then. But to assert that art is an exploration of consciousness is vacuous, unless one understands that consciousness has a structure, a thematics, a history. The choice of materials is never accidental or extraneous.

Is that what you were arguing in your essay in the New York Review of Books *(February 6, 1975) on Leni Riefenstahl and fascist aesthetics?*

Yes, that's one assumption behind the essay. It seemed to me all too easy to say that Riefenstahl's work is beautiful. The question is: What kind of beauty? In the service of what ideas, what forms of consciousness, what emotions? Not only ideas but emotions—joy, fear, whatever—have a history. There is such a thing as fascist emotions, a fascist aesthetic impulse.

How do you feel about Adrienne Rich's attack in the New York Review of Books *(March 20, 1975) on your Riefenstahl piece for its "unwillingness" to discuss Riefenstahl as a product of a patriarchal society? Do you feel put upon by feminists who demand that you take another "line" in your writing?*

Since I'm a feminist too, the situation can hardly be described as a difficulty between me and "them." As for Rich's argument, I said what I thought about that in my reply (in the same issue of the NYRB) to her letter—that it's not as if Nazi Germany were a patriarchal society and other societies aren't. What society is not patriarchal? Riefenstahl's work is explained by Nazism, not by the attitudes of Nazis toward women.

Yet many people see Riefenstahl's work as purely aesthetic, beautiful films.

There is no such thing as an "aesthetic" work of art—as there is no such thing as the engagement or exploration of consciousness as such. Neither consciousness nor the aesthetic is something abstract. We're not being honest about our experience if we ignore the iconography of consciousness. You can't look at the Rembrandt self-portraits and see them just as an arrangement of forms, as studies in brown. There's a face there.

Isn't this way of looking at art radically different from the one you espoused in "Against Interpretation"?

No. I never argued that all art should be looked at abstractly; I argued for the intellectual importance of its being experienced sensuously. "Against Interpretation" was a polemic against one reductive way of accounting for art, much more common a decade ago: treating a work as if it were equivalent to the account that could be given of its "meaning." This practice seemed to me misguided—first of all, because a great deal of art doesn't mean very much, in any non-tautological sense of meaning. (Of course, a work may not have a "meaning" and still contain "referents" outside itself, to the world.) And because it weakens and corrupts our direct appreciation of a work's "thingness." Instead of relying so much on questions about what elements in a work of art mean, I thought we could rely more on questions about how they function—concretely, sensuously, and formally—in the work.

I categorically refuse not to see meaning in a work. Otherwise it doesn't pay for me to go to see something. I have to approach the problem that is put before me and make it worthwhile for my own experiences.

I categorically refuse to ask art to "pay for me." Nor does it have to touch me personally, as people say. Isn't pleasure "worthwhile"? Among other things, art is an instrument of pleasure—and one doesn't have that much pleasure in life. And pleasure can be quite impersonal. And complex.

Are you positing a hierarchy of art—the kind that gives pleasure and the kind that makes you think? Are they mutually exclusive?

Hardly—since thinking is one kind of pleasure, both solemn and playful. But I don't want to minimize the fact that the role of pleasure in art raises all sorts of serious questions. I find it impossible to keep moral feelings out of my desire for pleasure. That is, part of my *experience* of pleasure is that there are facile pleasures, as there are facile ideas. Since art is a form of flattery, I find myself also responding to the quality of an artist's refusal. The history of art is not only part of the history of pleasure. It is also a series of renunciations.

Why should art have to renounce anything?

Because every leading idea—every leading style—needs a corrective. As Oscar Wilde said, "A truth in art is that whose contrary is also true." And a truth *about* art is one whose contrary is also true.

What do you hope for when you go to the theatre?

Passion. Intelligence. Intensity. Lyricism. Theatre—and poetry and music— supply a lyricism not to be found in life.

Why not?

Because life is too long. For life to be like *Tristan and Isolde*, the average human life should last two months instead of seventy years.

Is intensity the same as pleasure?

It's better. Sexier, more profound. As you see, I'm an incorrigible puritan.

You seem to be excluding humor.

I'm not. But I get restless when the treatment of the emotions in art takes second place—it does in so much of modernist theatre—to the dramaturgy of surprise, to a negative desire, the desire to avoid the expected.

Are you suggesting that surprise is not a worthy element in the performing arts?

After a century-and-a-half of surprises in the arts—during which time the ante has been upped steadily, so that people are harder and harder to surprise—it seems to have gotten much less satisfying. Most instances of outrage or shock now are gags.

You have written in one essay that "the history of art is a series of successful transgressions." If, as you say, the ante of shock and surprise is always being upped, what is left to transgress?

The idea of transgression, perhaps ... Transgression presupposes successful notions of order. But transgressions have been so successful that the idea of transgression has become normative for the arts—which is a self-contradiction. Modern art wished to be—maybe even was, for a brief time—in an intractable, adversary relation to the established high culture. Now it is identical with high culture, supported by a vast bureaucracy of museums, universities, and state and private foundations. And the reason for this success story is that there is a close fit between many of the values promoted by modernism and the larger values of our capitalist consumer society. This makes it difficult, to say the least, to continue thinking of modernist art as adversary art. And that's part of what lies behind the disenchantment with modernism I spoke of earlier.

You seem discouraged by this situation.

Yes and no. Rebellion does not seem to me a value in itself, as—say—truth is. There's no inherent value in transgression. As there is no inherent value to being interesting. My loyalty is not to the transgression but to the truth behind it. That the forms of life in this society, having become increasingly permissive, corrupt, vulgar, and disgusting, thereby deprive artists of the taboos against which they can, comfortably, heroically, rebel—that seems far less dismaying than the fact that this society itself is based on lies, on untruths, on hallucination.

What should artists do now?

In a society that works and enriches itself by means of organized hallucination, be less devoted to creating new forms of hallucination. And more devoted to piercing through the hallucinations that nowadays pass for reality.

This conversation with Susan Sontag was first published in *Performing Arts Journal*, Vol. II, No. 2 (Fall, 1977) and reprinted after her death with my new prefatory note in *PAJ: A Journal of Performance and Art*, Vol. XXVII, No. 2 (PAJ 80), May 2005. It was conducted by Gautam Dasgupta and me at the author's home in New York City the year after we had founded PAJ, in February 1977. Subsequently, it was published in *Conversations on Art and Performance*, Bonnie Marranca and Gautam Dasgupta, eds. (Baltimore: Johns Hopkins University Press, 1999) and in *Conversations with Susan Sontag*, Leland Poague, ed. (Jackson: University of Mississippi Press, 1995).